Russian Factory Women

Women workers in the shell-assembling section of the Sormovo metal-working plant. Nizhnii Novgorod Province. From *Illiustrirovannaia istoriia SSSR* (Moscow, 1977), p. 228.

ROSE L. GLICKMAN

Russian Factory Women

Workplace and Society, 1880–1914

UNIVERSITY OF CALIFORNIA PRESS
Berkeley • Los Angeles • London

University of California Press
Berkeley and Los Angeles, California

University of California Press, Ltd.
London, England

© 1984 by
The Regents of the University of California
First Paperback Printing 1986
ISBN 0-520-05736-8
Printed in the United States of America

2   3   4   5   6   7   8   9

Library of Congress Cataloging in Publication Data

Glickman, Rose L.
Russian factory women.

Bibliography: p.
Includes index.
1. Women—Employment—Soviet Union—History.
2. Factory system—Soviet Union—History.   I. Title.
HD6068.2.S65G54 1984   331.4'87'0947   83-6968

To my daughter, Eve

Contents

Illustrations

Tables

Preface

The reordering of social groups—the emergence of class—has been a universal consequence of capitalist industrialization, transcending all the national peculiarities that distinguish the course of industrialization from one country to another. No less an important consequence was the alteration of the functions and roles of the sexes within class. The most common observation about the influence of industrialization on sex roles is that men became the primary producers of goods and services for the market in exchange for wages, while women, divested of their obligation to produce for domestic consumption or the market, were confined to the home, there to reproduce and to adorn the domestic hearth. Paradoxically, historical curiosity has been weakest about the most significant exception to this generalization, that is, about those women whose lives, at least on the surface, looked more like men's—women who, whatever their domestic role was, were drawn into the workshops and factories of the new industrial economies.

Women workers were long unexplored territory on the historical map for two reasons. The first was the general lack of interest in the history of all women. While the neglect of women's history has been rapidly and successfully redressed in the wake of the women's movement, women workers remain a shadowy presence, blotted out, as it were, by women who left clearer traces and who most resemble the historians who study them.

The second reason is that earlier historians of labor tended to perceive the working class as a homogeneous entity and to be preoccupied with its economic, institutional, and narrowly political expressions. In the last two decades historians have begun to resurrect the human and individual dimensions of the working class, to investigate the subjective experience of different kinds of workers. In the confluence of both these tendencies—the legitimization of women's history and the recognition of diversity among workers—the woman worker has finally begun to emerge as a distinct individual. For whatever women workers had in common with women of other classes or with men of their own class, they experienced industrialization in ways different from both. They can be subsumed neither in the history of women as a whole nor in that of the working class as a whole.

This book is about Russian women workers between 1880 and 1914, the formative years of Russian industrial capitalism. It is an examination of the significance of gender within class; of the woman worker's relationship to male workers, to the work process, to changes in family relations; and on the larger canvas, of her relationship to broad economic and political changes of the period. The historian of working-class women has a foot in two camps and must confront the dilemmas inherent in both. As one who studies women, I have tried to steer a course between two powerful temptations: the temptation to find a "hidden history," a record of women bolder, more assertive, more intelligently conscious of their oppression than others have acknowledged; and, conversely, the temptation to emphasize the most dismal aspects of women's undeniable oppression and thereby to evoke pity for them. As a historian of Russian labor, I have tried to avoid writing the history of women workers with the revolutionary "outcome" of 1917 in mind, while recognizing at the same time that the shadow cast backward in time by the events of that year cannot be completely ignored. For many decades historians of Russian labor, in an effort to explain 1917, divided workers simplistically into "backward" workers and "conscious" workers, a polarization that obscured as much as it explained. To the extent that the presence of women workers was acknowledged at all, they were placed unequivocally among the "backward" elements. Here the conflicts of the historian of women become enmeshed with those of the historian of Russia, producing yet another temptation, that of finding some golden mean, which may correspond as little to reality as the extremes it seeks to avoid. I hope that my analysis, elaborated in the following pages, reveals that the historical record of women workers in Russia is richer, more interesting, and more complex than can be captured in simple generalizations about backwardness and consciousness.

Whatever success I have had in resolving my dilemmas is in no small part thanks to my friends and colleagues. Reginald Zelnik not only read too many incarnations of the manuscript, but has been critic, source of encouragement, sober counselor on small and large matters for the whole of my scholarly life. My debt and gratitude to him are incalculable. Kenneth Kann read the manuscript in progress. I am the grateful beneficiary of his fine skills and sensitivity to the social historian's problems. Alistair McAuley and Mary McAuley read early versions of several sections of the manuscript, rescuing me from a number of serious pitfalls. Victoria Bonnell, Nicholas Riasanovsky, and Steven Smith read the penultimate draft, and with their valuable criticism encouraged me to think again and revise more than I would have wished. Zelda Bronstein, Ruth Rosen, John Spier, and Jerry Surh have shared with me bibliography, ideas, and ruminations on a multitude of issues directly and tangentially related to the preparation of this book. I also wish to thank all of these friends and colleagues for many years of intellectual nourishment, and collegial and personal support.

Financial aid for the research and writing of this book came from the International Research Exchanges Board (IREX), the American Philosophical Foundation, and the Mabel McLeod Lewis Foundation. Librarians and archivists at the following institutions made the research possible and pleasant: In Leningrad, the Central State Historical Archive, the Leningrad State Historical Archive, the Saltykov-Shchedrin Library, the Library of the Academy of Sciences; in Moscow, the Lenin Library; and the libraries of the University of Helsinki, the University of California at Berkeley, and the Hoover Institution.

R.L.G.

Berkeley, California

1

THE WORLD OF RUSSIAN LABOR

To understand how and why the experiences and characteristics of women workers were different from those of men we must begin with the world that men and women inhabited together, with the collective experience of the Russian working class in the process of its formation. In so doing, we must be cognizant of the distinctive features of Russian industrialization. Despite many important parallels with Western industrial development, Russia's industrialization proceeded at its own pace through the tangled landscape of its own traditions and culture.

Industry became a significant component of the Russian economy long after industrialization and its social and political consequences had drastically changed many parts of the West. In the middle of the nineteenth century Russia was poor and backward, her economy agrarian, and her social structure semifeudal. The land was owned by the state and a small landowning gentry and tilled by enserfed peasants who constituted the great majority of the population. Such industry as there was existed mainly to satisfy the state's military needs. Russia's ignominious defeat in the Crimean War was a shocking demonstration of the West's industrial and technological superiority, and the Russian autocracy was forced to acknowledge that Russia could not maintain her position among the major European powers without a comparable industrial base. Thus, in 1861 the autocracy emancipated the serfs, to create a free and mobile labor force in the first step toward stimulating industrial development. In the ensuing decades industry, and with it an industrial work force, grew rapidly, if fitfully. By 1914 there were roughly 3 million workers in a population of approximately 170 million people.[1]

There are no models of harmonious industrialization. The metaphor of revolution speaks for the dislocations inherent in the transition from agrarian to industrial society. In the Western European countries that made this transition over long periods of time, in some cases over two centuries, the entire society adjusted, however painfully, to changing economic forces. Russia's industry, however, grew rapidly in the crevices of an edifice not designed to accommodate it. The speed and concentration of industrial development in a society that remained otherwise overwhelmingly agrarian produced a singular disequilibrium between the old and the new and gave to Russia's emerging working class its particular characteristics.

For almost a century students of Russian labor have wrestled with the problem of defining the Russian working class, which differed in so many ways from its European and American counterparts.[2] While other nations drew heavily

1. For studies of Russian industrial development to 1917, see: William L. Blackwell, *The Beginnings of Russian Industrialization, 1800–1860* (Princeton, 1968), and *The Industrialization of Russia* (New York, 1970); Alexander Gerschenkron, *Economic Backwardness in Historical Perspective* (Cambridge, Mass., 1962); Arcadius Kahan, "Government Policies and the Industrialization of Russia," *Journal of Economic History*, 27 (1967), no. 4; M. C. Kaser, "Russian Entrepreneurship," in *The Cambridge Economic History of Europe*, vol. 7, pt. 2 (Cambridge, 1978); P. I. Liashchenko, *History of the National Economy of Russia to 1917* (New York, 1949); Roger Portal, "The Industrialization of Russia," in *The Cambridge Economic History of Europe*, vol. 6, pt. 2 (Cambridge, 1965); M. I. Tugan-Baranovskii, *Russkaia fabrika v proshlom i nastoiashchem* (St Petersburg, 1898), translated into English as *The Russian Factory in the 19th Century* (1970) by A. and C. Levin; T. H. Von Laue, *Sergei Witte and the Industrialization of Russia* (New York, 1963).

2. See, for example, Olga Crisp, "Labour and Industrialization in Russia," in *The Cambridge Economic History of Europe*, vol. 7, pt. 2 (Cambridge, 1978); E. M. Dement'ev, *Fabrika, chto ona daet naseleniiu i chto ona beret* (Moscow, 1893); L. M. Ivanov, ed., *Rabochii klass i rabochee dvizhenie v Rossii, 1861–1917* (Moscow, 1966), and *Rossiiskii proletariat: oblik, bor'ba, gegemoniia* (Moscow, 1970); Robert Johnson, *Peasant and Proletarian: The Working Class of Moscow in the Late Nineteenth Century* (New Brunswick, N. J., 1979); Arcadius Kahan, "The 'Hereditary Workers' Hypothesis and the Development of a Factory Labor Force in 18th and 19th Century Russia," in C. A. Anderson and M. J. Bowman, eds., *Education and Economic Devel-*

on peasant populations in the early stages of their industrialization, Russia was unique in the degree to which the path between agrarian life and factory life was traversed in both directions at once. Until the twentieth century the majority of factory workers were peasants who worked in the factory during the dormant agricultural seasons and returned to the land for planting and harvesting. The male factory worker frequently left elderly kin, wife, and children behind to care for the land during his seasonal work in the factory. Even workers who eventually abandoned the land to live year round within the factory radius, who married in the factory or brought their families with them from the village, often returned to the village for the important rituals of their lives—births, deaths, christenings, and the numerous holidays in the Russian religious calendar. The larger portion of their work lives and incomes may have derived from the factory rather than the land, but their identity, their emotional commitments, and an important part of their social lives remained in the countryside. By the early years of the twentieth century, the number of second- or third-generation workers with no ties to the countryside—known as hereditary workers—increased. But the rapid growth of the industrial labor force from the 1890s to 1914 could not have occurred through the utilization of only the labor of hereditary workers, and new peasant recruits were constantly nourishing the factory's growing appetite for working hands.

What, then, were Russian workers? Were they, for example, peasants who happened to work in the factory? Or were they proletarians in the classical sense of the word,

_____

opment (Chicago, 1965); Gaston V. Rimlinger, "The Expansion of the Labor Market in Capitalist Russia: 1861–1917," *Journal of Economic History,* 21 (1961), no. 2; M. K. Rozhkova, *Formirovanie kadrov promyshlennykh rabochikh v 60-nachale 80kh godak XIX v.* (Moscow, 1974); T. H. Von Laue, "Russian Labor Between Field and Factory," *California Slavic Studies,* 3 (1964), and "Russian Peasants in the Factory, 1892–1904," *Journal of Economic History,* 21 (1961), no. 1; Reginald E. Zelnik, "The Peasant and the Factory," in Wayne S. Vucinich, ed., *The Peasant in Nineteenth Century Russia* (Stanford, 1968), and "Russian Workers and the Revolutionary Movement," *Journal of Social History* (1972–73), no. 6.

that is, industrial wage earners, possessing neither captial nor tools? Although both alternatives have had enthusiastic proponents among historians, more recently a new perspective has emerged which perceives the Russian working class as a special hybrid with few analogues in other countries that had undergone industrialization. For we do not have sufficiently reliable statistics to ascertain with any precision the proportional relationship of hereditary workers to workers with strong peasant ties. We can only say that the small but growing contingent of fully assimilated workers existed side by side with workers who still defined themselves as peasants or who had ambivalent and vaccilating identities, depending on the degree of physical contact and emotional attachment to their peasant roots, as well as on their experiences in the factory.

Whatever the degree of transformation from peasant to proletarian Russian workers may have achieved, regional bonds were strong and persistent among them. The peasant's decision to seek factory work was influenced, first, by the capacity of the land to support life and, second, by the availability of factory work among other wage-earning options. Although the numbers of peasants in the late nineteenth century who could sustain themselves by agriculture alone diminished steadily throughout the Empire, agrarian conditions as well as the distribution of factories varied considerably from region to region, and peasants who worked in factories were preponderantly, if not exclusively, from the same provinces throughout our period.[3] The factory itself helped to perpetuate regional homogeneity by actively recruiting groups of workers from the same village or locality. Workers who ventured alone from village to factory gravitated toward their fellow villagers when they reached their destination. In a buyer's market, where the demand for work far exceeded the supply of jobs, finding work without help of contacts could be humiliating and difficult.

---

3. Barbara Anderson, *Internal Migration During Modernization in Late Nineteenth Century Russia* (Princeton, 1980); Crisp, pp. 376–378; Johnson, pp. 31–35.

One worker who tried it described his experiences in the city of Ekaterinoslav in the 1890s:

> Usually the job seekers gathered at the factory gates in the early morning and at lunch time, waiting for the factory administrators, whom they would ask for jobs. The seekers almost always exceeded the number of jobs. . . . The bosses, feeling in command of the situation, would speak to no one, or worse— when the applicants gathered at the gates in crowds of a hundred or more, the bosses, for their own amusement, would order the watchman to pour water on them.[4]

It is not surprising that job seekers preferred to avoid such humiliation by utilizing their regional connections. The same Ekaterinoslav worker related, "It seems that in this business many of my countrymen were very useful. . . . Although I did not know them personally, they had been acquainted with my grandfather and grandmother or were related to them in some way. They tried to help me in every way."[5]

To be sure, for some workers, mainly the highly skilled, occupational bonds would gradually replace village allegiances. The skilled St Petersburg worker, for example, who acquired his skills through a long and sustained apprenticeship in a city factory, felt himself to be very different from his recently arrived fellow villagers and preferred the company of other urbanized St Petersburg workers. But for most, seeking work through fellow villagers was only the first important link in a chain that reinforced the workers' ties to their rural origins. Workers tended to cluster with their fellow villagers for long periods of time, sometimes for the whole of their work lives, to live, to eat, and to entertain themselves.[6]

Work contracts reflected the worker's peasant ties. Generally, they were drawn up twice a year; one work period

4. K. Norinskii, "Moi vospominaniia," in *Ot Gruppy Blagoeva k "Soiuz Bor'by"* (*1886–1894*), 1921, p. 24.
5. Ibid., p. 22.
6. Johnson, pp. 67–79.

ran from the autumn, after the harvest, to Easter, and the second ran from Easter to July, the month of the greatest exodus back to the fields. Within these contractual periods, the working day was long and arduous. Many factories ran twenty-four hours a day, and night work was a standard feature in the worker's life. In 1885 the government passed a law prohibiting night work for women and for children under the age of seventeen in certain industries. The night shift was defined as 10:00 P.M. to 4:00 A.M., and consequently it only minimally mitigated the arduous day for the worker. A workday of sixteen to eighteen hours was common until it was reduced by law to eleven and a half hours in 1897.[7] These gains were offset by the employer's virtuosity in devising ways to add to the length of the working day. The least offensive was obliging workers to clean their machines before leaving the factory after the work shift had allegedly ended. Another more onerous practice was to require overtime work, sometimes unpaid. In the formal sense, overtime was a voluntary option, but few workers could refuse without risking their jobs. According to the law of 1897, the amount of overtime had to be written into the contract and paid. Most often observed in the breach, this law in any case left workers who were paid piece rates unprotected even by a legal fiction.

The most devious and widespread method of bringing down the worker's real earnings was the system of fines. In principle, fines were levied to penalize workers for infringements of factory discipline, to impose external constraints on a labor force that had not yet internalized the imperatives of industrial productivity; in practice, they ate into wages and assaulted the worker's dignity. Fines began with the workday. Most factories were built like walled fortresses, guarded by watchmen and surrounded by gates that

---

7. For studies of labor legislation in prerevolutionary Russia, see: A. N. Bykov, *Fabrichnoe zakonodatel'stvo i razvitie ego v Rossii* (St Petersburg, 1909); F. C. Giffen, "Prohibition of Night Work for Women and Young Persons," *Canadian Slavic Studies*, 2 (1969); V. Ia. Laverychev, *Tsarizm i rabochii vopros v Rossii (1861–1917 gg)* (Moscow, 1972); V. P. Litvinov-Filanskii, *Fabrichnoe zakonodatel'stvo i fabrichnaia inspektsiia v Rossii* (St Petersburg, 1900).

opened only to swallow up or disgorge their human con-
tents at the beginning and end of each shift. A St Petersburg patternmaker writing in the 1890s relates:

> Order at the factory was strict. . . . Let us begin with the enor-
> mous metal gates which, like a clock mechanism, slammed shut
> in the morning at the beginning of the workday and again after
> lunch. If you did not run in on time, the heavy gates would
> rattle to a close before your very nose—and then you had to
> wander about for half a day, losing a ruble as a fine for
> tardiness.[8]

Fines for tardiness could cost the worker a significant
portion of the daily wage. But tardiness was only one form
of "truancy," as it was called. There was a more inclusive
category of fines: for absence due to illness not verified by a
doctor's report, absence for drunkenness, for unauthorized
holidays, for marriages, births, and deaths, absences to care
for ailing family members, and, for women workers, absences for taking time out to feed nursing infants. Fines
were built into the production process, often for conditions
beyond the worker's control. Many factories set impossibly
high production quotas for full payment of wages and
made deductions for the uncompleted work. Workers were
fined for damaging or losing tools, for not creating perfect
products from shoddy materials. By law, fines were to be
clearly defined and enumerated in the so-called workbook
given out to the worker with the contract, but it was not
unusual for factories to impose fines for infringements
never mentioned in the books. As a factory inspector noted,
"It would actually be hard to imagine a worker who could
meet all the demands set for him, who would not be subject
to fines and deductions no matter what his effort and skill."[9]

Management's contemptuous attitude toward workers
was expressed in fines imposed for disobedience, insolence,
bad language, immoral behavior, and bad character. When

---

8. Semen Kanatchikov, *Iz istorii moego bytiia* (Moscow and Leningrad, 1929), p. 7.
9. P. A. Peskov, *Fabrichnyi byt vladimirskoi gubernii. Otchet za 1882–1883* (St
Petersburg, 1884), p. 68.

the government suggested that fines for "rudeness and disobedience" be eliminated, employers claimed that this
would "undermine discipline and deprive factory owners of
the means to maintain and enforce order and respect for
stewards of their establishments."[10]

Humiliation was a daily experience for workers. At many
factories, they were rudely searched as they entered and left
the factory premises, allegedly to prevent theft. Equally degrading were physical and verbal abuse and the absence of
what was called "polite address." The Russian language, like
other European languages, has a polite form of address
used in formal situations and to superiors, and a familiar
form used to address intimates, children, servants, and ani-
mals. Workers were obliged to address supervisory personnel in the polite form (*na vy*), while they themselves, as a
matter of course, were addressed in the familiar (*na ty*)—a
practice which they felt to be demeaning, a vestige of the
former master-serf relationship.

Russian factories, large and small, technologically primitive or sophisticated, were notorious for neglecting the
workers' health and safety. While knowledge of advanced
industrial safeguards, processes, and machinery was available to and understood by Russian industrialists, they frequently preferred outmoded and physically demanding
hand processes because labor power was plentiful, and it
was cheaper than investment in machinery. With monoto-
nous regularity factory inspectors deplored working conditions: the noxious fumes or dust in certain industrial processes aggravated by inadequate ventilation; the hazardous
overcrowding of machinery on the factory floor; the primitive toilet facilities that created foul-smelling and unhy-
gienic environments. In addition to health and safety hazards in the factory, disease of all kinds spread rapidly and
easily within the factory enclosure. Yet, like all of Russia's
poor, workers had little access to medical care. In the countryside, local governments lacked the resources to provide

10. Laverychev, p. 62.

the rural population, agrarian or industrial, with regular professional medical personnel, not to speak of hospitals and medication. In cities, where doctors were more plentiful and medical services of better quality, workers could rarely afford to take advantage of them.

In 1866, in response to recurrent cholera epidemics, the government issued an edict requiring factory owners to provide one hospital bed for every one hundred workers. Subsequently, countless "obligatory rulings" were enacted by the local arms of the central bureaucracy, which, on paper, set reasonably high standards for medical care. But there were no provisions for enforcing these rulings. Twenty years after the first edict, factory inspectors found that medical care for workers was a fiction. Whether a factory worker had access to minimal first aid, diagnosis, and medicine or hospital care for enduring illness continued to depend entirely on the factory owner's benevolence. In the Central Industrial Region, where factory owners had a stronger tradition of paternalistic concern for workers than elsewhere, some form of medical care was more common, although properly trained doctors were rarely available on a regular basis. Usually workers were treated by a "feldsher," a kind of paramedic whose expertise was often barely greater than the patient's. St Petersburg factories were scandalously derelict in providing medical care. By the turn of the century only one large factory employed a doctor on a regular basis; he received patients two hours daily, which meant, of course, that he was not available to treat accidents that occurred in his absence. Among 668 Moscow factories in 1904, only 246 had outpatient clinics, and of these only 170 had fully trained doctors.[11]

Venereal disease, especially in the cities, was a grave social and medical problem, for workers served as an effective transmission belt back to the countryside. Both diagnosis and treatment were woefully lacking, as the following description

11. S. N. Semanov, *Peterburgskie rabochie nakanune pervoi russkoi revoliutsii* (Moscow and Leningrad, 1966), pp. 123–144.

of a factory medical examination in the 1890s indicates; the worker-narrator tells how the workers were examined for venereal disease before their periodic pilgrimages back to the country:

> The examinations were made primitively and coarsely and can hardly be said to have yielded results. When we went to collect our earnings at the bookkeeper's office, a doctor was waiting there. We lined up, pulled down our trousers, and showed the necessary part of our bodies to him. He poked around with a pencil, conveyed the results of his "examination" to the book-keeper, and if we were clean we were given our pay. Certainly at the plant there were many workers with venereal disease, but I do not know of a single case discovered by that doctor during the examinations.[12]

Before 1903 only 28 percent of Russian workers were covered by some kind of accident insurance; like medical care, the provision of accident benefits and pensions was at the discretion of the individual factory owner. The fortunate workers whose employers joined private insurance companies were nonetheless poorly remunerated for temporary or permanent disability. Payments were so low that, as one observer remarked, they were less than the selling price of a medium-sized cow.[13] In 1903 the government passed an accident insurance law for industrial workers. It did not cover workers at state factories or in transport, construction, and agriculture. Workers who lost the ability to work because of an injury incurred on the job were entitled to two-thirds of their wages. A factory owner who could prove that an accident was the result of the worker's "malicious intent" or "carelessness" was relieved of all financial obligation, and while the worker could appeal through the courts, this was a long, costly process which few could afford.

That workers tolerated this array of indignities—filthy, overcrowded, and dangerous workplaces; insecurity; and

12. Kanatchikov, p. 44.
13. K. A. Pazhitnov, *Polozhenie rabochego klassa v Rossii* (St Petersburg, 1906), p. 101.

humiliating treatment—speaks for their low self-esteem, reinforced by the hard economic facts of life in a market
glutted with working hands. It is important to keep in mind
that at whatever stage workers were in the transformation
from peasant to proletarian between 1880 and 1914, the
legacy of serfdom weighed heavily upon them. Many adult
workers in the 1880s and 1890s had lived their formative
years as serfs. By the turn of the century far fewer workers
had endured serfdom directly, but expectations of oppression and habits of servility were not easily obliterated in one
generation.

* * *

The worker's home was rarely a refuge from the factory.
In 'rural factories workers sometimes lived in their native
villages. But most rural factories were obliged to provide
housing for their workers and, as more workers abandoned
the land at the outset of the twentieth century, for workers'
families as well. Factory owners were as reluctant to invest
in housing as in safe, hygienic workplaces. In the 1880s one
factory inspector reported enthusiastically that several factories in the Central Industrial Region had constructed
small, individual stone houses for married workers, each
with a chicken coop and a small kitchen garden. They were
no worse than the average peasant dwelling—better, indeed, than many—and the workers were pleased with them.
The inspector therefore assumed that factory owners would
be inspired to house workers in this fashion in the future.[14]
Contrary to his optimistic prediction, this kind of living arrangement remained an anomaly.

The majority of factory dwellings in rural areas and small
towns consisted of barracks, which were, in the words of
Maxim Gorky, "like the dwellings of prehistoric peoples."[15]
Barracks usually contained several large rooms, crammed

---

14. Peskov, p. 88. See also, F. P. Pavlov, *Za desiat' let praktiki* (*otryvki vospominanii, vpechatlenii i nabliudenii iz fabrichnoi zhizni*) (Moscow, 1901), pp. 57–58.
15. Quoted in N. K. Druzhinin, *Usloviia byta rabochikh v dorevoliutsionnoi Rossii*
(*po dannym biudzhetnykh obsledovanii*) (Moscow, 1958), p. 86.

full of wooden bunks either freestanding or in tiers.
Workers frequently slept in their beds in shifts. Bedding
was rare, and workers slept on hay or on their own clothing.
There was no other furniture, no toilet or washing facilities.
Ventilation was similarly remarkable for its absence. A communal kitchen for the entire barrack population might be
placed on one floor or in a separate hut. In the most fortunate circumstances, married workers and their families
were housed in rooms apart from single workers, several
families to a room. One observer, commenting on an especially lavish barrack, which boasted a communal kitchen on
each floor as well as toilets consisting of a hole in the cement, noted that there as elsewhere "the family's life, even
its most intimate aspects, goes on under the gaze of others.
In the best cases the beds of a married couple are surrounded by curtains. The children, including adolescents,
sleep together without distinctions of sex and age."[16]

Worse yet than barracks were barns built by the workers
themselves, which were, in the opinion of one factory inspector, "more like dog kennels or chicken pens than like
dwellings for human beings."[17] To be housed at all, however badly, was still an improvement over the conditions in
some factories, notably in the textile industry, where
workers worked, ate, and slept by the side of their machines. Factory owners made a virtue of this arrangement,
claiming that the workers were, after all, "village people
who have not yet lost their country habits and attitudes;
they view sleeping on the loom as reminiscent of their own
homes."[18]

In cities, workers had greater choice in housing. But since
most workers could not afford public transportation, they

16. A. Iu. Kats, "Naselenie Pokrovskoi Manufaktury (dmitrovskogo uezda) i
ego zhilishchnye usloviia," *Svedenie o zaraznykh bolezniakh i sanitarno-vrachebnoi organizatsii moskovskoi gubernii* (1910), no. 10, p. 664.
17. Peskov, p. 89.
18. P. A. Peskov, *Sanitarnoe issledovanie fabrik po obrabotke voloknistykh veshchestv v
gorode Moskve.* Vyp. 2. Trudy kommissii, uchrezhdennoi g. moskovskim General-
Gubernatorom, Kn. V. A. Dolgorukovym, dlia osmotra fabrik i zavodov v Moskve
(Moscow, 1882).

lived mainly in factory slums close to the factory.[19] A typical factory neighborhood in St Petersburg was described as

> an entire forest of factory chimneys, throwing out clouds of black smoke obscuring the already grey Petersburg sky. The factory buildings, houses, streets, and bustling crowds of people were covered with a thick layer of soot. From everywhere rushed the massive rhythmical sounds—the rattle of huge rollers, the penetrating clank of iron bars, the heat of steam hammers which shook the earth . . . and above all these sounds in the air hung the uninterrupted hum of huge steam boilers lying on the ground like giant caterpillars.[20]

In neighborhoods like this, which were similar to factory districts earlier in Europe, workers lived according to their means: in a room shared with many others, a small corner of a kitchen rented from a family of workers who could not afford to keep an entire apartment for themselves. Even in private apartments, sharing a bed was the norm. A worker from Moscow of the 1890s described his quarters in the following way:

> My room and board was not far from the factory in a huge stinking house populated by haulers, cabbies, and day-laborers. We were fifteen men renting the apartment as a collective. Some were bachelors, others had wives in the countryside who looked after the land. I was put in a small dark room without windows—in other words, a closet. It was filthy and stuffy, full of cockroaches and bugs and smelled acutely of "humanity." In this closet stood two wooden cots. My fellow villager and guardian slept on one, and his son and I on the other.[21]

The housing situation deteriorated further in the twentieth century. Rents began to escalate in the 1890s and continued to rise thereafter. In St Petersburg, for example, although the number of apartments doubled between the

---

19. James Bater, "Spatial Mobility in Moscow and St Petersburg in the Late Imperial Era," paper delivered at conference, The Social History of Russian Labor, University of California, Berkeley, March 1982. Pp. 15–21.

20. Kanatchikov, pp. 68–69.

21. Ibid., p. 10.

1860s and 1900, the number of inhabitants per apartment increased by the expedient of the "corner habitation," the subdivision and resubdivision of apartments, tranforming every available space into sleeping quarters. In 1904 two-thirds of single workers and two-fifths of married workers lived in such "corners," and conditions were similar in Moscow and other cities.[22]

The nadir of living accommodations was the flophouse, which emerged on a fairly large scale in the late 1870s. Subsidized by charitable organizations and designed to provide cheap night shelter for the temporarily homeless, by 1910 flophouses had become a permanent institution, often housing people for long periods of time. In St Petersburg they provided 6,200 beds and, entirely against city ordinances, in fact housed many more people than the number of beds. Filthy and overcrowded, the flophouse was a breeding ground for recurring typhus and cholera epidemics.[23]

The highest priority in the urban worker's budget was housing, and within the limits described, the quality of housing improved as income rose. But even the highly skilled worker had difficulty making ends meet. From the 1880s to the outbreak of World War I, nominal wages rose considerably, but the cost of living rose faster. In 1910 budget studies showed that a family in St Petersburg required 600–700 rubles per year to purchase basic necessities, yet the average wage of metalworkers, one of the best paid sectors of the labor force, was 516 rubles per year, and in the lowest-paying industry, food processing, the average was 268 rubles.[24] The wage scale and the cost of living were higher in St Petersburg than in other cities, but the relationship of one to the other was similar throughout the Russian

22. James H. Bater, *St Petersburg: Industrialization and Change* (Montreal, 1976), p. 336. See also M. I. Pokrovskaia, "Vopros o deshevykh kvartirakh dlia rabochego klassa," *Vestnik Evropy* (1901), no. 7, pp. 188–203.
23. Bater, *St Petersburg,* pp. 337–338.
24. See M. Davidovich, *Peterburgskie tekstil'nye rabochie* (Moscow, 1919). For workers' wages as well as other aspects of the workers' standard of living, see also Iu. I. Kir'ianov, *Zhiznennyi uroven' rabochikh Rossii* (Moscow, 1979), and E. E. Kruze, *Polozhenie rabochego klassa Rossii v 1900–1914* gg (Leningrad, 1976).

Empire. The fundamental characteristic of the worker's budget was disequilibrium. Most workers were in debt all their lives.

Normally, the rural factory, far from town facilities, ran a shop which sold basic provisions. The shops were profit-making enterprises for the factory owners, who took advantage of their captive consumers to charge inflated prices for products of poor quality. Workers bought provisions on credit, and their debts were deducted from their wages, another mechanism for keeping them indebted to the factory. The high prices and poor quality of food in the shops, the burden of eternal indebtedness, often made the company store the first target of looting and destruction during periods of labor unrest.

Unmarried workers attempted to cope with the problems of survival by forming living and eating collectives, known as artels. Artels were frequently composed of workers from the same village or region. As quantity and quality of food were determined by the wages of the artel's members, there was a division within village groupings into workers whose earnings were roughly equivalent. Workers in artels ate noticeably better than those who fended for themselves, but, as a serious student of workers' lives commented, the workers' diet consisted of "an excess of carbohydrates, insufficiency of fat, and protein starvation."[25] The daily fare and communal dining habits of a worker's artel were described as follows:

> At 11 A.M. every day, as soon as the bell for dinner break rang, we ran eagerly to the apartment and immediately sat at the table on which already steamed an enormous basin of cabbage soup. All fifteen of us ate from a common bowl with wooden spoons. Bits of meat floated in the soup. First we gobbled the liquid, and as it disappeared we waited tensely for the signal. Someone tapped a spoon on the rim of the bowl and pronounced the awaited "go to it!" Then the race for the few floating bits of meat began. The most adroit got the most meat.

25. Druzhinin, p. 68.

After the cabbage soup we had buckwheat groats with pork fat or fried potatoes.[26]

The conditions of the Russian worker's life, especially in the cities, did not lend themselves to traditional family life. The extended family of peasant culture could not survive in the factory world, and workers' families were small and for the most part nuclear. Workers who retained close ties to the village left their children or sent them to be cared for by kin in the countryside. This practice disrupted even the new form of family life that emerged with urbanization and industrialization, but it was the only alternative for workers who could afford neither the housing, the feeding, nor the care of their children. Workers who had severed their ties to the land paid older children or elderly women to look after small children if they could afford it. Most simply left children untended; involuntary neglect contributed heavily to Russia's extraordinarily high infant mortality.[27]

The squalor and poverty of the Russian workers' lives, the long hours of arduous labor for which they were so miserably remunerated, left them with little time, energy, or money for recreation. Nor were amusements and social amenities readily accessible. The rich cultural offerings of the cities were beyond their means and probably not to their taste. Even simpler pleasures were hard to come by. Literacy, for example, was very low in the Russian Empire, lagging far behind most other European nations. In 1897 only 21.1 percent of the entire population was literate. Among industrial workers literacy was impressively higher than among peasants—50.3 percent—and by 1914 literacy among workers had increased still further.[28] A tiny minority of highly skilled workers were educated as well as literate and developed their literary gifts, as we have seen from workers' memoirs quoted here; but for the majority of so-called literate workers literacy meant little more than the

26. Kanatchikov, p. 10.
27. See David Ransel, ed., *The Family in Imperial Russia* (Urbana, Ill., 1978).
28. A. G. Rashin, *Naselenie Rossii za 100 let* (Moscow, 1956), pp. 284–310.

ability to scratch out one's name and read a simple text. A worker's account pithily sums up the cultural ambience of a St Petersburg factory neighborhood in the 1890s:

> The entire working-class population of Smolensk tract lived in crowded, filthy, and primitive conditions. The city government extracted huge taxes from the workers, but completely ignored their well-being. Throughout the tract there were many taverns, beer halls and churches, but not a single cultural establishment. For 60,000 people there were only two shabby theatres.[29]

Little wonder, then, that alcoholism was endemic among workers:

> Twice a month on Saturday payday, our artel became the scene of a wild debauch. Some workers, upon getting their wages, went directly from the factory to the tavern and the saloon; others, more dandyish, came home to change clothes. But everyone would return home late at night or on Sunday morning morose, sullen, frequently battered, and with hangovers.[30]

A great problem among the peasantry as well, alcoholism was more clearly observable among workers clustered in the factory ghettos. The dislocations inherent in the transition from agrarian to industrial life, the wrench from daily concourse in kinship circles, and the aridity of the worker's environment were blamed for the widespread consumption of vodka, primarily by male workers. But workers' alcoholism was the alcoholism of the poor. One observer, irritated by the moralistic judgments made by the upper class, noted that the workers' absolute expenditure on alcohol was actually quite small: "This undermines the opinion that workers would be in clover if only they did not drink. With the sum of money they spend on vodka, you cannot buy much clover."[31]

29. Kanatchikov, p. 79. See also Pavlov, pp. 77–79.
30. Kanatchikov, p. 11.
31. I. M. Shaposhnikov, "Biudzhety rabochikh odnoi iz fabrik bogorodskogo uezda v sviazi s pitaniem i zabolevaemost'iu," *Svedeniia o zaraznykh bolezniakh i sanitarno-vrachebnoi organizatsii moskovskoi gubernii* (1910), no. 1, p. 17.

If the soil of factory and city life was barren of the nutri-
ents necessary to preserve traditional family life and familiar relationships and recreations intact, the steady two-way
flow between factory and village provided at least intermittent relief. It is no wonder that workers clung to the village
long after it had ceased to play a significant part in their
economic survival. Peasant diversions, transplanted to the
new environment, may not have survived with their original
vigor, but surely continued to palliate the workers' hardships and disorientation in the factory. Young people must
have courted, sung, and danced in the barracks courtyard
as they had in the village. The church, perhaps declining in
the power to succor, remained a significant element in the
lives of many. Yet, over time, some features of factory life
became appealing substitutes for what was lost. Workers
returning to the village were reported to display proudly
their German accordions, their city fashions and dances,
and their new urban sophistication. While in the main illiterate or semiliterate, workers increasingly surpassed their
peasant kin in the ability to read and write, and a new world
of possibilities began to take shape with literacy. However
powerful the sway of rural habits, tastes, and commitments
on Russian workers, however incomplete their proletarianization compared with workers of the West, factory life was
molding a new identity. Their growing intolerance for the
bleak and wretched conditions of factory life attest to an
emerging sense of their collective interests and of their
worth as workers.

The history of Russian workers' attempts to improve
their lives in the face of tenacious resistance has something
in common with the history of all industrializing countries,
for the reluctance of government and industry to ameliorate the workers' condition was not unique to Russia. Russian social and political traditions, however, created special
obstacles to the formulation of workable solutions to the
problems of the burgeoning working class.

For centuries Russia's autocracy had been the sole source
of legislation in every area of life. The theoretical justifica-

tion for unfettered autocratic rule was that the tsar was an independent force, a stern but benevolent master whose task it was to stand above society's contentious elements in order to reconcile them. The elements beneath the tsar that constituted society, however, were not equal to one another. The landowning class was meant to execute the tsar's will over the peasantry and to be, like the tsar, a stern and benevolent master. If the landowner erred in his obligation to dispense benevolence as well as discipline, the serf had no right to insubordination, but did have the right to appeal to the ultimate arbitrator, the tsar. The assumptions that governed the relationship of tsar and landowner to peasants were applied wholesale to workers.[32] Given their ties to the land, it was argued, workers did not constitute a separate class for which it was necessary to alter the traditional hierarchy or to legislate separately. This argument was undermined by growing and persistent labor unrest. The autocracy's goals then came into conflict with one another: how to maintain the traditional hierarchy, support and encourage industry, and at the same time, assuage workers' discontent. Balancing these goals was a precarious business, but in principle (and increasingly in practice) the government grudgingly acquiesced to legislation in favor of workers; it did so in part because it perceived the demands of workers to be just, and in part because of the hope that economic concessions would prevent the translation of economic into political discontent. Industrialists, on the other hand, generally opposed concessions to the workers which threatened their purses or their control of the worker. Neither the tsar's dilemma nor the conflict between government and industry were resolved.

But, until 1905, they were in perfect accord on one point: workers should not be allowed to take autonomous and collective action in their own defense, nor should they partici-

32. Kahan, "Government Policies"; Gaston V. Rimlinger, "Autocracy and the Factory Order in Early Russian Industrialization," *Journal of Economic History*, 20 (1960), no. 1, and "The Management of Labor Protest in Tsarist Russia, 1870–1905," *International Review of Social History*, 5 (1960).

pate in the debates over the legislation considered to protect
them. All effective forms of workers' self-help and expression, including the strike, were forbidden and punishable as
crimes. Nonetheless, in the absence of legal channels for
peaceful settlement of grievances, the Russian workers' only
recourse was to withhold their labor. From the 1870s
workers engaged in strikes at the risk of severe punishment—loss of job, exile, or prison terms at hard labor.
Strikes ranged from isolated spontaneous outbursts of rage
against low wages, fines, living conditions, illegal firings,
and other abuses, to longer and more organized protests
demanding substantive changes in industrial relations.
From the 1890s strike activity, encouraged by socialist agitation, increased to such an extent that the government was
forced to modify its prohibition against workers' associations, hoping to do so, however, without relinquishing its
age-old paternalistic authority. In the early 1900s government agents were empowered to create workers' associations designed to give workers carefully controlled and limited scope for the expression of their economic grievances.
This curious experiment, known disparagingly as police socialism, was, predictably, popular with workers and irritat-
ing to industrialists. Before long, the government, too, had
second thoughts and brought an end to it. In 1904, however, the government permitted a similar workers' association to be formed in St Petersburg under the guidance of a
priest, Father Gapon.[33] This time workers' aspirations over-
ran the confines of the government's intentions. At a particularly sensitive moment—with opposition to the tsar
growing over the shoddy prosecution of the Russo-Japanese
War and in the middle of a strike of major proportions in
St Petersburg—the workers of the Gapon organization
mounted a massive demonstration. On January 9, 1905, a

---

33. For police socialism, see J. Schneiderman, *Sergei Zubatov and Revolutionary
Marxism* (Ithaca, N.Y., 1976); W. Sablinsky, *The Road to Bloody Sunday* (Princeton,
1976); Gerald Surh, "Petersburg's First Mass Labor Organization: The Assembly
of Russian Workers and Father Gapon," *Russian Review*, 40 (1981), nos. 3–4; and
"Petersburg Workers in 1905: Strikes, Workplace Democracy and the Revolution,"
Ph.D. diss., University of California, Berkeley, 1979.

huge contingent of workers and their families came before the tsar's palace with a petition for redress of grievances. The tsar's troops opened fire on the peacefully assembled workers, an event aptly called Bloody Sunday. It unleashed the revolution of 1905.

In October of 1905, workers of all varieties—artisanal, industrial, and intellectual—erupted in a massive Empire-wide general strike described by Lenin as the dress rehearsal to 1917.[34] The strike demands of 1905, fulfilling the autocracy's worst fears, went far beyond bread-and-butter issues as workers joined with other elements in society whose discontent had long festered in the oppressive social and political climate of tsarist Russia. This dramatic expression of opposition to the status quo provoked, among other things, a grudging acknowledgment on the part of autocracy and industry that Russia's workers, whatever their ties to the land, whatever their degree of illiteracy, ignorance, and naiveté, could no longer be pacified by dilatory policies and paternalistic, half-hearted legislation. The inchoate working classes were coalescing into an independent force that had to be recognized for its potential disruptive power if not for its human needs.

In the first chaotic months of the 1905 revolution workers formed hundreds of unions. Recognizing the inevitability of workers' participation in the issues that affected their lives, the state soon granted legal status to workers' organizations. Further, a legislature was created, the first in Russia's history, and although the franchise was limited, it gave the newly formed political parties that spoke for workers a public forum. Neither unions nor the legislature, however, were destined to play the same important role in Russian workers' fate as they did in the West. The ebb and flow of legal and autonomous activity was compressed into little more than one decade and, at that, under deteriorating conditions. Once the revolutionary fervor of

---

34. For the 1905 revolution, see Laura Engelstein, *Moscow, 1905: Working Class Organization and Political Conflict* (Stanford, 1982); Solomon M. Schwarz, *The Russian Revolution of 1905* (Chicago, 1967); Surh, "Petersburg Workers in 1905."

1905 waned, and state and industry no longer felt threatened by acute unrest, they reverted to traditional postures. Militant workers, who participated in unions and strikes, remained vulnerable to loss of job, blacklisting, administrative exile, and prison. The combination of obstruction and harassment and persistently adverse economic conditions sapped the vitality of the strike movement, unions, and political activity. True, in the interrevolutionary years, government and industry attempted to hammer out their differences on the labor question. Committees of government representatives and industry met independently and jointly, proposed and counterproposed. Since their fundamental perspectives and the attendant dilemmas had not seriously changed under the impact of the events of 1905, the results were minimal. The Russian worker remained overworked, ill-fed, badly housed, poor, and insecure.[35]

In 1912, workers once again turned to the strike as the most effective expedient for gaining control over their lives.[36] The outbreak of World War I interrupted the revitalized strike movement as it did all aspects of Russian life, and for awhile held workers' discontent in abeyance. But the dislocations and economic privations of the war were especially trying for workers. Their rage and discontent found more radical, direct, and satisfying release, first in the February Revolution of 1917, which destroyed the tsarist order, and then in the October Revolution, which initiated a radically new era in social, economic, and political relations.

* * *

35. S. I. Antonova, *Vliianie stolypinskoi reformy na izmenenie v sostave rabochego klassa* (Moscow, 1951); Victoria Bonnell, *Roots of Rebellion: Workers' Politics and Organizations in St Petersburg and Moscow, 1900–1914* (Berkeley, 1983); Leopold Haimson, "The Problem of Social Stability in Urban Russia, 1905–1917," *Slavic Review*, pt. 1 (1964), vol. 23, no. 4; pt. 2 (1965), vol. 24, no. 1; Geoffrey Hosking, *The Russian Constitutional Experiment* (Cambridge, 1973); Ruth Roosa, "Workers' Insurance Legislation and the Role of the Industrialist in the Period of the Third State Duma," *Russian Review*, 34 (1975), no. 4.

36. Arutiunov, G. A., *Rabochee dvizhenie v Rossii v periode novogo revoliutsionnogo pod'ema. 1910–1914 gg* (Moscow, 1975); Kruze, E. E., *Peterburgskie rabochie v 1912–1914 godakh* (Moscow and Leningrad, 1961).

In the foregoing account I have outlined the broad social and economic forces that shaped Russia's factory work force and that provided workers with a framework of shared experiences and characteristics. Within this framework, however, there were significant differences among workers, which, however blurred, overlapping, and complex, we must unravel to make sense of the distinction of gender that will preoccupy us in the following pages. With due regard for the perils of oversimplification, I will attempt to structure the differences among workers in a rough hierarchical order according to the degree of skill they possessed.

The highly skilled worker was at the top of the hierarchy. As institutionalized vocational training in tsarist Russia was in its infancy, most workers learned their skills on the job through long periods of apprenticeship. Literacy, whether a prerequisite for or a consequence of skill, was very high among skilled workers. Skilled workers earned relatively high wages and could afford a more comfortable life within the limits described earlier. Equally important, they commanded respect from management, for they were hard to replace and were therefore not easily threatened with insults, fines, or firing. Less-skilled workers respected them as well, for their literacy and sophistication, their competence and control over the work process. The skilled workers' bonds to the peasant village, already weakened through long apprenticeship, were often severed as these workers developed a sense of pride and identification with occupation and, with more money, leisure, and literacy, a more comfortable assimilation into the factory or urban environment. Those who had lived in the city for a long time were often indistinguishable from other lower-class urban dwellers. They wore their shirts with starched collar tucked into neatly pressed, narrow trousers, and "on holidays some even wore derby hats. . . . They carried themselves solidly with a sense of their own worth, swore only indoors under great pressure or on payday when they got drunk—some not even then."[37]

---

37. Kanatchikov, p. 17.

The greatest proportion of workers were unskilled or semiskilled. They did poorly paid jobs that required neither literacy nor long training. Competing with similarly illiterate and unskilled peasant job-seekers, they were easily replaced and consequently had little leverage with management. For the most part, unskilled workers retained lively connections to the countryside, sending a large portion of their meager wages to kin in the village, returning to the land for seasonal work and for recreation. Rewarded with neither decent wages, pride in the work process, nor respect, with one foot in the factory and one in the peasant world, the unskilled worker was more likely to have an amorphous and vacillating sense of identification with the factory than the skilled worker.

While all industries required a range of skilled and unskilled labor, heavy industries, especially metal processing and engineering, employed a far greater proportion of Russia's skilled workers. Skilled workers were a minority among the largely unskilled and semiskilled workers in light industry and were employed mainly to maintain and repair machinery. Thus, despite some mingling of the skilled and the unskilled in factories as well as in their neighborhoods and taverns, the differences of skill and its concomitants—literacy, urbanization, competence, and sophistication—were profoundly internalized by workers themselves. A skilled worker left an account of his visit to a textile factory in the 1890s, which he undertook as if he were conducting an anthropological expedition, complete with a "disguise" to help him pass unnoticed among the natives. His graphic description underscored the gap he perceived between his own milieu of skilled, urbanized workers and that of the unskilled textile workers:

> The whole crowd of lads and girls reminded me of a village in the provinces. The girls were striking for the color of their attire, which was completely different from city wear . . . and the lads wore their trousers tucked into high boots . . . grey

homespun shirts cinched at the waist with raggedy belts. Others simply wore rags tied around their bare feet.[38]

Another skilled worker recalled more succinctly that workers in light industry seemed to him "to be almost another race of workers."[39]

Women workers were a "race" within a "race," as it were, a special subcategory on the lowest rungs of this hierarchy. The female contingent of the Russian industrial labor force underwent significant alterations in the period under consideration. It grew in absolute size and in proportion to the male labor force, which in itself speaks of important changes in the peasant world from which women came and in the factory world which accepted them, indeed sought them out. The characteristics we have singled out to describe the entire work force changed for women workers as well: literacy, relationship to the land, urbanization, accumulated work experience. Yet, throughout our period women remained exclusively among the unskilled and semiskilled workers. Further, they were confined mainly to jobs in light industry, for it was only in the last years of tsarist Russia that they joined the ranks of unskilled labor in heavy industry. In other words, gender transcended all other distinctions among workers to keep women in a special place within the factory world.

The strength and tenacity of gender to influence the woman worker's destiny is something of a chicken-and-egg problem, requiring that we sort out carefully the interaction of tradition and cultural legacy with changing economic and social forces, the interplay between palpable physical determinants, such as the double burden of wage work and domestic responsibilities, and the psychological influences of the work experience itself. We must look as well outside the factory into the values of the larger culture which be-

38. I. V. Babushkin, *Vospominaniia Ivana Vasil'evicha Babushkina, 1893–1900* (Moscow, 1955), pp. 29–30.

39. A. Fisher, *V Rossii i v Anglii* (Moscow, 1922), p. 17.

queathed to factory owner and male worker alike an attitude of condescension to women and to the responses of women workers to the subordinate status which they shared with women of all classes. As a woman worker lamented in 1908: "We women have two burdens. At the factory we serve the boss, and at home the husband is our ruler. Nowhere do they see the woman as a real person."[40] We turn now to the study of the special characteristics of women workers in the hope that the real person will emerge.

40. Tsentral'nyi Gosudarstvennyi Istoricheskii Arkhiv v Leningrade (hereafter TsGIA), f. 150, op. 1, d. 154, l. 139 (*Stanok tekstil'shika [1908], no. 1*).

2
PEASANT WOMEN AND THEIR
WORK

Most women workers in Russia began life as peasants. They
abandoned traditional agrarian life, as did men, because the
land would no longer support Russia's burgeoning population in the decades after the emancipation of the serfs. Although the underlying impulse to leave the land was the
same for men and women, the woman came to the factory
according to a rhythm that was governed by her sex and
her role in the peasant household and economy. She came
with different life and work experiences, different expectations and aspirations, which tempered her experiences as a
factory worker and marked them off in significant ways
from those of her male counterpart. We must, therefore,
briefly examine the life of the peasant woman, her status in
the family and the community, and more specifically, her
place in the peasant economy: the work that women had
traditionally performed in the countryside and how it
changed during the period under consideration.

The core of peasant life from which all relationships radi-
ated and which determined values, obligations, rewards,
and behavior was land. And land was a male attribute. Although the land was not the private property of any individual male, the right to the land devolved from father to
son or, in the absence of sons, to other male relatives. Similarly, the homestead, kitchen garden, farm implements, and
domestic artifacts were the collective property of the household and passed indivisibly from one generation of males to
the next. Women had rights only over their dowries, which

consisted primarily of clothing and kitchen utensils, occasionally a sheep or a cow. As a student of Russian peasant society put it, "Peasant law did not consider women, strictly speaking, members of a household. . . . Therefore, a woman did not hold property rights over a household if male members of a family lived."[1]

Marriage was virtually universal and patrilocal. The peculiarities of patrilocalism in Russian contributed to the woman's instability and contingency within the household:

> As a girl the essence of her existence is to leave her own family for a strange one, that is, to marry. When she is married— taken [*vziata*], that is—from [her own] family, she is bound to the [new] family only by her husband; should he die, she can return to her kin. She may, of course, remain in her husband's family, but in both cases only to work according to her strength in return for sustenance. In other words, there is no solidity to the woman's position, no organic knots to bind her to the family. This is one of the reasons why the woman is at the bottom of the family. Her entire significance . . . consists of undertaking every task assigned to her in the household economy and providing it with new members—most important, sons, who are its real representatives. Girls are accepted only as a necessary evil.[2]

The multiple-family household, controlled by the male parent, was the most prevalent form of family organization until the revolution. The patriarch's authority over the household's life from the smallest detail to the largest included the right to sexual intercourse with daughters-in-law, a practice sufficiently common to merit a special word in the Russian language—*snokhachestvo*. Adult sons had a consultative voice in common family affairs and dominance over their wives. As for the woman, "She may not participate in

1. Theodore Shanin, *The Awkward Class* (Oxford, 1972), p. 222.
2. Aleksandra Efimenko, *Izsledovaniia narodnoi zhizni* (Moscow, 1884), pp. 68–69. A married woman's return to her own kin was not welcomed. Her labor was rarely valued, and her sons were superfluous, since they were not entitled to be counted in land redistribution. See also Peter Czap, "Marriage and the Peasant Joint Family in the Era of Serfdom," in David Ransel, ed., *The Family in Imperial Russi* (Urbana, Ill., 1978).

the governance of common [household] affairs. Every male has the right to participation once he is of age: she, in the final analysis, is considered lower than any adult male."[3]

The rigid patriarchy of peasant society was hardly unique to Russia. In Russia, however, the peasant woman was subordinate, not just to one father or one husband, but to the entire male community. Peasant households were organized into communes and governed by elders, male heads of households who acted in the name of the entire commune. They conducted all transactions with individuals and with the state on behalf of the commune's members; they redistributed land among member households periodically, collected taxes, allocated military obligations, and adjudicated in a variety of ways. The peasant courts (*volostnoi sud*), which were the courts of original and final jurisdiction over all civil and some criminal disputes between peasants, consisted of judges chosen from among male peasants. Women were represented neither in the commune nor in the courts.[4]

Thus, the peasant woman had neither direct access to land, the most vital component of subsistence, nor a role in the conduct of domestic or communal life. She was mute and powerless, a condition expressed in a pithy peasant proverb: *Kuritsa ne ptitsa, da zhenshchina ne chelovek*—a hen is not a bird, a woman is not a person. Her contribution to family survival was nonetheless great. Commentators on peasant life in the prerevolutionary period sometimes speak of the woman's role in peasant economy as "supportive" or "auxiliary," a formulation that derives from a modern definition of work as an activity rewarded with money.[5] Survival in agrarian society, however, was consequent on the indivisible contribution of the family as a unit. In an economy that was for the most part at subsistence level and that relied on domestic production for many necessities, such a functional

3. Efimenko, p. 76.
4. Peter Czap, "Peasant Class Courts and Peasant Customary Justice in Russia, 1861–1912." *Journal of Social History* (1967, Winter).
5. Sula Benet, ed. and trans. *The Village of Viriatino* (New York, 1970), p. 18.

distinction of the peasant woman's work is misleading and inappropriate. Let us look then at the peasant woman's work.

The multiple-family household often included as many as four sons and their families and could be as large as twenty-five or thirty people.[6] Domestic obligations were allocated among the unmarried daughters and the daughters-in-law by the wife of the male head of household. The mother-in-law, however, commanded only the activities of the women, for like all other women, she had no power in the male establishment and was herself under the thumb of the patri-arch. The mother-in-law's power and abuse of power over the women in the household was notorious, and for good reason. As the popular peasant saying described the daughter-in-law's lot: "And who carries the water? The daughter-in-law. And who is beaten? The daughter-in-law. And why is she beaten? Because she is the daughter-in-law."[7] According to the mother-in-law's dictates, the women took turns doing all the domestic tasks, first and foremost those that served the needs of the entire household: cleaning and maintaining the hut, grinding the grain, baking the bread, preparing the daily food, and preserving food for the future. They looked after the livestock and prepared butter and cheese. Sometimes the patriarch assigned the dairy work to the daughter-in-law lowest in his favor as a punishment, for it was heavy and demanding work. The kitchen garden, which produced the larger part of the household's food, was also the women's responsibility.

After attending to the common needs of the household, each woman worked for her own family. She cared for her children, dressed herself, her husband, and her children from head to foot. In some families she was also obliged to provide clothing for the mother-in-law and her husband's unmarried sisters and brothers. No mean task, it often in-volved the initial preparation of material from the sheep or

6. Ibid., p. 92.
7. Efimenko, p. 79.

communal hemp field. Each woman took complete care of her allotment in the household's hemp field from sowing to harvesting, and then prepared garments from the cloth which she spun and wove.

The peasant woman's responsibilities were not limited to the hut and its environs, for the survival of the household depended on her labor in the fields as well. By tradition field work was strictly divided between men and women. Generally, men kept the bees and sheep and ploughed and sowed the land. Women were responsible for fertilizing and weeding before the harvest. During the harvest they mowed the hay (sometimes jointly with the men), stacked it, turned and bound the sheaves. In some regions of the Empire even the joint obligations, like mowing, were traditionally divided by sex; women mowed the hay with a sickle, and men with the scythe.[8] But the sexual division of field labor was not designed to allocate less work to women, nor were these sexual divisions invulnerable to the influence of changing economic forces.

In our period Russian agriculture was suffering from serious underproduction. The land, exhausted by centuries of primitive cultivation, was unable to support a rapidly growing population. The peasant's impoverishment, already observable in the 1870s, was exacerbated in the last two decades of the century when the state initiated a vigorous program of industrialization, for which the peasant bore the cost. Thus, by the 1880s the peasant household was rarely self-sufficient. The land provided neither the surplus necessary for payment of taxes nor food for the peasants, and they were forced to buy goods that they had once produced themselves. Wage labor became a necessity and directly in-

8. V. A. Aleksandrov, ed., *Narody evropeiskoi chasti SSSR*, vol. 1 (Moscow, 1964), pp. 174–189; Benet, pp. 14–17, 95; Efimenko, p. 80. The interplay of tradition and relative physical strength in determining men's and women's agricultural tasks in England is discussed in Eve Hostettler, "Gourlay Steell and the Sexual Division of Labour," *History Workshop* (1977), no. 4, and Michael Roberts, "Sickles and Scythes: Women's Work and Men's Work at Harvest Time," *History Workshop* (1979), no. 7.

1.   *Women barge-haulers. Nizhnii Novgorod Province, 1910.* From
     Illiustrirovannaia istoriia SSSR (Moscow, 1977), p. 188.

fluenced the position and role of the peasant woman in the
household and in the larger economy.[9]

As agricultural production declined and the market intruded into the rural economy, the raison d'être of the
multiple-family household was undermined. Although the
multiple-family household remained the dominant form of
family organization to the end of our period, gradually it
became more common for married sons and their wives to
disengage from the larger household. The smaller family
was probably a welcome relief for both men and women.
The literature abounds with attestation to the tyranny of
the parental generation. The control and independence
that the peasant woman acquired may well have been adequate compensation for the increase in her work load. One
of the few nineteenth-century sources that investigated the
peasant woman noted that in the multiple-family house-

9. See Lazar Volin, *A Century of Russian Agriculture* (Cambridge, Mass., 1970),
pp. 57–76.

hold "she is simply a machine for the execution of predetermined and preallocated family tasks," while "in the smaller family the woman does not work less—perhaps even more, as peasant women themselves acknowledge, especially if they have small children . . . but she controls and manages her own work."[10] Moreover, in the multiple-family household the individual wife's importance was diluted by the other available work hands. In the small family the husband depended mainly on her labor, and her stature must have been enhanced accordingly. She was no longer only one daughter-in-law among many. To abuse the wife unduly, to kick her out of the family (not uncommon in the multiple-family household), or to lose her labor for other reasons could be a catastrophe for the small family.

But we can only speculate about the nature of these changes. The evidence is rare and impressionistic and our own judgment is clouded by the uncomfortable tensions between present-day romanticization of larger extended families and the acceptance of the nuclear family as the norm. Moreover, traditional attitudes and relationships are fiercely tenacious and capable of withstanding serious alterations in the material and economic bases from which they derive. In important ways, the woman's position in both the family and the peasant community remained as it had been. The small family gave her neither greater rights to land inheritance—or even to land use in her own right— nor the right to the slightest participation in village affairs. Patriarchy may have been of a gentler variety with only one male superior to contend with, but patriarchy it remained, down to the husband's prerogative to beat his wife, fully sanctioned by tradition and customary law. His liberal utilization of this prerogative appears to have been preserved intact: "Beating [the peasant woman] is not [considered] an abuse of power, but completely legal and natural to such an extent that the absence of beating is considered abnor-

10. Efimenko, pp. 91, 94.

2.   *Printing cotton from wooden blocks. Northern Russia, 1906.* From
Kiril Fitzlyon and Tatiana Browning, *Before the Revolution* (London,
1978), p. 127.

mal."[11] That observation, made in 1884, could have easily
been made in 1914 as well.

The changing economy led to more obvious and tangible
changes in the peasant woman's work obligations. Paradoxically, industrialization and the concomitant decline in peasant agriculture increased her share of field labor. The peasant was enormously reluctant to forsake the land entirely,
clinging to it as long as it yielded something, however minimal, to family survival. A 1912 *zemstvo* report stated:

> To cast off agriculture completely, to reduce it to nothing, is a
> decision very few [peasants] can make. But to leave it in the
> hands of women to carry on some way or other is a decision the
> majority come to.... Therefore, women not only plough,

11. Ibid., p. 81.

plant, rake, and gather the hay and grain, but often execute the social obligations of men as well.[12]

From all parts of the Empire, transcending the kaleidoscope of regional variations, came reports of women's growing responsibility for the land as men left to seek outside earnings: "Children and old men who remain at home cannot cope with the field work by themselves. Women must take the most active role even in such purely male work as ploughing and haymaking."[13] In 1891 a colorful example was provided in a report from Kostroma province, a province with relatively poor agriculture and many factories: "The stronger representatives of the local peasantry [men] have been driven from here by need, and we find ourselves in a mythical kingdom of amazons."[14] Here, the report continues, women were fulfilling all the duties reserved for men in earlier times, such as the heavy field work, road repairs, and tax collection: "Even in the inns and taverns these days the shrill, drunken voices of women drown out the hoarse bass notes of men's."[15]

The erosion of traditional divisions of agricultural labor was linked to less flexible sexual divisions in the world of wage labor. Men were more likely to see wage labor that took them from the land than were women—not only because women were responsible for child-rearing and therefore less mobile, and certainly not because peasants considered work to be inappropriate for women. Men left the land first, quite simply, because they could earn more than women. Nonetheless, peasant women were forced to earn

12. *Statisticheskii ezhegodnik kostromskoi gubernii za 1911*, chast' 1 (Kostroma, 1913), p. 78. The *zemstvos* were district and provincial councils in thirty-four of Russia's fifty provinces. Governed by elected boards of peasant and gentry landowners, they were designed to look after local needs, such as education, roads, medical care, agriculture, etc. The *zemstvos* hired appropriate professional personnel and published reports (7,000 between 1864 and 1914) on a great variety of local conditions.

13. *Materialy dlia otsenki zemel' vladimirskoi gubernii*, t. 2, *Vladimirskii uezd*, vyp. 3 (Vladimir na Kliazme, 1912), p. 4.

14. D. N. Zhbankov, *Bab'ia storona* (*Statistiko-etnograficheskii ocherk*) (Kostroma, 1891), p. 1.

15. Ibid., p. 3.

3.   *Spinning. Village of Izvedovo.* From Robert H. Allhause, ed.,
     Photographs for the Tsar (New York, 1980), p. 15.

money as well. Predictably, they looked first to occupations
that could be reconciled with their domestic and agricultural obligations.

The picture of women's remunerative work in the countryside must be pieced together from a jumble of inchoate
information. The main sources of information are the volu-
minous *zemstvo* studies and the works of individuals who
were devoted to the preservation of peasant crafts. The
data range from sophisticated statistical compilations to

communiques from "volunteer correspondents"—village priests, rural intelligentsia, barely literate peasants. The overriding bias in these studies is the compilers' profound opposition to the changes that were occurring in the country-side. Their populist proclivities frequently led them to exaggerate and romanticize the virtues of occupations that permitted peasants to remain on the land, that kept traditional sex roles intact, and to magnify and distort the negative results of emigration to the cities or of any change in traditional village life. By their own admission, and to their consternation, the state of quantitative information about peasant wage work was a shambles, and estimates varied wildly according to fantasies about what ought to be.[16] Still, a clear if only occasionally quantifiable picture emerges of the kinds of remunerative work that women did, the factors that influenced their choices, and the ways in which both changed.

The varieties of women's work were not distributed uniformly throughout the Empire, and depended on the geographical and economic characteristics of each region. For our purposes the country is best divided into three major areas: the Central Industrial Region, the province of St Petersburg, and the black earth provinces. While this threefold division does not exhaust the country's geographical, climatic, and socioeconomic regions, it encompasses the kinds of wage-earning alternatives available to peasant women throughout the Russian Empire.

The Central Industrial Region was densely populated, and all arable land had been under the plow for more than a century.[17] Long before the spurt of population growth in the mid-nineteenth century, the land had ceased to support the local population, and by 1900 only 6 percent of peasant

16. In a summary of estimates of the number of peasants engaged in *kustar'* production, three major proponents of peasant crafts gave the figures 3 million, 7 million, over 15 million, respectively. See A. D. Pogruzov, *Kustarnaia promyshlennost' Rossii. Ee znachenie, nuzhdy i vozmozhnoe budushchee* (St Petersburg, 1901).

17. The Central Industrial Region consisted of the provinces of Moscow, Vladimir, Kostroma, Tver', Nizhnii Novgorod, and Kaluga.

families survived by the cultivation of their plots alone.[18] In
the Central Industrial Region, one of Russia's most heavily
industrialized regions, factories were dispersed throughout
the countryside as well as concentrated in the city of Moscow. It also had a long and vigorous tradition of *kustar'*
production, that is, independent domestic production of
handmade finished products for an undefined market
which, since the growth of industry, included putting-out
work from the factories.

Table 1 shows the most representative women's crafts in
Moscow province in 1882, the number of women engaged
in each, and the range of yearly income for each.[19]

Women's *kustar'* production fell into three groups: In
Group I the woman worker was completely independent;
she bought or made her own materials, owned her tools,
and sold to merchants either directly or through an inter-
mediary. In Group II a merchant provided the materials
and tools and bought back the finished product. Group III
was work that was given out by factories to peasant women
"because they [peasant women] could be paid less than
women working in large factories where the identical work
is done on machines."[20]

In the 1880s the knitting of woolen gloves and stockings
occupied the greatest number of women:

18. *Moskovskaia guberniia po mestnomu obsledovaniiu 1898–1900*, t. 4, vyp. 2
(Moscow, 1908), pp. 1–3; Jerome Blum, *Lord and Peasant in Russia* (New York,
1964), p. 330: "Data for 1783–1784 for the province of Tver', directly northwest
of Moscow, showed that cash income from agriculture of the peasants covered
only 40–50 percent of the money they needed to meet expenses."

19. This table, as well as much of the information that follows, is taken from
an extraordinary study commissioned by the Moscow provincial *zemstvo*. The author was part of a movement that argued in support of rural industries as a means
to mitigate the disruptive effects of industrialization on traditional peasant life.
She and her colleagues hoped to influence the government to train peasants in
domestic artisanal work sufficient to keep peasants rural and at least partly agricultural. This volume is the result of her exhaustive study of women's occupations in
Moscow province, which does not, however, discuss service occupations or "certain
others [peasant women] who work as metal craftsmen, blacksmiths, stonediggers
[i.e., traditionally male occupations]." *Sbornik statisticheskikh svedenii po moskovskoi
gubernii*, t. 7, *Zhenskie promysly*, vyp. 4 (Moscow, 1882), p. i. M. K. Gorbunova,
compiler. (Hereafter referred to as Gorbunova.)

20. Ibid., p. iii.

Come autumn or summer early in the morning on a market day. On the roads that lead from the countryside to Moscow you will see a strange spectacle. You will see row upon row of wagons loaded down with grass, hay, wood, potatoes, and other vegetables, and driving or walking beside them women talking

TABLE 1 Women's *Kustar'* Production: Moscow Province, 1882

Group	Number of Women	Range of Yearly Earnings (rubles)
Group I		
Making lace	959	37–60
Embroidering crosses and stars for vestments	47	40–60
Knitting stockings and gloves	12,240	15–29
Weaving fishnets	373	11–17
Weaving rope sandals	53	41–132
Weaving reins	204	20–56
Plaiting bast sandals	87	37–47
Group II		
Making lace with gilded threads	330	21
Making glass beads	125	17
Sewing kid gloves	3,025	32–45
Knitting fringes	378	30
Gluing cigarette tubes	8,765	32–40
Plaiting belts	574	19
Plaiting straw hats	42	60–70
Weaving nets	25	25–30
Knitting kerchiefs	42	17–34
Group III		
Unwinding cotton	10,000	10–25
Cutting muslin threads	12	30–50
Darning and trimming	29	40–100

SOURCE: *Sbornik statisticheskikh svedenii po moskovskoi gubernii*, t. 7, *Zhenskie promysly*, vyp. 4. M. K. Gorbunova, compiler (Moscow, 1882) pp. iv–v.

loudly among themselves as their hands move and their fingers
flash. They are knitting stockings. You will see women carrying
sacks with jugs full of milk and cream, knitting as they walk.[21]

Under the best of circumstances women took the wool
from their own sheep. But as sheep raising declined, the
wool had to be purchased. In both cases, the women were
independent of middlemen for materials, tools of production, or access to the market. The knitter was poorly paid
for her efforts, and the work was performed "in addition to
her customary family contributions: field work, housework,
satisfying the demands of custom, dressing herself, her husband and her children. She is an essential member of the
family. . . . In times of need [her earnings] even pay for
bread or a cow or sheep."[22] Knitting was completely subject
to the vagaries of urban demand and therefore occupied
mainly women who lived within a 30-verst radius from Moscow city. As urban tastes changed and factory-produced
stockings and gloves triumphed over the handcrafted articles, the latter slowly dropped from the woman's repertoire.
In 1889 knitting was still singled out as a major woman's
craft, but by 1898–1900 it was not even mentioned in the
zemstvo reports.[23]

The second largest occupation, unwinding cotton, was a
job put out by the factory; "Despite the existence of machines for this work, most of the cotton used in cotton-
weaving factories is unwound by hand by peasant women in
the countryside."[24] The work of unwinding cotton thread
had several convenient features for the peasant woman.
The factories that put out the work were widely distributed
throughout the province and easily accessible. This was important because it eliminated the middleman, who could
otherwise eat into the woman's earnings. Simple enough for
a six-year-old child, unwinding required nothing more than

    21. Ibid., p. 143.
    22. Ibid., p. 146.
    23. *Statisticheskii ezhegodnik moskovskoi gubernii za 1889* (Moscow, 1889), p. 4;
Moskovskaia guberniia po mestnomu obsledovaniiu 1898–1900, pp. 92–94.
    24. Gorbunova, p. 279.

a bobbin and a roller, which could be purchased for a pittance or made at home. The work could be done in the peasant hut without encroaching on living space; it required neither the cleanliness, good vision, nor concentration of the more skilled crafts.[25] Yet unwinding cotton was not considered a desirable occupation, for the work was dirty and poorly paid. Women were driven to it either by the decline of better-paying crafts or by their lack of skill—two factors that increased over the years. It was always the choice of last resort. By 1900 more than twice as many peasant women in Moscow province were unwinding cotton as in 1882.[26] But from then on the craft declined steadily, so that by 1912 it had become a "victim of machinery."[27] Similar victims of mechanization were flax and wool spinning, also putting-out processes. Employing 12,000 women in 1882, flax and wool spinning had been swallowed up by the factory by the turn of the century.[28]

Some crafts followed an interesting trajectory from the factory to the village and back again to the factory. The craft of sewing kid gloves is one example. In the 1780s small glove factories using serf labor had begun to appear around Moscow (and St Petersburg) in response to urban demand. After the emancipation of the serfs the preparation of leather was so perfected that it became cheaper to put out the prepared leather to peasant women to sew the gloves together. This craft, although not highly skilled, was more demanding than many others. It required a degree of cleanliness not easy to come by in the peasant hut, agile fingers (in wet weather it was not possible to sew the gloves, because the fingers tended to swell), and good vision. Still, it was a desirable occupation because it paid well—until the factories began to reclaim it. In 1882, 3,000 women in Moscow province sewed kid gloves at home.[29] By 1900 only 575

25. Ibid., pp. 279–284.
26. A. S. Orlov, *Kustarnaia promyshlennost' moskovskoi gubernii* (Moscow, 1913), p. 7.
27. Ibid., p. 8.
28. Ibid., p. 7.
29. Gorbunova, pp. 174–184.

women were thus employed, and in 1904 *zemstvo* statisticians noted that even that vestige of a formerly important village craft had totally vanished.[30]

Another example of the fluctuating relationship between the factory and women's cottage industry was the manufacture of hollow tubes, called *gil'zy*, for cigarettes. Although *gil'zy* had originally been manufactured in tobacco factories, in the 1880s it had become cheaper to put the work out to peasant women. *Gil'zy* could be made at home with a few inexpensive materials after a few weeks of training. A middleman would buy or rent a hut in the village, which became the *"fabrichka,"* or little factory. Here he instructed the women and girls and then sent them back to their homes with paper cut to size for the hollow tube, cardboard to make the mouthpiece, a small copper cylinder (*bolvanchik*) around which the paper was wound, and a small primitive instrument for inserting the mouthpiece into the paper tube. Young boys were hired to pack the finished *gil'zy* into large cartons to be transported to Moscow. If the middleman (occasionally middlewoman) was not a factory representative, the work in the *fabrichka* was more complicated, for the boys had to cut the paper for the hollow tubes and the cardboard for the mouthpieces. It was not unusual for women to spend thirteen hours a day at this work for thirty-five weeks a year.[31] In 1889 *zemstvo* correspondents from Moscow province agreed that "all women do it with the exception of the elderly whose fingers are no longer dexterous."[32] By 1904 the reports stated that "the hand gluing of cigarette tubes has been replaced by machines in the factory, and now only a few women insert the mouthpieces into finished tubes that they receive from the factory."[33]

A host of luxury crafts catering to urban taste were brought from the city of Moscow to a small number of

30. Orlov, p. 7. *Statisticheskii ezhegodnik moskovskoi gubernii za 1904* (Moscow, 1905), p. 15.

31. Gorbunova, pp. 203–230.

32. *Statisticheskii ezhegodnik moskovskoi gubernii za 1889,* p. 19.

33. Orlov, p. 7. *Statisticheskii ezhegodnik moskovskoi gubernii za 1904* (Moscow, 1905), p. 15.

women in the village. The crafts of lace-making with gilded threads, embroidering crosses and stars for vestments, and knitting fringes to be sewn onto fashionable garments all had a transient life in Moscow province in the 1880s. Subsequently, other minor crafts appeared and disappeared in rapid succession in response to the ephemeral dictates of fashion.[34] But by 1911 the demand for domestic handwork of every kind had diminished radically as "the machine continues to bear down relentlessly on home industry, primarily for women and child workers."[35]

Male peasant wage earners were rather evenly distributed throughout the provinces of the Central Industrial Region. By contrast, the distribution of women workers was irregular and contingent on a greater variety of local conditions. To illustrate, let us compare three districts (*uezdy*) in Vladimir province which, like Moscow province, had a rich *kustar'* tradition and a heavy concentration of industry.

Shuiskii district was one of the most highly industrialized areas of Russia. It contained within its borders Ivanovo-Voznesensk, known as the "Russian Manchester," as well as the city of Shuia and the industrial villages of Teikovo and Kokhma. Altogether the factories in Shuiskii district employed at least 100,000 workers.[36] Outside earnings, mostly from factory work, predominated heavily over agricultural earnings in the peasant budget, and 26 percent of the peasant women were wage earners. Half of the women who worked for wages were employed in the factories and came mostly from households whose land did not produce crops. The other half, nine-tenths of whom had heavy field-work obligations, engaged in domestic hand-weaving (only three-fourths of male domestic *kustar'* workers simultaneously worked the land).[37] Domestic production was strictly divided between men's and women's work in Shuiskii district.

34. Gorbunova, pp. 8–9, 45–56, 89–91.
35. *Statisticheskii ezhegodnik moskovskoi gubernii za 1911*, chast' 2 (Moscow, 1912), p. 17.
36. The information for Shuiskii district comes from *Materialy dlia otsenki zemel' vladimirskoi gubernii*, t. 10, vyp. 3, *Shuiskii uezd* (Vladimir, 1908), pp. 1–25.
37. Ibid.

Most men made goods from sheepskin, work that paid very well in comparison with women's primary work, domestic hand-weaving on a putting-out basis.

Vladimir district was less industrialized and agriculturally more prosperous than Shuiskii district. Nonetheless, male emigration for outside work was extremely high even in households with relatively large parcels of land, mainly because of the shortage of livestock. But only 7 percent of the district's peasant women were wage earners. Women could not be spared for wage-earning work, since the burden of working the land fell on their shoulders. Half of the women wage earners worked in factories. The other half were divided between agricultural day labor and domestic service, because Moscow was too far from Shuiskii district to stimulate *kustar'* production.[38]

Pokrovskii district exhibited yet another configuration. Like Shuiskii and Vladimir districts, it was highly industrialized, and less than 7 percent of the men were engaged exclusively in farming. Of the remainder, two-thirds emigrated to the factories, "so that all the field work is the women's obligation when the men go out for summer earnings."[39] In spite of the remarkably heavy burden of field work, 47 percent of the district's women were domestic wage earners. Putting-out work from local cotton factories remained available as late as 1908, and domestic silk weaving occupied many women because "machine weaving cannot yet be applied to silk and . . . the factory is still in competition with *kustar'* production."[40] However, half the silk weavers were men because silk weaving was a skilled craft requiring two years of apprenticeship. Wages were high, 70–90 rubles per year compared with 20 rubles per year for cotton weaving, a woman's craft. Another option for women, found only in this district, was tearing the nap from woven velveteen, a fulling process that could not yet be

38. Ibid., t. 2, *Vladimirskii uezd*, pp. 160–165.
39. Ibid., t. 12, *Pokrovskii uezd*, pp. 1, 12.
40. Ibid., p. 17.

done by machine. In the 1880s it had been men's work. But remuneration was very small, and it passed into women's hands when factory work became available to men.[41]

Throughout the Central Industrial Region, then, uniform and growing economic distress forced most men into wage labor. The women stayed on the land as long as something could be scratched from it. Nonetheless, in addition to playing a large and often major role on the land, women worked for money. Whether they did and what they did depended on the local economic landscape—in other words, on whether urban markets or local factories made work available to them.

In the province of St Petersburg peasant women had a substantially different array of wage-earning alternatives. Here the climate was harsher, the land stingier, and the population sparse compared with the Central Industrial Region. Although the province was highly industrialized, industry did not go out to meet the peasant in the countryside as it did in the Central Industrial Region. Factories were almost entirely concentrated in and near St Petersburg city, and only peasants who lived close to the city worked in factories. Proximity to the city was, however, instrumental in determining women's contribution to family survival, but *kustar'* production, so prominent in the Central Industrial Region, played a negligible role, a few women here and there making gloves and weaving fishing accoutrements.[42] The great majority of women engaged in and dominated the sale of agricultural and dairy products, mainly to the city of St Petersburg. Of the 4,110 families in St Petersburg district who owned cows, 3,507 sold milk products.[43] The sale of produce from kitchen gardens to the city or, in the summer, to the resort population was exclusively women's work, as was the collection and sale of wild berries, mushrooms, and flowers. Women had complete responsibility not

41. Ibid., pp. 42–46.
42. *Materialy po statistike narodnogo khoziaistva v s-peterburgskoi gubernii* (St Petersburg, 1887), p. 270.
43. Ibid., p. 238.

only for growing and gathering, but for carrying the produce to the St Petersburg markets as well.[44] Calculating
their earnings is not possible, since in this type of wage-
earning activity the contribution was lost in the household
total.

The outlying areas of the province were popular holiday
places for the inhabitants of St Petersburg city and also
drew a large number of peasant immigrants from other
parts of Russia, looking for factory work in the city.[45] Thus,
second in importance among the local peasant women's
earnings was the renting of summer accommodations to
vacationers and to immigrants, as well as the provision
of a number of related services such as cleaning and
laundering.[46]

These occupations were created by St Petersburg's rapid
growth in the decades after the emancipation of the serfs.
The city's growing appetite for food and services was never
satisfied by the meager resources and sparse population of
St Petersburg province, but it provided a stable seasonal
market for those peasant women with the resources to accommodate it. Like women's work in the Central Industrial
Region, it allowed women to remain close to the household.
The important difference between the two areas was the
absence in St Petersburg of factory putting-out work and
domestic *kustar'* production. St Petersburg city was a great
textile-producing and tobacco-processing city, so it must be
assumed that the absence of putting-out work in the province was due to the better organization, more sophisticated
machinery, and greater labor productivity that distinguished St Petersburg from Moscow. Why the city failed to
provide a stimulus and a market for other kinds of hand-

44. Ibid., p. 244.

45. The immigrant (*prishlye*) peasant population had no land and rarely came
to St Petersburg province with children or elderly family members. Therefore, a
larger proportion of immigrant women than indigenous women were wage
earners and factory workers. Twenty-two percent of immigrant wage-earning
women were in the factory, and 14 percent of the indigenous wage-earning
women. Ibid., p. 270.

46. Ibid.

made items as Moscow did is not clear. It cannot be fully explained by the long tradition of local *kustar'* production in the Central Industrial Region. As we have seen, much of the *kustar'* work there originated not in age-old peasant crafts, but in the city or factories. In principle, the urban demand of St Petersburg city could have encouraged something similar in the surrounding countryside. Yet, it did not.

In St Petersburg, as in the Central Industrial Region, women stayed closer to home than men, as a result of their domestic responsibilities and because the responsibility for working the land fell to them as men increasingly sought outside earnings. In the Central Industrial Region, staying close to home was compatible with factory work because of the wide dispersion of factories in the countryside. In St Petersburg province the factories, clustered in and near St Petersburg city, were not a sufficiently powerful magnet to pull women away from the land and the hut. Although the percentage of women abandoning the land for some kind of city work increased between 1887 and 1912, the basic pattern did not change.[47]

The more prosperous agricultural areas of Russia, the so-called black earth provinces, had, in some cases, no industry, and in others, relatively little.[48] In these provinces fewer peasants sought outside earnings, since the land yielded, if not abundance, at least reasonable subsistence. Urban markets for *kustar'* products were few and not easily accessible. Consequently, women's work was largely on the land. In 1884 the *zemstvo* report of Saratov province indicated that the "outstanding characteristic of peasant women is the great variety of their occupations. Divisions of agricultural work into men's and women's hardly exist, unless we

47. *Promysly krest'ianskogo naseleniia s-peterburgskoi gubernii. S-Peterburgskii uezd* (St Petersburg, 1912), p. 51.
48. The black earth provinces in the southern steppe region of Russia stretched from west to east almost the entire width of the European part of the country. They contained Russia's most fertile land and included the following provinces: Kursk, Orel, Riazan', Tula, Tambov, Voronezh, Penza, Khar'kov, Ekaterinoslav, Kiev, Podol', Saratov, Simbirsk, Kazan', Viatka, and Perm.

count mowing and ploughing as men's work and care of the kitchen gardens as women's. But this is not a systematic division, and one can find many places where men and women exchange jobs."[49] Even most remunerative work was related to the land, mainly the selling of various edibles.[50] The major nonagricultural option for women was the knitting of woolen socks and gloves, which in some parts of the province occupied women the year round, interrupted only by the most necessary field work. Women took the wool from their own sheep and were responsible for selling the finished product in the city of Saratov or to itinerant merchants. The average income for knitters was 15–20 rubles per year.[51] As the demand for hand-knit articles declined in competition with cheaper factory-made goods, women found new occupations. In the famine year of 1892, for example, the weaving of goat down for headkerchiefs, a great luxury item, was brought to two of the most agriculturally productive districts of Saratov province and took a firm hold. "The female population of the countryside has joyfully seized on this new auxiliary occupation. Almost all the women and girls spin on hand wheels, while adolescents and children clean and comb the down."[52] But local opportunities for outside earnings were so few in this agricultural province that peasants were forced to emigrate when the land did not provide adequate subsistence. Men and women left the countryside in equal numbers. In 1904 a survey of *kustar'* production in the city of Kuznetsk, the most important *kustar'* center of the province, indicated that the city's working population was equally divided between men and women.[53]

In the black earth province of Khar'kov, there was yet

49. *Sbornik statisticheskikh svedenii po saratovskoi gubernii*, t. 3, chast' 1, *Promysly krest'ianskogo naseleniia saratovskogo i tsaritsynskogo uezdov* (Saratov, 1884), p. 129.
50. Ibid.
51. Ibid.
52. *Issledovanie kustarnykh promyslov saratovskoi gubernii*, vyp. 5, *Balashovskii i serdovskii uezdy* (Saratov, 1913), p. 1.
53. *Issledovanie kustarnykh promyslov saratovskoi gubernii*, vyp. 1, *Gorod Kuznetska* (Saratov, 1904), p. 2.

another configuration of opportunities to earn money. As in Saratov, very few of the inhabitants—only 10 percent—sought outside earnings. But here industry was growing, and the city of Khar'kov offered nonindustrial urban work opportunities as well. Between 1897 and 1912, peasant wage-earning work changed in the following way:[54]

	1897	1912
Percentage of population in *kustar'* production	5.3	2.0
Percentage of women *kustar'* workers	55.0	28.0
Percentage of men *kustar'* workers	45.0	67.0
Percentage of population in the factory	0.5	3.8

By 1912 peasants in the factory far exceeded those who stayed behind to work locally in *kustar'* production: 130,000 in the former and 34,389 in the latter; the opportunities for female *kustar'* work had suffered most. Obviously, many women were going to the factory, or at least to the city, as the steady increase in passports given out to women indicates.[55] But for those who remained behind there was a significant shift in available work. In 1891 *zemstvo* statisticians noted that in this basically agricultural province, weaving had always been a very important woman's job:

Women have guarded this craft as a necessary way to cover their needs by the labor of their own hands, since by custom all clothing which is not made at home must be acquired somehow by the woman alone. Neither husband nor father give a kopek. Therefore, the year round, women have no rest. In every home there are one or two weaving looms. Each woman works for herself; the mother, the bride, the daughter. All winter they prepare wool and hemp. Spring, summer, and autumn they weave woolens, linen, belts, foot-cloths. . . . With this they dress themselves, their husbands, and their children

54. *Kustarnye promysly v khar'kovskoi gubernii po dannym issledovaniia 1912 g.* (Khar'kov, 1913), pp. 1–3.
55. In 1897, 28,149 passports were issued to women. By 1905 that figure had grown at a very steady rate to 37,600. This was a 25 percent increase, while passports issued to men had increased by only 19 percent. *Kratkii ocherk mestnykh i otkhozhikh promyslov naseleniia khar'kovskoi gubernii* (Khar'kov, 1905), p. 100.

and sell the surplus at an average of twenty-five rubles per year per household.[56]

In 1891, then, all women wove; by 1912 only 76.7 percent did. But as weaving declined a variety of small *kustar'* occupations emerged to take up the slack. The most important was the production of spinning cards and looms, a craft that had not existed at all in 1891. By 1912 it was entirely in women's hands. The second was a significant increase of women tailors, from 4 percent in 1891 to 15.7 percent in 1912, catering to urban demand. Further, women had moved into some traditionally male occupations such as basket making, coal working, and shoemaking, albeit in small numbers.[57] Thus, even in the provinces with more sustaining agriculture where outside earning was a small part of family survival, women had a growing wage-earning role, determined in these provinces, as elsewhere, by land conditions and urban demand.

Despite the diversity of regional conditions that influenced the proportions of peasant women wage earners and the kinds of work they did, we can make some generalizations about the nature of women's work in the countryside. The most ubiquitous consequence of the changing economy between the 1880s and 1914 was that women took increasing responsibility for working the land to free men for outside wage work. Where male earnings could not assuage growing peasant need, women too sought remunerative work. But unlike men, they engaged first in a variety of occupations that could be combined with household and field obligations. The traditional division between men's and women's work on the land, collapsing under the impact of altered economic forces, was transmitted intact to the world of remunerative labor. Women's work invariably required relatively little training and skill. While it enabled women to move easily from one occupation to another, it

---

56. *Doklad v khar'kovskuiu zemskuiu upravu o kustarnykh promyslakh po khar'kovskomu uezdu* (Khar'kov, 1891), pp. 27–28.

57. *Kustarnye promysly v khar'kovskoi gubernii*, p. 6.

also invariably commanded less money than men's work—and less respect. Indeed, the more skilled *kustar'* production that men did exclusively, like blacksmithy, metal working, carpentry, and stonecutting, was called by another name, *remeslo.*

Women earned less even in those rare occupations that they shared with men. Agricultural day labor, which employed both sexes throughout European Russia, is a good example. In 1887 a *zemstvo* statistician was astonished to discover a farmstead with "an extremely original organization: here men received two rubles and two poods of flour per month and women receive two rubles and one and one-half poods of flour per month."[58] Such near equality of wages was unusual enough to merit special attention. According to a 1907 survey of agricultural wages, women earned from one-fifth to two-thirds of men's wages, depending on the region.[59] As a *zemstvo* report observed in 1908:

> Women's remunerative labor is not only technically simpler [than men's] and closer to the domestic hearth, but is also very low on the social ladder. As a result, the social position of the woman worker is lower and more difficult than men's. For this reason women's work is considered less valuable and is paid less than male labor. Women do not have equal rights with men in labor as they do not have equal rights in social life.[60]

For some decades expanding urban markets and putting-out work from factories enhanced the opportunities for peasant women to combine household and field work with wage work. But by the turn of the century the factory's tentacles began to choke off the demand for handmade crafts and, concomitantly, encroached on the work that it had itself created, that is, the various putting-out processes.

58. *Materialy po statistike narodnogo khoziaistva v s-peterburgskoi gubernii,* vyp. 5, chast' 2 (St Petersburg, 1887), p. 269.
59. "Otsenka zhenskogo i muzhskogo truda na sel'skikh rabotakh," *Zhenskii Vestnik* (1907), no. 2, pp. 48–49.
60. *Materialy dlia otsenki zemel' vladimirskoi gubernii,* t. 10, *Shuiskii uezd,* vyp. 3 (Vladimir, 1908), p. 33.

Many factories that closed during the slump of the first years of the twentieth century abolished their putting-out departments when they reopened, and the manual work previously done by peasant women in their homes was absorbed within the factory walls to be performed on mechanized apparatuses.[61] A limited amount of putting-out work remained available, however, for the absolute numbers of peasant women thus employed, province by province, remained stable between 1902 and 1910.[62] Many peasant women—perhaps most—continued to seek work that was compatible with remaining on the land. Whether it was the exchange of one putting-out process for another, whether it was an occupation abandoned by men for better-paying factory work, or whether a new urban taste surfaced, they eagerly accepted whatever came their way. The salient point is that such work no longer accommodated peasant need. Over the years as more peasant women had to, or wished to, earn money, domestic *kustar'* production simply occupied relatively fewer women, and they went to the factory in ever increasing numbers.

* * *

Unfortunately, the subjective dimension of the peasant woman's life and work cannot be deduced from quantitative information on agriculture and labor. Nor has she left memoirs or other tangible sources from which we can make direct judgments. We must therefore rely on the perceptions of the observers of rural life, who only infrequently recorded the voices of women themselves, but whose observations, sometimes direct and at other times oblique, evoke an impressionistic picture of how the peasant woman experienced her life.

For the most part, those who observed and reported on rural work were biased in favor of preserving village life intact. It would have violated tradition to suggest that the

61. *Svod otchetov fabrichnykh inspektorov za 1906* (St Petersburg, 1908), p. iv.
62. *Svod 1902*, pp. 34–35; *1906*, pp. 41–42; *1907*, pp. 44–45; *1908*, pp. 44–45; *1909*, pp. 44–45.

peasant woman do nothing but care for children and hut, since field work had been an indivisible component of her existence from time immemorial. Nor was the transformation of production for home consumption to market production regarded as a threat to rural stability and the stability of sex roles. New crafts introduced to the village were hailed as a good thing, for they replaced dying crafts and permitted women to continue working in the village. One *zemstvo* reporter even concluded that the peasant woman's work was not only an economic necessity but morally uplifting as well: "Debauchery is a rare exception among the women of more prosperous [peasant] families, but is entirely normal among the poorer families."[63] In other words, the peasant woman's solid economic contribution to family survival was fully accepted and encouraged. The goal of the proponents of *kustar'* production was to train peasants (men as well as women) in those village industries that might weather the onslaught of industrialization and retard the erosion of village life. Therefore, the conditions under which peasant women worked, the extra burden they bore, and the physical effects of various kinds of work were irrelevant. In fairness to the observers, they seldom put forth the kind of saccharine and sentimental stereotypes of the jolly, healthy farm woman which appeared so often in Western European literature. The distortions are rather in the absence of analysis.

Most observers assumed that women's wage work could easily be slotted into the crevices of her daily activities. It is more likely that women worked many hours a day in addition to their normal obligations. Often women themselves were at a loss to calculate how much time they spent on a craft: "We have no hours, we just do not know," they would say and then explain that since candles were expensive, they simply arranged their working hours to fit the available light.[64] Even the paltriest of earnings could cost the woman

63. *Promysly vladimirskoi gubernii*, vyp. 3, *Pokrovskii i Aleksandrovskii uezdy* (Moscow, 1882), p. 113.
64. Gorbunova (see n. 19 above), p. 42.

ten to fourteen hours a day.[65] Some kinds of *kustar'* work,
like sewing kid gloves, were harmful to the eyesight and
could only be done for a limited number of years. Women's
kustar' work was rarely skilled, creative, or innovative. Most
of it was, as one *zemstvo* observer noted, a "daily, monoto-
nous grind, requiring long, exhausting hours. Such work
not only exhausts the body, but dulls the mind as well."[66]
Once a process had been assimilated, it was simply repeated
mindlessly as long as demand remained—and sometimes,
however futile, longer.[67] Given the constraints of their lives,
their poverty, illiteracy, and lack of skill, it is not surprising
that as eagerly as peasant women seized new opportunities,
they were rarely capable of creating them or ferreting them
out. For the most part, peasant women were the passive
beneficiaries of benevolent chance. It was not uncommon
for an entire village to ply a craft that had been introduced
fortuitously by a woman from another village who married
a local peasant.[68] The following report from the Ministry of
Education illustrates the obstacles faced by even the most
energetic of peasant women:

> The peasant women of Iashchery [a tiny village in St Peters-
> burg district] appealed to the Zemstvo for help in learning how
> to make lace. As their households live in extreme poverty, they
> wish to make some contribution. They invited a teacher, Mrs.
> Pushkareva . . . , rented a space in the village and began to
> make lace. In the first year the women were able to sell part of
> their work. In view of the current winter unemployment this
> kind of work would be a great advantage to them, but they do
> not have the means to pay a teacher [for further training] or to
> rent a space.[69]

65. Ibid., pp. 89–91, 180–184, 209.
66. *Statisticheskii sbornik po iaroslavskoi gubernii*, vyp. 14, *Kustarnye promysly* (Iaroslavl, 1904), p. 46.
67. *Statisticheskii ezhegodnik kostromskoi gubernii 1909 g.*, vyp. 1 (Kostroma, 1912),
p. 55.
68. Gorbunova, passim.
69. TsGIA, f. 741, op. 8, d. 11, l. 2.

Cooperation was rare among peasant women engaged in *kustar'* production. Occasionally they would render one another certain kinds of services. For example, factories issued only one packet of cotton at a time to women who unwound cotton thread, thereby limiting the amount of money they could earn. Sometimes when a women decided to stop unwinding temporarily she would pass her work-book on to a friend so the latter could have more work.[70] There were many crafts that would have lent themselves to cooperative marketing, especially those that depended on a middleman to fetch materials and return the finished prod-uct to the factory. The middleman, who absorbed some of the producer's already meager earnings, could have been circumvented if the women took turns going to the Moscow markets or the factories. But apparently it never occurred to them.[71] Their isolation and illiteracy also left them prey to the calculated errors of merchants and factories; because the women were unable to read what was written in their workbooks, how much material had been given them, and what the prices were, they were easily cheated.[72]

A thin stratum of peasant women became *khoziaiki*, that is, they abandoned production and worked as middlemen between merchant and producer. From all reports, *khoziaiki*, or any kind of intermediaries, were exploitative in many ways. Women workers often had to accept whatever form of payment the middleman chose to hand out. Payment in kind could be in the form of useful goods, like bread or tea, but frequently it was in useless goods which then had to be sold back to the shops at half the market price. The only way to mitigate the exploitation was to work through several middlemen so as not to be dependent on one.[73]

Women were indeed aware of their exploited position,

---

70. Gorbunova, p. 280. The author noted that while this kind of service was rare, even rarer was the fact that it was rendered free.
71. Ibid., p. 175.
72. Ibid.
73. Ibid., pp. ix, 97.

but this was balanced by "their gratitude, even when [the middleman] cheated them all the time. . . . Some women sincerely looked upon the *khoziaiki* as their benefactresses, for they did not know how they would feed themselves without the work."[74] One could also question whether they resented the fact that their earning power was consistently and significantly lower than men's, not only because they were concentrated in lower-paying occupations but even when they did work identical to men's. There is, however, no evidence for this. It can safely be assumed that the patriarchal mentality was so deeply ingrained in peasant women as well as men that they never questioned what must have seemed to them a law of nature. But it is clear that when there was a choice, jobs that paid women directly were more appealing to them than whose in which earnings accrued to the family unit, at least among unmarried women. In Moscow province, for example, women lace-makers would help the family make brushes when lace-making was slow. "But they do this reluctantly because they do not get their earnings 'in hand' . . . and have to wait until the father doles out the money."[75]

A few *zemstvo* observers, less intent on preserving the village intact at any price, perceived that the sharp distinction between men's and women's work made women "the victims of extreme exploitation."[76] To be sure, these divisions were sometimes based on relative physical strength, but by no means invariably. More often, the divisions were based on patriarchial definitions of what was appropriate to women. After the turn of the century, then, the more sensitive *zemstvo* observers approved women's increasing choice of factory work over domestic production. For, to the peasant women, long accustomed to contributing to their own and their family's survival, "It is a misfortune

74. Ibid., p. 17.
75. Ibid., p. 5.
76. *Materialy dlia otsenki zemel' vladimirskoi gubernii*, t. 10, p. 33.

not to work. . . . It is painful and distressing to sit without occupation; bread is dear."[77]

Among Russian peasants, qualities attributed to women and prized by other classes, like beauty and grace, were at most of secondary importance. The most desirable wife was one who even as a girl had demonstrated her capacity for work. Work, paid and unpaid, was the focal point of existence for peasant women as well as men. The specific economic niche occupied by peasant women, assigned them by tradition and modified by the exigencies of an industrializing economy, thus provided them with a legacy of expectations quite favorable to the move from farm to factory. To work hard, to contribute to their own survival and that of their families, was in no way a transformation of their destiny.

Peasant women also brought with them to the factory a legacy of subordination: in the family hierarchy, in community governance, in occupational divisions, in remuneration and rewards, and in status. A romantic view of precapitalist and early capitalist society postulates that when the family was the basic unit of production the woman "had a respected role within the family, since the domestic labor of the household was so clearly integral to the family as a whole."[78] The logic in this assumption is belied by historical reality. True, in our discussion of the peasant woman's world we have not speculated on the informal arrangements that may have been negotiated in subtle and unarticulated ways but not reflected in the codifications of law or inheritance relationships. The bonds of love and affection, of loyalty and other emotional commitments, may have palliated the humiliating effects of patriarchal dominance. We have alluded to but not explored the possible enhancement of the woman's position as multiple-family households fragmented into smaller family units, as peasant women took on

---

77. Gorbunova, p. 5.
78. Eli Zaretsky, *Capitalism, The Family and Personal Life* (New York, 1976), p. 29.

greater agriculture and wage-earning burdens. These sub-
tleties of her life remain to be investigated, if indeed there
is evidence of them in unexplored sources. It is unlikely,
however, that either informal familial accord or the influence of the changing economy seriously dented the double
legacy of work expectations and subordination that characterized the woman's life as a peasant. It is now our task to
examine the interplay between this legacy and the conditions of her new life as a factory worker.

3

IN THE CITY—IN THE MILL

From the foregoing examination of the working life of peasant women, it is clear that factory work was not a sudden transformation of the female role among those strata from which factory women came. Between village crafts and factory, however, there were other wage-earning alternatives, especially for women who made their way to the cities.

In the decades after the emancipation of the serfs, St Petersburg and Moscow, Russia's two largest and most industrialized cities, gradually swelled with peasant migrants. By the turn of the century both cities numbered over a million inhabitants, of which more than half were peasants. The proportion of women among them increased steadily: from 30 percent of St Petersburg's immigrant population in 1869 to 48 percent by 1914.[1] Of the total female population in the two capitals, one-half lived by independent means. Peasant men and women who came to Moscow and St Petersburg did not, of course, have a free choice of ways to earn a livelihood. Even if they came to the cities determined to find factory work, it was not always available. Although both cities were great industrial centers, in St Petersburg of 1910 and Moscow of 1912 only about one-third of the labor force was in factories.[2] Thus the city presented a great array of wage-earning possibilities outside the factory. For women some occupations, like domestic service, were clearly nonin-

1. James H. Bater, *St. Petersburg: Industrialization and Change* (Montreal, 1976), pp. 309, 313, 396.
2. Ibid., p. 255. *Istoriia Moskvy*, t. 5 (Moscow, 1955), p. 18.

dustrial. Other occupations, like tailoring, fell into a gray area between industrial and nonindustrial, artisanal in technology and industrial in organization. For the purposes of our discussion we will simply call all work outside the factory nonindustrial as we examine the alternatives available to working women in the city.

The single largest employer of women in both cities was domestic service, and it absorbed more and more women as time went on. In 1864 the number of male and female domestic servants in St Petersburg was almost identical: 55,381 men and 55,307 women.[3] By 1890, although the city had grown enormously, the number of male domestics remained the same. But the number of women domestics had increased to 87,777—a third of all working women.[4] In Moscow in 1902, 28 percent of the working female population was in domestic service.[5] The proportion of women domestics in Moscow decreased slightly to 25 percent by 1912 because of growing opportunities for women in the textile factories, but there were still twice as many women domestic servants as factory workers at that time.[6]

Routinely, only half of the women who registered for domestic jobs with private agencies found places. So great was the supply of applicants that prospective employers could well afford to wait for peak periods of immigration— just after Christmas and Easter—to have their pick of women "unspoiled by city life."[7] Indeed, the great majority of women domestics were newly arrived peasants.[8] Nor was the preference for fresh country girls a simple whim. A woman with skills or more sophistication about the choices that, at least in principle, city life offered was less willing to tolerate the dismal, demanding, and poorly paid work of a

3. *Statisticheskii ezhegodnik S-Peterburga 1892*, p. 83.
4. *S-Peterburg po perepisi 15 dekabria 1900 goda*, vyp. 2 (St Petersburg, 1903), pp. 38–93.
5. *Perepis' Moskvy 1902 g.*, chast' 1, vyp. 2 (Moscow, 1906), pp. 90–115.
6. *Statisticheskii ezhegodnik g. Moskvy i moskovskoi gubernii za 1914–1925*, vyp. 2, *Statisticheskie dannye po gorodu Moskvy* (Moscow, 1927), pp. 68–74.
7. *Promyshlennost' i Zdorov'e*, kn. 2 (1904), pp. 128–129.
8. Ibid.

servant—*belye nevol'niki* (white slaves), as they were called.[9] All observers agreed that domestic service was the least desirable, the most degrading of all women's work. Domestic servants were deprived of a private life; they were permitted neither visitors, including legal husbands, nor holidays.[10] On call to satisfy the employer's whim from dawn to midnight, bedded in a kitchen corner or a corridor, fed on the dregs of the family meal, prey to the sexual advances of the household's adult males, domestics averaged five rubles a month in earnings by the turn of the century.[11] They were excluded from even the minimal protection that labor legislation offered factory women. As a conscience-stricken upper-class woman confessed in 1906, "We prefer the most ignorant, the better to exploit her. The illiterate, oppressed, inarticulate creature will not protest, of course, and will make her peace with everything."[12]

In addition to live-in service, a large number of women worked as laundresses, cooks, bath-house attendants, and charwomen on a day-to-day basis for private and public institutions as well as for individual families. Thus, peasant women pouring into the cities, far in excess of what factories and workshops could absorb, could escape beginning their work lives as domestic servants only as individuals but not as a group.

The next largest group of nonindustrial women workers, about 8 percent of the female working population in Moscow and St Petersburg, worked in the needle trades.[13] Before 1882 ready-made clothing had been imported from abroad because of the absence of tariffs, and the needle-worker had been an independent artisan who created a

9. Evgenia Turzhe-Turzhanskaia, *Belye nevol'niki* (*Domashniaia prisluga v Rossii*) (Smolensk, 1906).

10. L. N. Lenskaia, *O prisluge* (Moscow, 1908), p. 11.

11. Turzhe-Turzhanskaia, pp. 5–7; M. I. Pokrovskaia, "Peterburgskaia rabotnitsa," *Mir Bozhii* (1900), no. 12, pp. 31–32.

12. Turzhe-Turzhanskaia, p. 6.

13. This figure is taken from *S-Peterburg po perepisi 15 dekabria 1890 goda*, chast' 1, vyp. 2 (St Petersburg, 1891), pp. 26–50; *S-Peterburg po perepisi 15 dekabria 1900 goda; Perepis' Moskvy 1902 goda; Statisticheskii ezhegodnik goroda Moskvy i moskovskoi gubernii za 1914–1925*.

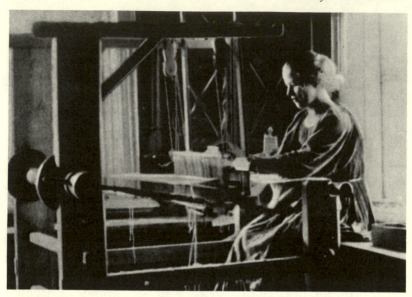

4. *At the weaving loom. Village of Privetluzh'e, 1911.* From *Illiustrirovannaia istoriia SSSR* (Moscow, 1977), p. 187.

whole product to specific order. When tariffs were imposed on imported clothing, the indigenous garment industry grew quickly in size and complexity, and the worker was gradually transformed into a hired laborer who specialized in making one part of a garment.[14] Women garment workers were divided between those who did plain sewing (*beloshveiki*), a female occupation, and those who could do the more skilled tailoring, which employed men and women. Tailoring required a relatively long period of training and apprenticeship, averaging two to three years. The most skilled tailors were employed in workshops attached to large fashionable stores. The majority of garment workers worked in workshops of five to fifty employees, while about one-third worked independently out of their own homes,

14. E. A. Oliunina, *Portnovskii promysl v Moskve i v derevniakh moskovskoi i riazanskoi gubernii. Materialy k istorii domashnei promyshlennosti v Rossii* (Moscow, 1914), pp. 15–17.

usually through jobbers for larger establishments. Russia had only two large clothing factories, which for the most part produced military uniforms. The workers in these factories had steady employment, but most seamstresses and tailors alternated between periods of frenetic overwork and unemployment: "In season there is unrelenting overtime and insane haste, so the tailor has no time for eating and sleeping. Out of season the tailor frequently cannot afford to buy food."[15] During the season—roughly from March to June and from September to the beginning of December—a thirteen-hour day without breaks was standard for the larger workshops, fourteen hours and more in the small ones. More often than not, overtime was unpaid, especially in the smaller workshops, where wages were paid at a set rate and divided between cash payment and room and board. The worker who lived at home was often required to take work home to finish after the thirteen-to-fourteen-hour day, for no extra remuneration.[16] E. A. Oliunina, who did a detailed study of Moscow tailors, observed:

> In the sixth week of Lent, I have frequently seen women workers coming to the dinner table and falling on the bench without the strength to eat, thinking only of how to rest for a quarter or a half hour to relieve their aching limbs and calm their aching heads.[17]

Oliunina remarked on the effects of this pace:

> Squandering her life's energy under the pressures of this difficult work, mainly the result of the length of the work day, by the age of thirty the woman worker is no longer capable of enduring the pressures of the workshop. This accounts for the generally young composition of the workshop.[18]

Living and working conditions in the workshops were as notorious as the exploitation and constant abuse of the workers by the mistresses or masters:

15. Ibid., p. 7.
16. Ibid., pp. 190–201; Pokrovskaia, pp. 31–32.
17. Oliunina, p. 195.
18. Ibid., p. 196.

5. *Moscow textile workers, 1890s.* From *Istoriia Moskvy* (Moscow, 1955), vol. 5, p. 41.

The premises are filthy, the walls covered with torn wallpaper. Bedbugs, lice, and cockroaches emerge from the filth. The temperature in the workshops is very high, since the heaters for the irons are either right in the workshop or adjacent to it in the corridor; the odor of the toilets permeates the room. It is stuffy and crowded. . . . The constant noise and buzz destroys the workers' nerves and at the same time one hears the coarse shouts and curses of the mistresses.[19]

The women often worked and slept in the same room, sharing beds and eating at their benches. Like all workers outside the factory, they had no recourse to the regulation of their conditions through legislation. As one observer remarked, "One needs a great deal of fortitude, fighting want and working twelve hours a day to resist the temptations of . . . vice, which pays much better."[20]

19. Ibid., p. 247.
20. Pokrovskaia, p. 36.

Male and female garment workers had to cope equally with the problems inherent in the organization of the needle trades: the miserable living and working conditions, the abuse and exploitation, the rhythms of a fickle and seasonal industry. But women suffered two further disadvantages, one common to all categories of work that employed both sexes, and one specific to garment workers. The first was in the inequities of remuneration. Women garment workers were paid far more than domestics, but only 64 percent of male garment workers' earnings; in both Moscow and St Petersburg the average yearly earnings of women was 150–200 rubles, a sum that barely covered the demands of basic survival.[21] In the slow months, garment workers inevitably fell into debt or were forced to return to the countryside. However—and this is the problem specific to this industry—more women than men in the needle trades were urban by origin, so that they had less of a protective cushion against unemployment than men, who could and did return to the countryside in the slow season. A far greater proportion of women garment workers than domestics were urban-born. In Moscow, for example, one-third of all seamstresses, regardless of skill, had been born in the city.[22] Nor is this surprising. In the countryside the number of women sufficiently skilled to do even simple sewing declined as ready-made clothing grew cheaper and more accessible. In 1882 an observer noted that in Moscow province "many village girls do not know how to sew and cannot put together even the simplest article of clothing."[23] To be sure, some peasant women found a market for rural *kustar'* skills, such as stocking-knitting, glove making, and embroidery. But the long period of apprenticeship in the needle trade was a major deterrent for the peasant women who needed

21. Oliunina, pp. 201–219.

22. *Perepis' Moskvy 1902 goda. Statisticheskii ezhegodnik goroda Moskvy.* Information on birthplace of garment workers in St Petersburg is not available, but it is reasonable to assume that the proportions of city-born to rural-born were similar, perhaps even higher.

23. *Sbornik statisticheskikh svedenii po moskovskoi gubernii*, t. 7, *Zhenskie promysly*, vyp. 4 (Moscow, 1882), p. ix. M. K. Gorbunova, compiler.

6. *Tobacco workers. Rostov-on-the-Don, late 1890s.* From Joel Carmichael,
An Illustrated History of Russia (New York, 1960), p. 202.

and sought immediate remuneration. And while peasant
immigrants predominated in all women's occupations, the
greater the requisite skill, the higher the percentage of urban-born, as table 2 indicates.

Yet another nonindustrial occupation employed more
women of urban than rural origin. Retail and commercial
enterprises sprouted and flourished with urbanization,
creating jobs that demanded a standard of appearance and
demeanor that city-born women were more likely to approach. Women were about 7 percent of the roughly three
million shop assistants in the early twentieth century, but
their absolute number—210,000—was significant.[24] In Moscow one-half of the female retail clerks were urban born
(see table 2). Working sixteen to eighteen hours a day, they

24. A. Gudvan, *Ocherki po istorii dvizheniia sluzhashchikh v Rossii.* Chast' pervaia
(Moscow, 1925), pp. 135–137.

TABLE 2 Percentages of Women in Moscow City Born in Moscow City, by Occupation, 1902 and 1912

Occupation	1902	1912
Domestics	5	4.5
Laundresses	9	10
Plain sewers (in workshops)	21	21
Plain sewers (independent)	38	—
Tailors (in workshops)	33	41
Apprentices (sewing)	28	30
Shop assistants	—	51

SOURCE: *Perepis' Moskvy 1902 goda* (Moscow, 1906), chast' 1, vyp. 2, pp. 90–115. *Statisticheskii ezhegodnik g. Moskvy za 1914–1925* (Moscow, 1927), vyp. 2, pp. 168–174.

earned an average of 180–200 rubles a year, half the earnings of their male counterparts. The pace in most retail establishments was debilitating, since for the most part the workday did not include time off for eating and rest. The specific problems of the woman shop assistant are succinctly summarized in the words of a woman shop assistant in 1908:

> As it is, we do not earn enough to live on, but on top of that the bosses insist that we dress fashionably. We cannot do anything about it because Petersburg is full of girls prepared to work fifteen hours a day for no more than a crust of bread. The bosses want only good-looking girls and are in a position to make whatever demands they feel like.[25]

What the bosses "felt like" was a euphemism. It meant that "they [shop girls] would . . . frequently have to prostitute themselves with a prospective employer to acquire a job in the first place, and what began as casual prostitution often became a permanent source of income."[26]

25. Ibid., p. 137.
26. Ibid., p. 136.

Women workers in more skilled and prestigious, but equally exploitative, white-collar jobs practiced casual and intermittent prostitution to augment their meager earnings as well:

> The combined effect of such long hours, low pay, and the high cost of living in the large towns is such that those girls with the least resistance gradually begin to follow the example of the shop girls. The income from an evening stroll helps many a cashier or secretary to make ends meet.[27]

But prostitution as a full-time occupation, like domestic service or factory work, was primarily a lower-class occupation and of no mean proportions. On the eve of the 1905 revolution in St Petersburg, a city of one and one-half million, the number of prostitutes was estimated at thirty to fifty thousand.[28] Official Russian designations of estate or class are too crude to allow us to quantify accurately the social origins of prostitutes, but it is clear that by far the great majority were peasant women.[29] Young, naive peasant girls entering the large cities at the railway stations were abundant quarry for the ubiquitous brothel recruiters, who had a well-organized system of purchasers and agents in the shops, inns, and factories as well. The life and fate of the Russian prostitute was too similar to her Western counterpart's to require special elaboration here.

Russia's smaller cities differed from Moscow and St Petersburg in economic structure and social composition, and the kinds of work available to women varied accordingly. In Odessa, for example, Russia's third largest city, the female population had grown to 48 percent of the total population by 1897.[30] The majority of the population was not peasant, as in Moscow and St Petersburg, but *meshchane*. The *mesh-*

---

27. Ibid., p. 139.
28. Richard Stites, "Prostitute and Society in Prerevolutionary Russia" (unpublished article), p. 12. See also Stites, *The Women's Liberation Movement in Russia* (Princeton, 1978), pp. 178–190.
29. Stites, "Prostitute and Society," p. 5.
30. *Pervaia vseobshchaia perepis' naseleniia rossiiskoi imperii. 1897 g.*, t. 47 (1903), p. vi.

7. *Tailor's workshop. Riazan' Province.* From E. A. Oliunina, *Portnovskii promysl v Moskve i v derevniakh moskovskoi i riazan'skoi gubernii* (Moscow, 1914), opposite p. 80.

chane—56 percent of Odessa's inhabitants—was a nebulous estate comprising primarily lower- and middle-class city dwellers and representing an extremely wide economic range from the wealthy merchant at the top to the impoverished street peddler at the bottom. While the poorest women among them were as likely to be employed as were peasant women, a much higher proportion would have been able to survive on the family income without working. Thus only 28 percent of Odessa's female population was gainfully employed, compared with the roughly 50 percent of Moscow and St Petersburg.[31] Further, Odessa was a great port and commercial city with little industry. Thus, a proportionately higher percentage of women wage earners were in domestic service—45 percent—and the rest were

31. Ibid., pp. vi–vii. Peasants were 27 percent of Odessa's population.

distributed among the needle trades, work as laundresses, and the selling of agricultural products.[32]

Kiev and Khar'kov had large peasant populations comparable to those of the capitals and therefore a correspondingly high proportion of women wage earners. But, like Odessa, these cities had relatively few factories of the kind that employed women; the proportion of women in domestic service was therefore similar to Odessa's—45 percent—and the rest were similarly distributed among needle-workers, laundresses, and agricultural traders.[33]

A small proportion of urban women, of course, were engaged in intellectual or semi-intellectual occupations, and in some cases they outnumbered men in professions such as teaching and lower medical personnel. With rare exceptions, these women came from social strata that neither fed into the working classes nor drew on them. While they were working women in the fullest sense of the term, they fall outside our consideration.

The nonindustrial occupations in which city women clustered were more often than not "women's work," extensions of women's age-old unpaid domestic work. Transformed into wage labor, these occupations continued to be performed by women workers. Because these occupations were low in skill and status, they were at the bottom of the wage scale, and for the same reasons attracted mainly peasant women newly arrived in the cities. It is perhaps relevant to include in this category women who lived by begging. In 1912, 69 percent of Moscow's 21,993 inhabitants who lived by begging or on institutional charity were female, and of them 71 percent had been born in the countryside.[34] In the occupations that women shared with men, like tailoring and sales work, women were shunted to the bottom of the wage scale even when their skill was equal to men's. Factory work and the factory milieu differed in many important ways from the work just described, but the patterns of occupa-

32. Ibid., p. xvi.
33. Ibid., t. 41, pp. v–xii; t. 16, pp. ii–v.
34. *Statisticheskii ezhegodnik goroda Moskvy*, p. 74.

tional distribution and rewards that characterized women's nonindustrial work were as pervasive and tenacious within the factory walls as without.

* * *

The continuum from nonindustrial work to the factory, from the village setting to the urban, is, in a sense, artificial. As we saw in chapter one, factory work in Russia was by no means an exclusively urban form of wage labor and was, in fact, more available in the countryside than in the city. Nor was factory work for women the end point on a straight path from village household crafts through urban nonindustrial work. It had been an alternative for women from the very beginnings of Russian industrialization, although, as for men, an extremely modest one given the torpor of industrialization from the early eighteenth to the mid-nineteenth century. Let us glance back briefly into the origins of female factory labor from the eighteenth century when Peter the Great attempted to turn Russia onto the road to industrialization.

The economic and social structure of eighteenth-century Russia was as sluggish in providing a labor force for factories as it was in stimulating private entrepreneurship. It is not surprising, then, that Peter the Great showed no special preference for male workers in his strenuous attempts to provide working hands for existing or potential factories. For example, in 1721 he ruled that women sentenced for various crimes should serve out their sentences in the factory. Labor scarcity did not end with his reign, and subsequent decrees ascribed prostitutes and even the idle, able-bodied wives of sailors, soldiers, and other service people to work in the factories.[35]

However, most factory labor did not come from piecemeal accumulations of "idle" or deviant individuals; it came from a portion of the serf population that was ascribed to factories

---

35. M. I. Tugan-Baranovsky, *The Russian Factory in the 19th Century,* trans. Arthur and Claora S. Levin (1970), p. 17.

with similar disregard for gender distinctions. Serf workers themselves may not have been indifferent to this kind of random ascription. To be sure, the evidence is meager, but worth relating for what it suggests about peasant attitudes as well as those of government and factory owners. In 1741 a government commission set out to investigate the poor output of wool factories. It issued a preliminary suggestion that the wives and daughters of male wool workers who stayed at home "idle or carousing" should be put to work in the factories. Those who refused should be fined for their "disobedience and insolence." The final resolution was modified and declared that wives and daughters should work only if they wished to, "for it may be that they have some other occupations for earning subsistence: in addition they are obliged to do their housework." In 1797 the workers at the large Osokin wool factory in Kazan' province refused to allow their wives and daughters to work and appealed to the ruling for support. The government decided in favor of the workers on the grounds that forcing women to work would destroy the peasant-worker economy:

> The peasant-workers with land would have to cut their sowing and livestock in half; the landless peasant worker would have to abandon all domestic wage-work; children and the elderly would be without care. The peasant woman cannot cope with everything at once, nor do the low wages of women help the peasant family to survive.[36]

But in 1836 the government reversed its decision and gave Osokin permission to force women to work.[37] In a similar case in 1859 at a factory in Voronezh province, the government supported the factory owner against the workers.[38] Thus it appears that factory owners were eager to put

36. K. Pazhitnov, "Iz kazennoi ekaterinoslavskoi sukonnoi i shelko-chulochnoi fabriki," *Arkhiv Istorii Truda,* 2 (Leningrad, 1924), pp. 211–213.

37. Tugan-Baranovsky, p. 116.

38. *Rabochee dvizhenie v Rossii v XIX veke: Sbornik dokumentov i materialov.,* t. 1, chast' 2 (Moscow, 1955), pp. 463–470. This collection of documents consists of four volumes published between 1950 and 1963. The editor-in-chief of vols. 1–3 was A. M. Pankratova; of vol. 4, L. M. Ivanov. (Hereafter, *Rab. dvizh.*)

women in the factory, the workers were opposed, and the government vacillated.

We cannot judge from these two examples the extent of peasant resistance to the employment of women. Further, since men spoke for their wives and daughters, we do not know whether women themselves were reluctant to work in the factory. The lean data on factory workers in general in this period reflect the serf status of the factory population. Just as only male "souls" were counted among the agricultural peasants, often only male workers in the factory were counted. But from scattered sources, women appear to have been employed in most industries, including those which required great physical strength, like mining and metallurgy.[39] In 1764 they were almost 20 percent of the workers in wool factories, Russia's largest textile industry in the eighteenth century.[40]

Peasant resistance to female factory labor, whatever its dimensions, clearly weakened as freely hired labor began to compete with ascribed factory labor: freely hired workers protested when women were kept out of the factory.[41] Unlike most of Russia's early industries, cotton manufacture developed independently of government needs and support at precisely the time when manufacturers were forbidden to buy serfs. Consequently, cotton manufacturers had to rely almost entirely on freely hired labor. By 1825 almost 100 percent of cotton workers were freely hired, and the majority of women who worked in factories were in cotton production.[42] On the eve of the emancipation of the serfs, women made up 20 percent of the total labor force of St Petersburg, but were 44 percent of cotton-spinning workers.[43]

39. Tugan–Baranovsky, pp. 9, 84, 87, 91, 92. A. G. Rashin, *Formirovanie promyshlennogo proletariata v Rossii*, (Moscow, 1940), p. 51; *Rab. dvizh.*, t. 1, chast' 1 (Moscow, 1955), pp. 482, 485, 683, 769.

40. K. A. Pazhitnov, *Ocherki istorii tekstil'noi promyshlennosti dorevoliutsionnoi Rossii* (Moscow, 1955), pp. 56–57.

41. *Rab. dvizh.*, t. 1, chast' 1, pp. 556, 726.

42. Tugan-Baranovsky, p. 70. Forty-eight percent of the entire factory labor force consisted of freely hired labor.

43. *Proekt pravil dlia fabrik i zavodov v S-Peterburge i uezde* (St Petersburg, 1860), in S. N. Valk, ed., *Istoriia rabochikh Leningrada*, 1 (Leningrad, 1972), p. 93.

In the 1880s information about women factory workers becomes far more abundant. This decade witnessed the emergence of the "labor problem" as workers began to protest the conditions of their lives with some persistence, and government and industrialists opened a serious, sustained dialogue about the regulation of industrial relations. The first major piece of protective legislation was passed in 1882 to limit child labor.[44] At the same time, a factory inspectorate was established to monitor compliance with this and future labor laws. Russia was divided into nine factory districts (*okrugi*), each with a small staff of junior inspectors and one senior inspector. Along with the enumeration of child workers and attempts to enforce the law, factory inspectors counted and observed women workers as well. Many of the factory inspectors interpreted their responsibilities broadly and went far beyond the government's narrow definition of their duties. It is mainly thanks to them that we have figures for women workers as well as sensitive descriptions of workers' living and working conditions in the mid-1880s.

The factory inspectors' reports of 1885 revealed that the proportions of women in the factory work force had scarcely changed since the emancipation, despite the significant if modest growth of industry. Women were roughly 22 percent of the total labor force, as they appear to have been for decades earlier, and as before, they far exceeded that figure in textile production.[45] As table 3 shows, they were from a quarter to a half of all textile workers in Russia, even in factory districts where their overall representation was low and textile factories were few, like Kiev, Khar'kov, and Kazan'. Textile production, Russia's major industry, was

44. The law of 1882 prohibited employment of children under the age of twelve and limited the work for children aged twelve to fourteen to eight hours a day.
45. Factory inspectors' statistics did not include state-owned enterprises. The government owned mainly St Petersburg metal and armament factories which employed male workers. Satisfactory estimates of the number of workers in these enterprises are not available. It is highly unlikely that the addition of these workers to the factory inspectors' statistics would change the proportions of women workers in this study. But the reader should be aware of the bias.

TABLE 3 Women as a Percentage of the Factory Labor Force in European Russia, by Factory District (*okrug*), 1885

Factory District (okrug) (with component provinces)	Percentage Employed in: Textile	Paper	Tobacco	All Industries
Moscow (Moscow, Tver', Smolensk, Tula, Riazan', Kaluga)	31.2	47.2	47.5	31.7
Vladimir (Vladimir, Vologda, Kostroma, Nizhnii Novgorod, Iaroslavl)	25.0	41.5	10.2	36.3
St Petersburg (St Petersburg, Olonets, Arkhangelsk, Estliand, Lifliand, Pskov, Novgorod)	45.6	28.8	84.3	36.5
Kiev (Kiev, Volynia, Podolia, Kherson)	32.2	27.4	22.7	10.1
Khar'kov (Khar'kov, Poltava, Ekaterinoslav, Chernigov, Oblast Voiska Donskogo)	54.7	27.3	56.9	22.6
Kazan' (Kazan', Perm, Viatka, Simbirsk, Ufa, Orenburg)	40.0	—	—	5.2
Voronezh (Voronezh, Penza, Samara, Saratov, Astrakhan, Kursk, Tambov, Orel)	25.6	48.9	47.3	18.2
Vil'na (Vil'na, Kovno, Grodno, Minsk, Mogilev, Kurliand, Vitebsk)	39.0	30.0	59.4	16.3
All Factory Districts Combined	36.7	35.9	46.9	22.1

SOURCE: Factory inspectors' reports for each district (all published in St Petersburg, 1886). The form of the title in each case is *Otchet za 1885 g. fabrichnogo inspektora . . . okruga.* Authors of the reports are: I. I. Ianzhul (Moscow); P. A. Peskov (Vladimir); K. V. Davydov (St Petersburg); I. O. Novitskii (Kiev); V. V. Sviatlovskii (Khar'kov); A. V. Shidlovskii (Kazan'); V. I. Miropol'skii (Voronezh); and G. I. Gorodkov (Vil'na). I have not included the Warsaw factory district, which contained the ten provinces of the Kingdom of Poland. Factory conditions in Poland were substantially different from those in the rest of European Russia and require separate analysis.

concentrated in the most highly industrialized factory districts: Moscow, Vladimir, and St Petersburg. In these districts women far surpassed their average representation in the labor force. They were also employed in other light industries such as tobacco and paper.

These averages do not reflect the considerable disparity in female employment from factory to factory. In St Petersburg, Moscow, and Vladimir factory districts, where industry was a stable feature of the economic landscape, factories were relatively large, and the indigenous population was already disposed to accept factory work as an alternative to agriculture and *kustar'* production. The factories here attracted peasant immigrants from other parts of Russia as well. The proportions of women workers in individual factories were consistent with their overall representation in the industry of these districts.[46] But in factory districts of low and less stable industrial concentration the proportions of women vacillated from factory to factory. For example, in the Kazan' factory district, where women were 40 percent of all textile workers, one of the two largest textile factories (590 workers) employed no women, and in the other (635 workers) women were a third of the workers.[47] Similarly, in the Kiev district, where the tobacco industry was the major employer of female labor, some factories employed no women while others employed primarily women.[48]

From 1885 to 1914 the salient feature of the history of women workers was the slow but steady increase not only of their absolute numbers in the labor force but of the percentage of their representation in the total as well. The increases transcended depressions and booms, war and revolution. Whether the total labor force increased or diminished, whether industry flourished or declined, the proportion of women in factories rose relentlessly.

46. See source note for table 3, for this note and nn. 47, 48, 51. Ianzhul, pp. 22–36; Peskov, pp. 18–23; Davydov, pp. 15–24.

47. A. V. Shidlovskii, p. 12.

48. Novitskii, pp. 42–44.

A portent of this phenomenon was apparent in the earliest observations of the factory inspectorate. In 1882 I. I. Ianzhul, the factory inspector for the Moscow district, predicted that the limitation of child labor would lead to greater employment of women.[49] Indeed, by 1885 the number of children in the factories of the Moscow district was only 32.5 percent of their number in 1882. Some of these child workers were not replaced, because of the economic crisis of the first half of the 1880s. Some were replaced by adolescent boys. But most were replaced by adult women. In cotton manufacture, the proportion of women rose from 35.4 percent of the work force in 1882 to 39.1 percent in 1885. In wool production they increased from 28.6 percent to 39.1 percent, and in tobacco, women replaced children almost entirely.[50] However, as late as 1885 the news of the child labor law had barely penetrated beyond Moscow province, and where it had, it was often either misunderstood or resisted by factory owners. Consequently, the number of child workers in other provinces of the Moscow factory district had not decreased as sharply as in Moscow province, nor, correspondingly, had the number of women workers increased appreciably. Similar observations came from the Vladimir factory inspectorate.[51] It was too soon, therefore, for the legislation to influence the total picture. By 1891, however, it was clear to the factory inspector of the Vladimir district that however small the increments of increase in female labor, they were adding up. He commented in his official report to the Ministry of Finance that "the percentage relationship between men and women [workers] is almost the same as it was last year. But since 1888 there has been a gradual tendency for the percentage of women workers to increase . . . and this is especially pronounced in the cotton industry."[52] In fact, throughout the Empire the

49. I. I. Ianzhul, *Fabrichnyi byt moskovskoi gubernii. Otchet za 1882–1883* (St Petersburg, 1884), p. 8.
50. Ianzhul, *Fabrichnyi byt moskovskoi gubernii. Otchet za 1885*, p. 51.
51. Peskov, p. 30.
52. TsGIA, f. 20, op. 13b, d. 28, l. 10.

proportions of women in the labor force increased slowly but surely. The increase was most significant in textile production. Even in the silk industry where the total number of workers shrank between 1901 and 1909, the percentage of women workers grew enormously (see table 4). This nineteenth-century pattern of distribution continued into the twentieth century. On the eve of World War I women had come to dominate the textile industry (see table 5) and to constitute the majority of workers in two of the major textile-producing provinces, Vladimir and Kostroma (see table 6).

Female factory labor increased in the great urban industrial centers, Moscow and St Petersburg, in accord with the specific economic structure of each city (see table 7). In 1882 P. A. Peskov studied the textile industry in Moscow city and noted a higher proportion of women in provincial textile factories than in the city's textile factories, 35.8 and 21.5 percent, respectively.[53] He attributed this to his skewed sample: the majority of the city's factories in his sample still depended on manual processes, which favored male employment, while the province's textile factories were more mechanized and hired more women. He was only partly correct. The discrepancy between city and countryside was mainly the result of migration patterns of the nineteenth century. In the nineteenth century the migration of peasant women to the city lagged behind male migration, for, as we observed in chapter two, women looked first for work close to home. Further, the conditions of urban life discouraged peasant immigrants from bringing their families to the city. However, by the twentieth century male and female migration to the cities was almost equal. In the textile industry the proportions of women in Moscow's textile factories equaled those in provincial factories by 1909. But within the total factory population the proportions of women workers remained higher in the province than in the city. This was because textiles were by far the dominant industry in the

53. P. A. Peskov, *Trudy,* p. 78 (see source for table 7).

TABLE 4 Female Employment in Vladimir Factory District, Vladimir Province, and Moscow Province (for various years)

District or Province	Years			
Vladimir Factory District	*1888*	*1889*	*1890*	*1891*
Percentage of total labor force	34.1	34.8	35.2	35.4
Percentage of cotton workers	38.4	38.5	39.0	39.4
Vladimir Province	*1885*	*1891*	*1897*	
Percentage of total labor force	36.3	35.4	39.0	
Percentage of all cotton workers	—	41.4	51.2	
Percentage of cotton weavers	—	49.0	52.0	
Percentage of cotton spinners	—	33.8	50.4	
Percentage of workers in printing, dying, bleaching		19.7	25.0	
Moscow Province	*1882*	*1897*	*1901*	*1909*
Percentage of total labor force	—	—	33.8	38.0
Percentage of cotton workers	43.8	45.5	44.5	48.5
Percentage of wool workers	33.2	31.4	33.5	41.2
Percentage of silk workers	37.8	43.0	54.8	62.3

SOURCES: TsGIA, f. 23, op. 29, d. 91, l. 4–6; *Otchet chinov fabrichnoi inspektsii vladimirskoi gubernii, 1894–1897* (Vladimir, 1899), p. 202, for Vladimir factory district and province.

F. F. Erisman, *Sbornik statisticheskikh svedenii po moskovskoi gubernii*. Otdel sanitarnoi statistiki (Moscow, 1890), t. 4, chast' 1, pp. 198–202; N. A. Troinitskii, *Chislennost' i sostav rabochikh v Rossii na osnovanii dannykh Pervoi Vseobshchei Perepisi Naseleniia Rossiiskoi Imperii 1897 g.*, t. 1 (1906), pp. 2–93; I. M. Koz'minykh-Lanin, *Deviatiletnii period fabrichno-zavodskoi promyshlennosti moskovskoi gubernii* (Moscow, 1912), pp. 2–20, for Moscow province.

(My calculations.)

province, whereas in the city there was a greater variety of industries, including some that employed mainly male workers.

In St Petersburg as well as Moscow the increase in female peasant migration was only slightly lower than male migration by the twentieth century, and the proportion of women

TABLE 5 Percentage of Women in Factory Employment, by Industry, 1885–1914

Industry	1885	1897	1900	1901	1910	1911	1912	1913	1914
Textiles	36.7	41.0	44.6	46.9	51.6	52.1	52.9	55.8	57.0
Cotton	—	42.9	46.0	—	53.6	54.2	55.2	56.2	58.6
Wool	—	31.6	36.0	—	38.7	38.9	39.3	40.8	43.9
Silk	—	50.8	50.4	—	66.0	68.1	67.9	66.7	66.0
Linen, hemp, jute	—	43.3	47.0	—	55.1	54.2	54.8	55.1	57.2
Mixed textiles	—	—	54.8	—	56.8	57.2	57.3	60.4	52.7
Paper	35.9	33.9	25.7	—	25.7	—	25.4	25.2	24.9
Wood	—	—	10.2	—	10.1	—	10.2	11.1	11.5
Metals	—	—	2.8	—	5.2	—	5.6	5.9	5.5
Minerals	—	—	12.8	—	17.6	—	17.7	18.3	18.2
Animal products	—	—	—	—	15.2	—	16.4	16.5	19.0
Food production	—	—	—	—	20.1	—	21.9	22.2	23.5
Chemicals	—	—	—	—	33.4	—	35.5	36.6	37.7
Oil	—	—	—	—	—	—	—	—	—
Others	—	—	—	—	9.9	—	8.4	—	8.1
Percentage of all factory women employed in textiles					71.6	71.0	69.9	68.3	67.5

sources: Otchet za 1885 g. fabrichnogo inspektora za. (St Petersburg, 1886). (For all factory districts, see table 1.). Svod otchetov fabrichnykh inspektorov za, 1900; 1901; 1910; 1911; 1913; 1914. N. A. Troinitskii, Chislennost' i sostav rabochikh (see source for table 4), pp. 2–93.

TABLE 6 Percentage of Women in the Total Factory Labor Force, by Province, 1901–1914

Province	1901	1903	1904	1905	1908	1910	1912	1913	1914
St Petersburg	24.7	24.9	24.2	25.9	29.8	29.3	29.1	29.5	29.5
Vladimir	43.9	45.3	46.3	46.3	48.1	51.0	51.7	52.0	55.0
Moscow	33.8	31.8	33.9	35.3	37.9	39.1	39.5	40.0	41.5
Kostroma	40.7	44.0	45.6	46.3	49.0	49.0	51.1	52.0	54.9
Kiev	12.2	14.7	14.3	15.0	17.6	17.0	16.8	18.4	20.0
Khar'kov	14.8	16.1	16.4	15.1	21.0	19.75	20.9	—	21.2
Saratov	22.2	12.0	11.0	13.5	14.0	14.9	—	—	15.2
Viatka	11.6	9.2	5.2	6.2	6.8	7.7	—	—	9.4

SOURCE: *Svod otchetov fabrichnykh inspektorov za 1901*, pp. 34–35; *1903*, pp. 38–39; *1904*, pp. 41–42; *1905*, pp. 39–40; *1908*, pp. 42–43; *1911*, p. xlvi; *1912*, pp. 22–23; *1913*, pp. xlvi; *1914*, p. 26.

The provinces in this table were chosen to include the highly industrialized provinces and two with insignificant concentrations of industry. The decline of women workers in the latter two, Saratov and Viatka, can be explained by the tendency in the agricultural provinces to give women more responsibility on the still viable land as men emigrated for outside work, as well as by the weak development of industry. The number of workers was small enough in Viatka and Saratov that if one factory of any size closed, the percentages were considerably skewed. The smaller percentage of women workers in St Petersburg throughout is due to the lesser importance of the textile industry compared with heavy industry in that province.

TABLE 7 Women as a Percentage of the Factory Labor
Force in the Cities of Moscow and St Petersburg
(for various years)

City		Years		
St Petersburg	*1890*	*1900*	*1910*	*1913*
Percentage of total work force				29.4
				(N=32,705)
Textiles	43.9	54.7	62.0	67.7
Tobacco	81.8	85.6		
Rubber	46.3	50.7		
Paper		26.6		
Animal products		25.5		28.2
Moscow	*1882*	*1902*	*1912*	
Percentage of total work force		27.6	30.3	(N=49,995)
Textiles	21.4	37.0	50.8	
Candy	18.7	38.8	42.7	
Chemicals			30.5	
Paper			25.0	
Food processing			25.6	
Tobacco		64.5	75.6	
Day labor			25.1	

SOURCES: For St Petersburg: *S.-Peterburg po perepisi 15 dekabria 1900 goda*, (St Petersburg, 1903), vyp. 2, pp. 38–83; *S.-Peterburg po perepisi 15 dekabria 1890 goda*, (St Petersburg, 1891), vyp. 2, chast' 1, pp. 26–50; E. E. Kruze, *Peterburgskie rabochie v 1912–1914 godakh* (Moscow and Leningrad, 1961), p. 78.
For Moscow: *Statisticheskii ezhegodnik g. Moskvy i moskovskoi gubernii za 1914–1925* (Moscow, 1927), vyp. 2, table 14; *Perepis' Moskvy 1902 goda* (Moscow, 1906), pp. 90–114; Koz'minykh-Lanin, *Deviatiletnii period fabrichno-zavodskoi promyshlennosti moskovskoi gubernii* (Moscow, 1912), pp. 2–20; P. A. Peskov, *Trudy kommissii uchrezhdennoi g. moskovskim General-Gubernatorom, kn. V. A. Dolgorukovym dlia osmotra fabrik i zavodov v Moskve*, vypusk pervyi (Moscow, 1882), p. 77.

workers concentrated in textiles rose correspondingly (see table 8). But St Petersburg was a great metallurgical center, and the proportion of women in the city's total work force was lower than in Moscow. In textiles, however, the percentages of women workers were higher. As there was virtually no industry in the province, women drawn to factory

TABLE 8 Participation of Women in Factory Employment:
Russian Empire, 1901–1914

Year	Total Employment	Number of Women Workers	Percentage of Women Workers
1901	1,710,735	453,357	26.8
1903	1,690,478	463,114	27.4
1904	1,663,080	458,527	27.6
1905	1,693,323	480,714	28.4
1906	1,723,177	509,476	29.6
1907	1,811,267	583,778	29.7
1908	1,808,144	546,346	30.2
1909	1,831,396	565,095	30.8
1910	1,151,955	606,588	31.7
1911	2,051,198	638,277	31.1
1912	2,151,191	667,307	31.0
1913	2,319,557	723,913	31.2
1914	1,970,860	662,620	31.7

SOURCE: *Svod otchetov fabrichnykh inspektorov za 1901*, p. iii; *1903*, p. iv; *1904*, p. iii; *1905*, p. vii; *1906*, p. vi; *1907*, p. vi; *1908*, p. vii; *1909*, p. xii; *1910*, p. xxxi; *1911*, p. xxvi; *1912*, p. lxv; *1913*, p. lxii; *1914*, p. xxxviii.

work had no choice of factory employment closer to home, as they had in Moscow province.

At the same time that women were becoming dominant among textile workers—58.6 percent by 1914—the industry was actually absorbing proportionately less of the total female work force. In 1910, 71.6 percent of all women workers were in textile factories; in 1914, 67 percent (see table 5 above). The shift into other industries was small but steady. In the two capitals, for the most part, women simply worked in greater numbers in industries where they had always worked. But in the regions of Russia weak in textiles, women workers began to move into industries that had formerly been exclusively male. Khar'kov province is a good illustration of this phenomenon. Typical of Russia's southern provinces, Khar'kov was heavily agricultural with a sprinkling of small-scale industries, among which textiles were insignificant. Between 1901 and 1914 women workers increased from 14.8 percent to 21.2 percent of the province's factory work force. In 1885, eleven of Khar'kov's industries had employed no women whatsoever. By 1911 only three excluded women: the building of engines, the construction of agricultural machinery, and the construction of assorted machinery. The increase of women workers was especially dramatic in four industries that had previously employed only men.[54]

	Khar'kov Province	
Industry	*Women Workers, 1885*	*Women Workers, 1911*
Pottery	0%	37.5%
Ceramics	0	41.5
Glass	0	29.0
Brick	0	16.0

By 1913, reports of women penetrating new industries poured in from all corners of the Empire. The *Svod otchetov fabrichnykh inspectorov* [Summary of Factory Inspectors' Reports] for that year pointed out that, although the percentage increase of women workers over the previous year was insignificant, it masked the fact that "the striving to replace men with women continues": In St Petersburg women were beginning to work on small-sized drilling machines; in Moscow province women were working on bridge-girding electric cranes; in Vologda and Ekaterinoslav provinces women were hired to work in sawmills for the first time; in Voronezh they had increased by 23 percent overall (men by only 5 percent), especially in candy factories and brick works.[55]

* * *

In 1885 approximately one in every five factory workers was a woman; in 1914, one in every three. The more signifi-

---

54. A. N. Opatskii, *Fabrichno-zavodskaia promyshlennost' khar'kovskoi gubernii* (Khar'kov, 1912). My calculations.

55. *Svod otchetov fabrichnykh inspektorov za 1913*, p. xliv.

cant increase took place between 1900 and 1914. Between 1901 and 1913—the peak year of Russian industrial growth before the outbreak of World War I—the total labor force had increased by 35 percent and the male sector by 27 percent. But women factory workers had increased by 59.6 percent (see table 8).

In all Western European countries the absolute and proportional increase in women workers had accompanied industrial expansion. In the 1880s factory inspectors and *zemstvo* statisticians assumed that Russia would emulate the course of industrialization in England and Germany and that sex ratios in the labor force would change accordingly. They assumed that the change would follow first from an evolution inherent in the dynamics of industrialization. As Ianzhul remarked in 1885, "As the techniques of industry improve and hand labor is replaced by mechanical devices, the demand for male labor will drop correspondingly."[56] According to this formulation, a simple technical consideration—mechanization—governed the rate of employment of women and children. A second prerequisite was the conscious intervention in the evolution of industrialization, namely, the enactment of legislation to limit child labor. An unpremeditated effect of such legislation would be an increase in the female work force as employers sought to replace one kind of cheap labor with another. In other words, children would be replaced by women.

The law of 1882 that limited child labor achieved maximal results by 1900. Between 1900 and 1914 child labor remained stable at roughly 1.5 percent of the labor force. There were simply no more children to replace. Adolescent labor, too, remained stable. Yet, from 1900 the proportions of women workers mounted at a greater rate than in the period between 1885 and 1900, when women had been replacing children in the factory. This increase meant that women were hired instead of men. As table 9 shows,

56. I. I. Ianzhul, "Zhenskii fabrichnyi trud," *Drug Zhenshchin* (1884), no. 5, p. 94.

TABLE 9 Percentage of Adult Workers in the Industrial
Labor Force by Sex: Russian Empire,' 1901–
1913

Workers	1901	1903	1904	1905	1908	1909	1912	1913
Men	66.7	65.9	65.9	62.4	61.1	60.3	59.5	59.0
Women	22.7	23.0	23.5	27.2	29.0	29.7	29.7	29.9

SOURCE: *Svod otchetov fabrichnykh inspektorov za 1901; 1903; 1904; 1905; 1908; 1909; 1912; 1913.*

between 1901 and 1913 male workers dropped from 66.7
percent to 59 percent of the adult factory labor force,
and women workers increased from 22.7 percent to 29.9
percent.

The twin explanations of mechanization and limited child
labor offered by nineteenth-century observers are necessary
but not sufficient to account for the expansion of the female labor force. As we have seen, the simple replacement
of children by women reached its limits, and still the female
sector of the labor force continued to expand. Mechanization made it *possible* for women to perform tasks previously
considered too difficult for them or for which they had not
acquired the skills. But it did not make it necessary or *inevitable* for employers to hire them. What, then, motivated
entrepreneurs to hire women instead of men when the
overpopulated countryside provided a veritable cornucopia
of potential male factory workers? The reason was that as a
process was mechanized and required less strength or less
skill it also commanded a lower wage. The fundamental
attraction of women workers for the entrepreneur was that
as child labor declined women were the remaining source of
cheap labor.

In the next chapter we will examine the conditions of the
factory woman's life, among which the question of wages is
central. Suffice it to say here that throughout our period the
wages of women were from one-half to two-thirds of men's

wages. The demand for cheap labor was not new. But as the tempo of industrialization accelerated, the quest for cheap labor quickened and the employment of women with it.

Official observers were curiously reluctant to acknowledge fully that employers preferred women workers because women would work for lower wages than men. For a number of years they cast about for other ways to explain the accelerated growth of female factory labor. In 1904, a year in which the total factory labor force shrunk by 21,254 workers but the absolute number of women workers increased by over 3,000, the senior factory inspector speculated that the increase must have been due to the Russo-Japanese War, which siphoned male workers from the factory to the army. A year later this explanation had already become untenable:

> In the last two years, especially in 1904, the decrease in the number of adult male workers can be explained to a degree by the . . . war. But all the factory inspectors have pointed out the employer's unquestionable [and continuing] preference for female over male labor wherever possible.[57]

When the war ended and could no longer serve as even a partial explanation, factory inspectors turned to the political and economic convulsions of 1905–1906 to explain the preference for women workers. In a somewhat bewildered tone, the senior factory inspector observed in 1907:

> The exceptional conditions of industry in 1905 and 1906 which forced factory owners to replace male personnel with calmer, more tractable and cheaper women . . . have abated. It might seem that with the pacification of the worker's environment . . . the reverse phenomenon would occur, i.e., . . . the cessation of ousting men to hire women. But in fact this has not occurred, and male labor is still being replaced by female labor. If this is not overtly manifested in the summary data for the Empire, it is because in September for the first time the oil industry of Baku was counted. It comprises 46,499 workers—all male.[58]

57. *Svod 1905*, p. ix.
58. *Svod 1907*, p. vii.

By 1908 it had become clear that the termination of episodic and temporary conditions, like war and revolution,
would not reverse the preferential hiring of women and
that women were hired instead of men "mainly because
they are significantly cheaper labor. . . . The substitution of
female for male workers allows the factory to economize on
wages."[59]

Women workers had other virtues as well to recommend
them to the employer. Factory inspectors often remarked
that women workers were desirable because of their
"greater submissiveness and greater reluctance to demand
higher wages."[60] To be sure, women workers were the
"calmer, steadier element,"[61] although, as we shall see, they
were by no means consistently passive. That they may have
been less inclined to make general demands of the employer was important, although the demands that concerned factory owners most were related to wages.[62]

Entrepreneurs, however, were not exclusively economic
creatures. They were susceptible to assumptions about
women common to the entire society, and their decisions to
hire women were undoubtedly conditioned by factors other
than gain. While the preference for cheap labor may have
been paramount and consistent, notions about the kinds of
work appropriate to women entered into their calculations
as well. Time and experience altered these notions. By 1913
when the senior factory inspector enumerated the industries that were employing women for the first time, he reported that manufacturers were finding that "women have

59. *Svod 1908*, p. 12. TsGIA, f. 23, op. 16, d. 75, l. 141.
60. *Svod 1901*, p. iv.
61. *Svod 1905*, p. ix.
62. Another reason for the desirability of women workers was suggested by G.
Schultze-Gaevernitz, a German economist who studied the Russian cotton industry
very carefully and published an important article on the subject in 1896: "Die
Moskau-Wladimirsche Baumwollindustrie," *Jahrbuch fur Gesetzgeburg, Verwaltung
und Volkwirtschaft*, 2 and 3 (1896). He postulated that employers hired women to
stabilize the labor force by weakening workers' bonds to the village. However, I
have found no evidence that employers, individually or as a group, were so aware
of the virtues of a married factory population that they deliberately hired women
on that account.

the same productivity as men and are also more precise and indulge in less truancy."[63] As assessments of women's abilities changed, the purely economic motivation for hiring them could be indulged with ever more frequency in wider areas of factory labor.

Thus, women marched unswervingly into the factory: their absolute numbers and proportions in the factory labor force increased, and they filtered into industries previously reserved for men. This quantitative dimension, however, is but one index of the transformation which the female factory force underwent. By 1914 women workers as an aggregate were different from their predecessors of the 1880s, and the profile of the female work force had changed in a number of important ways beyond the simple increase in size.

A pervasive and enduring assumption in Russia was that factory work was "something they [women] do just until they get married."[64] The indices we are about to examine do not undermine that assumption for a portion of women workers throughout the period under consideration. But they seriously weaken it as a useful generalization for a significant and growing portion of women workers. Between the 1880s and 1914 women workers evolved toward greater stability as workers, toward a greater degree of proletarianization.

The question of the stability of the female work force is a facet of the more inclusive problem that, as we saw in chapter one, bedevils the historian of Russian labor, namely, the degree to which the Russian factory worker can be called a true proletarian. To reiterate, since the great majority of factory workers came from the peasantry, to what extent had they extricated themselves from their physical, economic, and psychological involvement with the land, and to what extent did they identify themselves in all these ways as factory workers rather than as peasants who

63. *Svod 1913.*
64. M., "Zhenskii trud v fabrichno-zavodskoi promyshlennosti Rossii za poslednie 13 let (1901–1913)," *Obshchestvennyi Vrach* (1915), no. 9–10, p. 596.

happened to work in the factory? The question for women is even more complex, since their identity as factory workers was conditioned not only by their relationship to the land, but by the potential power of marriage to precipitate withdrawal from the labor force.

By the late 1890s the average age of women workers had risen significantly. An inevitable result of the limitation of child labor was that the lower end of the age continuum was virtually eliminated. Although true for the entire labor force, the shift was far more dramatic for women. As we can see from table 10, in Moscow province between 1880 and 1908, women under the age of fifteen decreased from 13.6 percent to 1.82 percent of the female work force. Female children were not replaced by women in the next closest age cohort, namely, by adolescents and younger adults. Instead, the most significant increase was of women in the adult years of greatest vigor, which were also the childbearing and child-rearing years. In the 1880s women between the ages of twenty and forty were 44 percent of the female work force; by 1908 that age cohort had increased to 58.3 percent and was roughly equal to the comparable male age span.[65] This distribution remained consistent to the end of our period in both rural and urban factories (see table 11). However, within this cohort the age structure was different for men and women, and reflected the distribution along the entire age continuum: it tilted toward the lower end among women workers and toward the upper end among men (see tables 10, 11, and 12).

A natural corollary of the changing age structure was that over the decades greater percentages of women factory workers were married. From tables 13 and 14 we see that between 1880 and 1908 the proportion of married women in the factory labor force increased from two-fifths to about one-half.

This increase might be ascribed to three factors: the impact

TABLE 10 Distribution of Male and Female Factory Workers, by Age: Moscow and Vladimir Provinces, 1880–1908 (percentages)

Province	Ages	1880		Ages	1908	
		Women	Men		Women	Men
Moscow	−12	2.6	3.0	−12	0	0
	12–14	11.0	4.9	12–14	1.82	1.3
	15–19	30.79	20.24	15–19	24.05	15.9
	20–24	16.29	15.29	20–24	20.73	15.88
	25–29	12.1	14.27	25–29	16.9	17.6
	30–39	15.63	21.29	30–39	20.9	26.36
	40–49	8.0	12.26	40–49	11.1	15.26
	50–59	2.97	6.14	50–59	3.7	6.11
	60+	.5	2.17	60+	.72	1.39

TABLE 10 *(continued)*

Vladimir		1897	
	Ages	*Women*	*Men*
	12–14	1.5	2.8
	15–19	27.0	19.6
	20–24	21.5	16.9
	25–29	16.3	16.2
	30–39	21.9	25.2
	40–49	8.0	13.0
	49–59	2.1	4.7
	60+	.46	1.9

SOURCES: For Moscow province: F. F. Erisman, *Sbornik statisticheskikh svedenii po moskovskoi gubernii,* Otdel sanitarnoi statistiki, (Moscow, 1890), t. 4, chast' 1, pp. 271, 199; I. M. Koz'minykh-Lanin, *Semeinyi sostav fabrichno-zavodskikh rabochikh moskovskoi gubernii* (Moscow, 1914), p. 16.
For Vladimir province: *Otchet chinov fabrichnoi inspektsii vladimirskoi gubernii, 1894–1897* (Vladimir, 1899), pp. 208–209.

TABLE 11 Distribution of Male and Female Factory Workers, by Age: Moscow and St Petersburg, 1900–1902 (percentages)

	Age	Men		Women	
Moscow, 1902	under 15	.9 ⎫		.8 ⎫	
	15–17	10.3 ⎬ 20.6		11.9 ⎬ 23.3	
	17–19	9.4 ⎭		10.6 ⎭	
	20–24	17.3 ⎫		21.3 ⎫	
	25–29	17.5 ⎬ 59.2		17.8 ⎬ 61.6	
	30–39	24.4 ⎭		22.5 ⎭	
	40–49	14.2 ⎫		11.2 ⎫	
	50–59	4.9 ⎬ 20.2		3.8 ⎬ 15.9	
	60+	1.1 ⎭		.9 ⎭	
St Petersburg, 1900	under 16	5.73		6.0	
(textile workers)	16–20	23.95		22.0	
	21–41	53.2		56.9	
	41–60	16.02		13.3	
	60+	.99		.8	

SOURCES: *Perepis' Moskvy 1902 g.* (Moscow, 1906), vyp. 2, chast' 1, pp. 2–7. *S–Peterburg po perepisi 15 dekabria 1900 goda* (St Petersburg, 1903), vyp. 1, p. 38.

of the child labor laws, changes in age/marriage propensities, and other changes in age/employment structure. Age/ marriage propensities appear to have changed very little, as women factory workers throughout this period married between the ages of eighteen and twenty-one.[66] Therefore, the increase in married women depended on some interplay between the responses of employers to the legislation prohibiting child labor and the behavior of potential women workers. As we have seen, children were not simply replaced by adolescents and young adults. If this had been the

66. If we calculate the hypothetical proportion of married women in the labor force using 1880 age-specific marriage rates and the 1908 age distribution, we obtain a figure of 52 percent. This implies that little of the observed change can be ascribed to age/marriage propensities.

TABLE 12 Age Distribution of Factory Workers, by Sex: Russian Empire, 1901–1913 (percentages)

Age Category	1901	1903	1904	1905	1908	1909	1912	1913
Women Workers								
Child	3.0	2.5	2.1	2.0	2.0	1.9	1.9	2.0
Adolescent	12.3	13.3	12.6	12.1	11.6	11.5	12.4	13.0
Adult	84.7	84.2	85.3	85.9	86.4	86.6	85.6	85.0
Men Workers								
Child	1.6	1.7	1.3	1.2	1.1	1.2	1.2	1.2
Adolescent	7.3	8.0	7.8	7.7	7.2	7.4	8.0	8.2
Adult	91.1	90.3	90.9	90.1	91.7	91.4	90.8	90.6

SOURCE: *Svod otchetov fabrichnykh inspektorov za 1901; 1903; 1904; 1905; 1908; 1909; 1912; 1913.*

TABLE 13 Age and Marital Status of the Female Labor
Force, Moscow Province, 1880s

	Percentage of Sample (N=35,890)			
Age	Unmarried	Married	Widowed	Total
under 15	13.7	0	0	13.7
15–19	27.7	3.0	0	30.7
20–29	7.5	19.9	1.0	28.4
30–39	2.1	11.1	2.4	15.6
40+	1.2	6.2	4.1	11.5
Total	52.2	40.2	7.5	100.0

SOURCE: F. F. Erisman, *Sbornik statisticheskikh svedenii po moskovskoi gubernii*, Otdel Sanitarnoi Statistiki (Moscow, 1890), t. 1, chast' 1, p. 271.

TABLE 14 Age and Marital Status of the Female Labor
Force, Moscow Province, 1908

	Percentage of Sample (N=34,583)			
Age	Unmarried	Married	Widowed	Total
under 15	1.8	0	0	1.8
15–19	21.9	2.1	0	24.0
20–29	10.4	26.3	1.0	37.6
30–39	2.4	15.8	2.7	20.9
40+	1.6	8.4	5.6	15.6
Total	38.1	52.6	9.3	100.0

SOURCE: I. M. Koz'minykh-Lanin, *Semeinyi sostav fabrichno-zavodskikh rabochikh
moskovskoi gubernii* (Moscow, 1914), p. 3.

case, the proportion of married women in the sample would
have increased by only 1.3 percent. If, however, we consider only the labor force over the age of fifteen and assume that the underage girls were replaced by women in
proportion to their share in the 1880 labor force, the share
of married women would have risen to 46.7 percent. In

other words, the simple elimination of underage girls would have led to some natural increase of married women, but not to the extent that actually occurred.[67]

Further, among both married and single women the proportion of those in peak childbearing years (ages twenty to twenty-nine) also increased. Between 1880 and 1908 the proportion of women factory workers who were married and in the peak childbearing years rose from one-fifth to about one-half. Although the percentage of single women in the factory declined from 52 to 38 percent, among them women over the age of twenty rose from 20 to 38 percent. This suggests the possibility, never discussed in the sources nor calculable from statistics, that many single women workers had family responsibilities. It was certainly the case that many widowed factory women, all of whom were over the age of twenty, had children to care for. Thus, the rise of married women and the simultaneous increase of women in the prime childbearing years, married and single, beyond what either the prohibition of child labor and age/marriage propensities would have produced, belies the belief in Russia that factory work for women was "something they do just until they get married." The argument often made that women were a casual segment of the labor force is difficult to sustain.

The evidence for proletarianization commonly explored in the literature of labor history does not include marital status. Marriage did not have the same implications for the male factory workers, since it never led to withdrawal from the labor force. The significance of marriage for the male worker was rather whether his family lived with him at the factory or remained in the countryside. The important question was the male worker's relationship to the land; his marital status and the location of his family were only possi-

67. Of the 11.8 percentage point increase in the share of married women attributable to the effect of child labor laws and other changes in age/employment structure together, from 1.3 to 6.5 percentage points can be attributed to the child labor laws, and 5.3 to 10.5 percentage points to other factors, that is, increases in the degree of commitment to factory labor or, in other words, increased proletarianization.

ble illustrations of that relationship. The question of ties to the land for women workers is more problematical, since land ownership was a male attribute. As we know, peasant women worked the land as part of their unquestioned traditional contribution to the family economy, and the de jure absence of land rights had no effect whatever on their daily obligations as long as they remained within the peasant household. We must therefore ask whether they carried that obligation with them to the factory to the same extent that men did.

Factory workers with active ties to the land returned to it mainly for planting and harvesting. This seasonal exodus to the family plot was called *ukhod*. The evidence for *ukhod* is sparse enough for male workers and even sparser for women. Many official calculations of *ukhod* took no notice of women's comings and goings, even in factories where they were heavily represented.[68] But the data we have show clearly that women workers were far less likely than men (roughly one-half to two-thirds) to return to the land for seasonal work (see table 15).

The explanations lay, first, in the conditions that led women to leave the land. It appears that factory women came predominantly from peasant families at the opposite extremes of prosperity. The more successful agricultural families, invariably large, could afford to dispense with the services of some women, both in the hut and in the fields. If families of this kind needed supplementary income, and they did so increasingly in our period, it was more economical to send superfluous women to the factory than to keep them at home engaged in less remunerative *kustar'* production. At the other extreme, factory women came from landless peasant families or from families too poor to work the land they possessed. In this case, of course, there was no reason for women or men to return to the land.[69]

68. See, for example, *Rab. dvizh.*, t. 3, chast' 2 (1952), p. 593.

69. *Materialy dlia otsenki zemel' vladimirskoi gubernii*, t. 12, *Pokrovskii uezd*, p. 11; and t. 10, *Shuiskii uezd*, p. 25. See also *Materialy po statistike narodnogo khoziaistva v s-peterburgskoi gubernii*, vyp. 2, *Shlissel'burgskii uezd* (St Petersburg, 1885), p. 215.

TABLE 15 Percentage of Male and Female Factory
Workers Participating in *Ukhod,* Moscow and
Vladimir Provinces, 1894–1909

	1901		1909	
Moscow Province	*Men*	*Women*	*Men*	*Women*
Industry:				
Cotton	9.3	4.0	5.7	3.1
Silk	22.0	15.0	19.3	5.7
Wool	19.0	16.0	—	—
Mixed Textiles	21.5	10.5	—	—
All Industries			5.6*	3.5

	1894–1897		1901	
Vladimir Province	*Men*	*Women*	*Men*	*Women*
All Industries	12.5	7.9	12.5	8.0

SOURCES: For Moscow 1901: TsGIA, f. 23, op. 29, d. 88, 1. 52–53; for 1909:
I. M. Koz'minykh-Lanin, *Ukhod na polevye raboty fabrichno-zavodskikh rabochikh moskovskoi gubernii* (Moscow, 1912).
  For Vladimir Province: *Otchet chinov fabrichnoi inspektsii vladimirskoi gubernii,
1894–1897* (Vladimir, 1899); TsGIA, f. 23, op. 29, d. 88, 1. 83 (my calculations).
  *This figure is brought down by the inclusion of male workers in heavy indus-
try whose rate of *ukhod* was very low (2.6%). For male workers exclusive of heavy
industry, the figure is 6.6%.

Second, as we see from table 16, from the ages of twenty
to forty-five—the ages of greatest vigor—male *ukhod* increased and female *ukhod* decreased. As these ages were
peak childbearing and child-rearing years, the factory
woman was held back from seasonal migration by domestic
obligations not shared by men.

Thus, the land played a dominant role in women's lives
only as long as they remained physically in the household,
to a greater extent than was true for men. Once women left
the land, the fact that their relationship to the land was
mediated by their relationships to male kin became the
more important element, and suggests the possibility that to

TABLE 16 Participation of Male and Female Factory Workers in *ukhod*, by Age: Moscow Province, 1908 (percentages)

	All Industries	
Age	Men	Women
12–14	3.5	1.9
15–19	3.8	5.0
20–24	6.0	5.2
25–29	5.3	2.5
30–34	5.9	2.3
35–39	5.3	2.0
40–44	7.0	2.8
45–49	6.0	.9
50–55	11.1	1.4
60+	5.6	0

SOURCE: I. M. Koz'minykh-Lanin, "Ukhod na polevye raboty fabrichno-zavodskikh rabochikh moskovskoi gubernii" (Moscow, 1912).

leave the land for work in the factory was a more decisive step for women than for men.

One of the most revealing indices of stability is, of course, *stazh*, the number of years a worker spent in the factory. Once again we must make assessments from evidence that is meager for all workers and more so for women. Further, a glance at table 17 shows that it is difficult to make comparisons for equivalent populations over time. With these caveats in mind, it appears that the majority of workers of both sexes did not spend the whole of their working lives in the factory, although male workers clearly surpass their female colleagues in *stazh*. For example, in Moscow province of the 1880s a third of both male and female workers worked in factories from seven to fifteen years. Another

TABLE 17   Percentage Distribution of Male and Female
            Factory Workers, by Period of Employment
            (*Stazh*): Moscow and St Petersburg Cities,
            1879–1908

| | Years in Factory | | | | |
Province and/or City	*−1*	*1–3*	*4–6*	*7–15*	*16+*
Moscow Province (1879–1885)					
Men	2.1	19.1	13.8	32.1	32.9
Women	2.3	31.3	17.2	34.1	15.1
Moscow City (1881)					
Men	6.2	12.2	10.2	26.4	44.5
Women	15.2	23.5	19.5	25.8	16.0

| | Years in Factory | | | | |
	−10	*10–19*	*20–29*	*30–39*	*40–50*
Moscow City and Province (1908)					
Men	51.75	21.46	14.5	7.4	1.9
Women	67.7	17.5	10.0	3.94	.9

| | Years in Factory | |
	6–15	*16+*
St Petersburg Cotton Industry		
(1900)		
Men	23.6	12.2
Women	24.9	11.0

SOURCE: P. A. Peskov, *Trudy kommissii uchrezhdennoi g moskovskim General-Guber-natorom, kn. V. A. Dolgorukovym dlia osmotra fabrik i zavodov v Moskve.* Vypusk pervyi (Moscow, 1882), p. 122; F. F. Erisman, *Sbornik statisticheskikh svedenii po moskovskoi gubernii,* Otdel sanitarnoi statistiki (Moscow, 1890), t. 4, chast' 1, p. 287; L. M. Ivanov, *Rabochii klass i rabochee dvizhenie v Rossii, 1861–1917* (Moscow, 1966).

third of male workers had a *stazh* of more than sixteen years, while only 15 percent of women had worked that long. This was due in part to the fact that until the early years of the twentieth century more women than men were likely to begin factory work over the age of twenty-five. In Moscow province, 20 percent of factory women had entered the factory at age twenty-five or older in the 1880s.[70] By 1908 only 8 percent of women began their factory work lives that late.[71] While women continued to lag behind men in accumulated years in the factory, a substantial proportion in the middle range was almost equal to men.

The final gauge of proletarianization, and perhaps the most subtle, is what was called *preemstvennost'*, or occupational heredity: that is, the occupation of a worker's parents. A worker whose formative years had been spent in the factory culture would be more likely to identify himself or herself as a factory worker than would one for whom not only factory work but factory life in the broadest sense was a new experience. In Russia, however, what appears to be a simple indicator is in fact complex. Given the two-way flow of factory workers between factory and countryside, it was common for workers, especially men, to leave their families behind in the village. Therefore, the unadorned fact that a worker's father had been a factory worker tells us only that. It is not evidence that the worker in question was acculturated into factory life from earliest childhood. It would have been far more revealing to know whether a worker's mother had worked in the factory, since many fewer women factory workers left their children in the

70. Erisman, *Sbornik*, p. 288 (see source for table 4). See also S. Gvozdev, *Zapiski fabrichnogo inspektora* (Moscow, 1911), p. 34. Peasant widows undoubtedly account in part for the greater proportion of women entering the factory at age twenty-five or older. Only in rare cases did widows retain the use of the land belonging to their deceased husbands. If they were not welcomed back by their own families, factory work remained one of the few ways of sustaining themselves and their children.

71. I. M. Koz'minykh-Lanin, *Gramotnost' i zarabotki fabrichno-zavodskikh rabochikh moskovskoi gubernii* (Moscow, 1912), p. 275.

village.[72] Unfortunately, the question was rarely asked. However, three surveys that queried women workers as well as men about their family origins indicate that men and women were hereditary workers in roughly equal proportions, namely, about one-third in both cases (see table 18).

The female work force has been juxtaposed to and compared with the male work force in order to avoid isolating women workers from the totality of which they were a part. We have also traced the evolution of the female work force irrespective of the characteristics that it shared with male workers. We must now attempt to weave together these two perspectives and to make some cautious generalizations about the nature of the female work force and the significance of its evolution.

Where they can be compared directly with men, women workers were different in two critical ways: as a group they were younger and worked fewer years in the factory. They either left the factory to marry or entered the factory later in life than men. This suggests that women had lower expectations of spending their lives as factory workers and a concomitantly weaker sense of themselves as factory workers. Leaving aside the comparison with men, however, in both of these ways women workers inclined toward greater stability over the decades we have examined. At the end of our period they were older as a group than at the beginning. More significant is the change in marital status, a condition that is irrelevant to the stability of male workers but of primary importance to the judgments we make about women workers. The increase in married women workers was only partly attributable to the changing age structure. Marriage was simply less and less a reason to leave the factory as well as a decreasing obstacle to entering the factory later in life.

Men and women in the factory came in the same propor-

---

72. According to a study of St Petersburg workers in 1901–1902, 27.3 percent of married male workers sent their children to the countryside, while only 14.7 percent of married women sent their children away. S. N. Semanov, *Peterburgskie rabochie nakanune pervoi russkoi revoliutsii* (Moscow and Leningrad, 1966), p. 51.

TABLE 18 Percentage of Workers with One or More
Parents at Factory

| | *Percentage of Workers* | |
Province	*Men*	*Women*
Moscow, 1908	44.4	35.0
Vladimir, 1897	37.6	36.3
Kostroma, 1911	33.3	33.0

SOURCES: I. M. Koz'minykh-Lanin, "Ukhod na polevye raboty fabrichno-zavod-skikh-rabochikh moskovskoi gubernii" (Moscow, 1912), and *Fabrichno-zavodskii rabochii vladimirskoi gubernii* (Vladimir, 1912), p. 32. *Materialy dlia otsenki nedvizhi-mykh imushchestv v gorodakh i fabrichnykh poselkakh kostromskoi gubernii*, t. 1, *Statistiches-kie svedeniia o seredskom fabrichnom raione, nerekhtskogo uezda*, vyp. 2 (1911). The *Materialy* data pertain to a highly industrialized district in Kostroma province and include four factories with 9,120 workers. Women were 55% of the workers. It is the only data compilation that takes into account all of the possible variations of succession:

	Men	*Women*
Workers with both parents at factory	17.8	18.6
Workers with father at factory	11.1	9.6
Workers with mother at factory	4.1	4.5

tions from factory families. Thus, parental occupation or acculturation into factory life was as compelling for women as for men, and hereditary workers were as likely to be female as male, whether the choice was made by the worker or the worker's parent. On the other hand, the ties that bound workers of peasant origin to the land were weaker for women, and this suggests that peasant women factory workers had more decisively severed their links to the village than had men.

Individually, each of the characteristics we have examined, absolutely or comparatively, would be a fragile peg on which to hang an argument about the growing stability and prole-tarianization of the female work force. It would be folly to assign an unequivocal value to each characteristic; to juggle them about as if weighing one integer against another would produce an equation. But taken together they point in the same direction. Despite the relative instability of the female work force, and aside from the portion of it that was clearly casual and episodic, a growing segment among women workers was as fully proletarian, as stable in the factory, as it was possible for a worker to be in tsarist Russia.

4

LABOR AND LIFE

Among the tangle of relationships that shaped the contours of the woman worker's life, two were especially important in differentiating her objective position within her class as well as her subjective experiences, her perceptions, and her responses. One was the undeviating relationship of her wages and earnings to men's. Whatever changed as her life unfolded—as she aged, as she perhaps married, had children, and was widowed, as her workplace changed, or as she participated in greater social and political events—this relationship remained constant. It was a pivotal relationship because women's lower wages were as much the result of a configuration of determinants as the cause of other fundamental features of her life and condition. We can, therefore, work in all directions from it to examine her place among factory workers. The second important factor was her marital status, which influenced the allocation of her earnings among life's necessities—in other words, her standard of living—as well as the more elusive emotional and psychological burdens and satisfactions that she experienced. Marital status was a more important factor in her life, materially and subjectively, than it was for male workers, and it transcended other important conditions, such as the kinds of work she did, whether she was an urban or a rural factory worker, the degree to which she had severed her ties to the countryside. Income and marital status form a matrix within which the other aspects of the woman worker's life were embedded, and will serve as a point of departure as we follow her through her life cycle.

In one of the first factory inspector reports, I. I. Ianzhul noted that the highest wage of the woman worker in the Moscow factory district barely surpassed the minimal male wage.[1] The factory inspectors' reports of 1885 made similar observations throughout European Russia.[2] A decade later, an official report of the Department of Trade and Manufacture stated that "the labor of women and minors . . . is paid significantly less than male labor. On the average women receive a half and children a third of men's wages."[3]

From the turn of the century the gap between men's and women's wages narrowed, especially in textiles, the industry that employed the largest segment of women workers and in which they were rapidly becoming the majority of workers. A woman weaver in Moscow province who earned one-half the male wage in 1884 was earning four-fifths of the male wage by 1908.[4] The smallest wage difference was in mechanized weaving. One small category of mechanized weaving even paid identical wages to men and women, namely, to weavers who worked four looms simultaneously. So small was this group of workers (2.2 percent of women and 4.7 percent of men who worked on mechanized looms operated four looms at once) that as a curiosity it starkly illustrates the general imbalance in wages.[5] In general, by 1914 women's wages were closest to men's in those indus-

1. Ianzhul, *Fabrichnyi byt*, p. 108.

2. Ianzhul, *Otchet*, p. 60; Gorodkov, pp. 31–32, 34; Sviatlovskii, p. 40; Davydov, pp. 153–173; TsGIA, f. 20, op. 3, d. 188²ᵃ, l. 30, 39, 41, 123, 132, 142; f. 20, op. 12, d. 265, l. 39.

3. Ia. Mikhailovskii, "Zarabotnaia plata i prodolzhitel'nost' rabochego vremeni na russkikh fabrikakh i zavodakh," in Ministerstvo Finansov, Departament Torgovli i Manufaktur, *Fabrichno-zavodskaia promyshlennost' i torgovlia Rossii* (St Petersburg, 1896), p. 466.

4. E. Mikhailova, "Polozhenie fabrichnykh rabotnits na moskovskikh fabrikakh i uezdnykh," *Drug Zhenshchin* (1884), no. 5, p. 117; I. M. Koz'minykh-Lanin, *Mekhanicheskoe tkachestvo v moskovskoi gubernii. Obrabotka khlopa* (Moscow, 1912), pp. 6–7. In 1884 the average monthly earnings in rubles for women and men weavers was 12 and 25, respectively. By 1908 it was 17.49 and 19.49 rubles per month, respectively.

5. Koz'minykh-Lanin, *Mekhanicheskoe tkachestvo*, pp. 12–15.

TABLE 19 Women's Average Wages as a Percentage of Men's Average Wages, by Industry, 1914

Industry	Women's Wages
Cotton	72.1
Wool	67.8
Linen	65.4
Hemp and jute	64.8
Mixed textiles	55.0
Paper, polygraphics	46.5
Wood	44.3
Metal	41.1
Minerals	44.3
Animal products	58.2
Food processing	58.9
Chemicals	64.0
Extractive industries	62.8
Remaining nonspecified	50.6

SOURCE: I. M. Koz'minykh-Lanin, *Zarabotki fabrichno-zavodskikh rabochikh v Rossii,* vyp. 1 (Moscow, 1918).

tries and processes within industries in which women workers predominated (see table 19).

The discrepancy between men's and women's wages was universal. It existed in agricultural labor, in artisanal labor, and in all countries. It is as much a contemporary as a historical phenomenon. Certainly in nineteenth-century Russia it was regarded by most people with equanimity, as an immutable law of nature, to be explained perhaps, but never to be questioned. The conventional rationale for women's lower wages was that they lacked the two essential prerequisites of better-paid work: strength and skill. To a degree the rationale was justified. That women were deficient in the strength to perform some tasks and in skills to perform others cannot be gainsaid. But these deficiencies do not explain the lower wages of all women. The relationship of strength and skill, on the one hand, and women's lower wages, on the other, is correlative rather than causal, and we must probe further into the social context for the more profound causal factors.

It would be folly to engage in a polemic over whether women are significantly weaker than men. The important thing is that they were thought to be, although the operative definition of strength was a result of traditional notions, not of scientific inquiry—a point that did not escape all observers. As V. V. Sviatlovskii, a factory inspector who was exceptionally sensitive to the position of women workers, remarked, "Whoever is acquainted with the hardiness and endurance for physical labor that characterizes Russian women of the agricultural regions will not be satisfied by this explanation and will look for a more profound one."[6] He pointed out with some irony that, despite their alleged weakness, women were hired to perform certain physically demanding jobs, such as wool cleaning, which were nevertheless notoriously poorly paid:

> Wool trampling in wet clay [a primitive method of washing wool] is also done by women. This harmful operation consists of the following: scores of barefooted women, skirts raised high, trample in large containers full of filthy wool mixed with water and clay. This work becomes especially arduous as the weather grows colder in the autumn. The result is considerable muscular pressure on the legs, often leading to inflammation of the vaginal tendons characterized by cracking, pain, and inflammation of the skin. . . . Men do the relatively light work on the . . . machines—which is not dangerous.[7]

The popular conviction that women workers suffered more than men from the "ruinous effects" of industry be-

6. V. V. Sviatlovskii, *Fabrichnyi rabochii (iz nabliudeniia fabrichnogo inspektora)* (Warsaw, 1889), p. 12.
7. Ibid. Throughout the period under consideration, women were 77% to 90% of workers employed in wool-cleaning. See, for example, Novitskii, p. 44; TsGIA, f. 20, op. 3, d. 188[2a], l. 123.

cause they had "more sensitive and delicate constitutions" was not a deterrent to hiring them for taxing or dangerous work, provided the work paid poorly.[8] Wool cleaning was only one of many such occupations. In 1901 a resolution was passed at a conference of factory inspectors designating fourteen industrial tasks sufficiently dangerous to restrict workers to an eight-hour day. Five of them employed mainly women.[9] Nor was lack of strength an advantage in gaining access to jobs, indeed to whole industries, which did not require strength. "After all," demanded Sviatlovskii, "what kind of strength is necessary for work as a typesetter or in bristle production, vinegar, mineral water, and many other industries in which women are never employed?"[10]

The logic of the argument about strength to explain women's lower wages requires that women should never have been employed to do physically demanding jobs, that they should have been at least predominant in work requiring little strength, and that the reverse be true of men. Logic in this case was contrary to reality.

The argument that lack of skill accounted for women's lower wages is more tightly woven. However, tucked into the crevices of many industries, certain skilled jobs, such as warping in textile production, were performed primarily by women workers.[11] "The work of the warper required great ability, which was acquired only in the process of prolonged work at the factory. The warper performed a preparatory operation, but was the fundamental figure in the weaving process."[12] Thus, as early as 1882 women warpers had a high seniority compared with other categories of both male and female workers. Their wages were also high—com-

---

8. I. I. Ianzhul, *Ocherki i izsledovaniia* (Moscow, 1884), p. 881.
9. TsGIA, f. 20, op. 13ª, d. 357, l. 95.
10. Sviatlovskii, p. 12.
11. *Rabochee dvizhenie v Rossii v XIX veke* (Moscow and Leningrad, 1950–1963), t. 3, chast' 2, pp. 562–563.
12. V. I. Romashova, "Obrazovanie postoiannykh kadrov rabochikh v poreformennoi promyshlennosti Moskvy," in L. M. Ivanov, ed., *Rabochii klass i rabochee dvizhenie v Rossii, 1861–1917* (Moscow, 1966), p. 160. In 1882 almost half the warpers had been at their job for twenty-five years.

pared, that is, with other women workers. In 1914 in Vladi-mir province the average earnings of the woman warper were 23 rubles per month, while women weavers earned an average of 16.8 rubles per month. (It should be noted that warpers were 1 percent of women textile workers in this province, while weavers were half the female textile work force.) But this relatively high wage for a woman warper was only seven-tenths of the highest wage of male weavers.[13]

In 1882 several Moscow factories manufactured a fine grade of wool and silk fabrics. The winding machines were operated almost entirely by women. Although the work re-quired "experience, skill, and certain delicate manipula-tions," it was among the lowest paying jobs in these facto-ries.[14] Similarly, in the largest plant in Nizhnii Novgorod province in 1912, "the most delicate and complex work in the upholstery section of the railway car shop" was per-formed exclusively by women.[15] Their skills were poorly remunerated. It is clear, then, that even when women did relatively skilled work, which sometimes paid more on the woman's scale of wages, they rarely achieved the average wage of less skilled male workers.

These exceptional women workers aside, we are left with the fact that most women did unskilled or semiskilled labor and that the universally lower wages of women reflected the way in which occupations were distributed among men and women. Women earned less because they did work which paid lower wages no matter who was doing it. The real ques-tion is why women did primarily unskilled labor. How did workers acquire skills and why were the avenues to the acqui-sition of skill for the most part closed to women?

One of the most important components of skill was liter-acy. The general level of literacy in Russia was abysmally low. In 1897 the rate of literacy for the entire Russian Em-pire was 29.3 percent for men and 13.1 percent for

13. *Rab. dvizh.*, t. 3, chast' 2, pp. 562–563.
14. A. V. Pogozhev, "Iz zhizni fabrichnogo liuda v stolitse," *Russkaia Mysl'*, kn. 5 (1885), p. 9.
15. TsGIA, f. 23, op. 16, d. 75, l. 179.

women.[16] Peasant women at that time fared badly—they were 9.8 percent literate, whereas peasant men were 25.2 percent literate,[17] bearing out the observation that "they [peasants] do not acknowledge in general that literacy is necessary for girls."[18]

Factory workers, male and female, fared considerably better than their rural brothers and sisters, although it is by no means clear that overall they acquired literacy as a by-product of working in the factory. It has been postulated that literate peasants were more likely to abandon the land for the factory in the first place.[19] In 1897 male workers were 56.5 percent literate, and women workers, 21.3 percent.[20] This was a more impressive advance for women than for men. For example, in the 1880s in Moscow province 33 percent of male workers were literate, while women workers were only 4.7 percent literate. By 1908 male literacy in Moscow province had risen to 76.2 percent and female literacy to 26 percent. It should be noted, however, that Moscow workers were not typical of Russian workers as a whole in this regard. Dividing women workers into age cohorts, we find a great leap forward among women under the age of twenty-five, which pushed the average literacy up for all women workers. Women under the age of twenty-five would have been of school age in 1885–1890, precisely the time when Moscow province made a strenuous attempt to provide elementary education on a broad scale. The attempt was not emulated by other provinces.[21]

Still, the factory woman's growing literacy was impressive, especially when compared with peasant women. On the eve of World War I, literacy among peasant women varied considerably by province, ranging from 3.8 percent in Penza

16. A. G. Rashin, *Formirovanie rabochego klassa Rossii* (Moscow, 1958), p. 580.

17. A. G. Rashin, *Naselenie Rossii za 100 let* (Moscow, 1956), p. 293.

18. *Sbornik statisticheskikh svedenii po moskovskoi gubernii*, t. 7, *Zhenskie promysly*. Vyp. 4. M. K. Gorbunova, compiler (Moscow, 1882), p. 285.

19. Barbara Anderson, *Internal Migration During Modernization in Late Nineteenth Century Russia* (Princeton, 1980), passim.

20. Rashin, *Formirovanie*, p. 593.

21. Ibid., pp. 587–588; Koz'minykh-Lanin, *Gramotnost' i zarabotki*, pp. iii–iv.

province to 25.9 percent in Moscow province.[22] At that time something over one-third of women factory workers were literate. Formidable as the gap in literacy between men (who were roughly 79 percent literate) and women remained, it had diminished significantly over the decades.[23] There is no way to assess the improvement in the quality of the woman worker's life that may have resulted from greater literacy. One thing, however, is certain: literate women workers were not rewarded with better wages.

Literacy was a clear advantage for men. In Moscow province, for example, literate male workers earned 13 percent more than the illiterate.[24] This was mainly due to the access literate men had to skilled occupations in heavy industry. Most workers came to the factory unskilled and acquired their skills on the job, although prior technical education expanded somewhat, at least for men, from the beginning of the twentieth century. Therefore, the opportunity to learn well-paying skills depended first and foremost on initial acceptance at the workplace; in other words, on the nature of the industry and the a priori preferences of the employer. The branches of industry that required literate and highly skilled workers simply did not hire literate women. The workers in machine-tool plants, metal works, engineering plants, as well as the skilled workers in light industry—the best paid workers in the industrial world— were uniformly male.

Traditional attitudes toward the woman's place in the family sometimes served to depress her wages. It was characteristic of early industrialization that workers, as in prein-

22. Rashin, *Naselenie,* p. 294.
23. Rashin, *Formirovanie,* p. 601. Rashin's data pertains to 1918. He calculated that in that year 44.2 percent of factory women were literate. However, this is a simple average. Breaking women workers down by industry, textile workers—67 percent of all women workers—were only 37.9 percent literate. The simple, overall average is seriously distorted by the very small percentage of women in the engineering industry, who were 59 percent literate. Therefore, I estimate that in 1914 roughly one-third of women workers were literate.
24. Koz'minykh-Lanin, *Gramotnost' i zarabotki,* pp. 13–14.

dustrial times, were hired as families rather than as individuals, especially in the textile industry. This practice declined as industrialization evolved from the earliest stages, although members of the same family—husbands and wives, parents and children—were often hired as individuals to work in the same factory. The notion of a family wage and of the woman's wage within it as a supplement to the husband's was sufficiently persistent to justify paying women less, long after the practice had declined and in places where it had never existed. As an official report of a strike in Ivanovo-Voznesensk in 1895 argued when it advised against acquiescing to the workers' demand for better wages, "Taking into account that the workers in this factory are all local residents . . . and whole families work in the factory, one can conclude without the slightest error that the underpayment of women is compensated by the overpayment of men."[25]

The woman worker's place in the family created yet another and more fundamental impediment to her earning power. Setting aside the disparity between men's and women's wages, women's earnings were further diminished by the burden of domestic responsibilities. The various types of absenteeism over which she had little control, such as caring for sick children or taking time off to nurse infants, were penalized twice over. Especially in the many industries that paid piecework rates, her earnings were brought down first by her absence and second through the fines levied on absenteeism.

Finally, it must be acknowledged that to some extent women were paid less because they would accept less. Women workers did not often articulate their aspirations for posterity. We must, for the most part, deduce their aspirations from records of their behavior. They did not behave in ways calculated to achieve parity in wages. In subsequent chapters we shall examine the participation of women workers in labor protest. Suffice it to say here that until the

25. TsGIA, f. 23, op. 30, d. 14, l. 10.

revolution of 1905 women rarely protested against the occupational distribution that kept them out of better-paid work or against their relatively lower wages.

Historians are legitimately wary of monocausal explanations of complex phenomena. But more is not necessarily better, and to collect many causes in the attempt to avoid what appears to be a simplistic explanation is not to guarantee the sought-for answer. In isolating the question of women's lower wages, we have examined the standard explanations. Each one has a degree of validity. But after we peel away successive layers of causation, we arrive at a core, a single factor that supports the entire structure. Women were less literate and less skilled than men because they were women. All women were excluded from well-paying jobs for which some women had the requisite strength or skill or accumulated seniority. Women earned less because they were women.

The final test of this hypothesis is in the relationship of the wage structure to mechanization. Mechanization was one of the special contributions of industrialization to the modern world. It is a tool which, as we now know, does not depend on capitalistic organization of production to be useful. Mechanization was the great equalizer. Machines reduced the human operative to a few essential characteristics shared by most human beings regardless of sex. But it did not equalize wages. Women working side by side with men, performing identical operations on identical machines, continued to receive lower wages. It was not the nature of the work that determined the difference in wages, but the sex of the operative.

There is no presumption here of conscious conspiracy against women. Men and women alike were the receivers of traditional attitudes and expectations, which with the passage of time were unquestionably altered, but not transformed, by industrialization. Men and women alike agreed that women's labor was worth less.

* * *

The higher wages of men did not provide for them a vastly better life than was available to women. To be sure, highly skilled unmarried male workers who no longer had financial obligations to relatives in the village had a good life in comparison with other workers, as we saw in chapter one. They could afford better housing, better food, and better clothing, and "some even had savings put aside for a 'black day.' "[26] There was no comparable category of women workers, for the jobs that provided even such minimal comfort and security to the relatively privileged male worker were not open to women. The point here, however, is not to belabor the difference between men's and women's wages, but to begin to explore how women survived on their wages.

In 1908 M. Davidovich carried out a careful and sensitive budget study of St Petersburg textile workers. The official estimate of the yearly income necessary for an unmarried worker's minimal subsistence in the capital was 230 rubles per year. The average single male textile worker with no ties to the countryside earned 335.24 rubles yearly; a bachelor with a family in the village, 314.30. The average yearly income of a factory girl living with her parents was 153.50, while the single woman worker living on her own earned 286.50 rubles per year.[27] Thus the single woman's wage fell miserably short of the marginal existence permitted by the male income, and consequently a larger percentage of her income went to purchase rudimentary necessities.

Although workers spent the largest portion of their incomes on food, their diet was dreary and inadequate in both quantity and quality. Aesthetics aside, quantitative hygienic norms of the time calculated a woman's nutritional requirements to be four-fifths of a man's. It is unlikely that the single woman worker ascended to such heights, for precise studies as well as impressionistic observations agreed unanimously that the unmarried woman worker ate less and more poorly than most other workers.

26. S. Kanatchikov, *Iz istorii moego bytiia* (Moscow-Leningrad, 1929), p. 17.
27. M. Davidovich, *Petersburgskii tekstil'nyi rabochii v ego biudzhetakh* (St Petersburg, 1912), pp. 5–6, 8.

In rural factories, most single workers organized eating cooperatives called artels. As the quality and quantity of food depended on the earnings of the artel's members, women formed their own artels, sometimes joined by adolescent and child workers.[28] Contrasting the relatively high meat consumption of men's artels with the low meat consumption of women's, a study undertaken in 1893 noted that "in fact, the members of women's artels never see beef in the literal sense, since whenever it is used—in minute quantities in the soup—it completely disappears. As the women say, they put beef in the soup 'for the taste.' "[29] The fare in women's artels consisted mainly of black bread and tea with occasional supplements of buckwheat groats, cabbage, and lard. The study estimated that women consumed one-third the meat and potatoes and one-fifth the bread of male workers.

To their detriment, single women in urban factories rarely formed eating artels. Whereas the artel provided men with a daily hot meal, the single woman survived on uncooked meals, for she rarely had access to cooking facilities. Women in Moscow were observed to "eat meat only on Sunday and holidays, while men eat meat every day of the week. . . . Women feed themselves on tea and bread, sometimes with a bit of sausage or eggs."[30] One-half to two-thirds of the single woman's earnings went to purchase food, yet, as observers were wont to conclude, she experienced chronic hunger.[31] A curious indulgence noted of the single woman worker in St Petersburg was that she spent

28. Ianzhul, *Fabrichnyi byt*, p. 94; F. F. Erisman, *Pishchevoe dovol'stvie rabochikh na fabrikakh moskovskoi gubernii* (Moscow, 1893), p. 4.

29. Erisman, p. 25; L. Katenina, "K voprosu o polozhenii rabotnits v tekstil'noi promyshlennosti," *Obshchestvennyi Vrach*, 1914, no. 3, p. 439.

30. P. M. Shestakov, *Rabochie na Manufakture T-va "Emil Tsindel" v Moskve* (Moscow, 1909), p. 4.

31. Davidovich, p. 13; I. M. Shaposhnikov, "Biudzhety rabochikh odnoi iz fabrik bogorodskogo uezda v sviazi s pitaniem i zabolevaemostiu," *Svedenie o zaraznykh bolezniakh i sanitarno-vrachebnoi organizatsii moskovskoi gubernii* (1910), no. 1, p. 25; M. I. Pokrovskaia (zhenskii-vrach), "Peterburgskaia rabotnitsa," *Mir Bozhii* (1900), no. 12, pp. 32–37; Erisman, p. 50; G. Naumov, *Biudzhety rabochikh g. Kieva* (Kiev, 1914), p. 67.

8.   *A worker's house in a Moscow factory district. Early 1890s.* From *Istoriia Moskvy* (Moscow, 1955), vol. 5, p. 233.

an inordinate portion of her food budget on sugar.[32] Perhaps she felt a greater need than others to sweeten her tasteless life.

The second greatest expenditure in the worker's budget was for housing. The costs and quality of housing in cities varied with the kinds of accommodation a given city had to offer. But the greater importance that unmarried women workers attached to the quality of their living space transcended the variations. In St Petersburg single women workers spent not only a far higher proportion of their income on housing than men—17 percent and 8 percent, respectively—but more in absolute sums as well.[33] Davidovich compared the official hygienic norm of 3.2 cubic meters per person with the average single male worker's dwelling of 1.9 cubic meters and the single woman's 2.5

32. Davidovich, p. 20.
33. Davidovich, pp. 9–10. In Kiev women allocated the same proportion of their earnings as men to housing, which meant a much smaller sum. See G. Naumov, p. 67.

cubic meters.[34] M. I. Pokrovskaia, a doctor who made strenuous efforts to publicize the appalling living conditions of urban workers, translated these figures into more descriptive terms:

> As a result of our investigations of workers' dwellings, we conclude that there is greater need for better housing for single women workers than for male workers. A young girl or woman worker always earns less than a man. Nonetheless, she often spends more on her dwelling than a man does. When renting a corner she rarely shares a bed, which the St Petersburg male worker does quite often. If two women workers occupy one bed, it is usually a mother and daughter, grandmother and grandchild, or two sisters. . . . Sometimes she takes some kind of a dark corner or kitchen . . . which she must share with a single man. This undesirable state of affairs is not common in St Petersburg, but frequently occurs elsewhere.[35]

Housing in small towns or rural factory settlements absorbed less of the worker's income. The great majority of workers were housed in factory barracks, which often did not provide separate sleeping quarters for the sexes. Ianzhul's description of barracks in Moscow province in 1883 required very little alteration in the twentieth century:

> In most factory housing there is total indifference to mixing sexes and ages: all the workers are squashed together in the very same barracks or tiny rooms (*kamorka*) . . . married and single, children and grown girls . . . in extremely crowded and filthy conditions.[36]

Where women slept in separate dormitories they showed the same concern for a modicum of comfort as urban women workers, and their quarters were observed to be "tidier than men's and the air much cleaner."[37] Factory housing was woefully lacking in the most rudimentary

34. Davidovich, pp. 9–10.
35. M. I. Pokrovskaia, "Vopros o deshevykh kvartirakh dlia rabochego klassa," *Vestnik Evropy* (1901), kn. 7, p. 193.
36. Ianzhul, *Fabrichnyi byt,* p. 118; Sviatlovskii, p. 118; Miropol'skii, p. 60.
37. Sviatlovskii, *Fabrichnyi rabochii,* p. 69.

amenities, to the point where in some factories men and women alike "bathed in a muddy puddle . . . in which the factory disposes of its waste and garbage."[38] But barracks were inexpensive, a factor of overriding importance for the woman worker; where workers were expected to rent private accommodations, women were routinely given half the housing allowance of men.[39] Private accommodations were no improvement over factory housing, consisting for the most part of "a spot big enough for a bed," and, into the bargain, it was "repulsive, crowded and dirty."[40]

Of all life's basic necessities, expenditure on clothing was the most flexible and the most vulnerable to the influences of the environment. The single woman in urban factories spent more of her income on clothing than all other workers. In a provincial city, like Kiev, she spent a larger proportion of her income but a considerably smaller sum than men, while in St Petersburg both proportion and sum were considerably beyond the male expenditure.[41] The single male worker in St Petersburg spent roughly 10 percent of his earnings to clothe himself. The woman worker newly arrived in St Petersburg, whose rustic expectations were still intact, spent 14 percent on clothing, while the woman worker of longer duration, "no longer satisfied with rough country underwear," spent 20 percent.[42] Lest the reader come away with an image of the single woman fecklessly squandering her pitiful income on clothing, the greater outlay meant that she was less inclined to buy used clothing (the norm for married workers), that she exchanged her country boots for city shoes, and that, unlike the married woman worker, she did not expect one outer garment to last twenty to thirty years.[43]

38. Ibid.
39. M. Zaiats, *Tekstili v gody pervoi revoliutsii, 1905–1907* (Moscow, 1925), p. 172.
40. A. Iu. Kats, "Naselenie Pokrovskoi Manufaktury (dmitrovskogo uezda) i ego zhilishchnye usloviia," *Svedenie o zaraznykh bolezniakh i sanitarno-vrachebnoi organizatsii moskovskoi gubernii* (1910), no. 10, p. 660.
41. Naumov, p. 67.
42. Davidovich, p. 11.
43. Ibid., p. 12; Shaposhnikov, p. 18.

The unmarried urban factory woman lived a singularly isolated existence. While many factory workers, male and female, came to urban factories as individuals, it was probably more common for women to relinquish not only kin ties, but regional and village connections (*zemliachestvo*) as well. *Zemliachestvo,* the tendency for workers to perpetuate relationships with others from the same village or region, forming living and eating artels, providing contacts for job-seekers, was weak among women workers. They were not, as a rule, hired from their districts or villages in large groups by factory subcontractors as were men, nor, in any case, was this the practice of industries in which women worked.[44] Thus, the single factory woman in the city did not form living or eating artels. She did not frequent the taverns, billiard halls, or teahouses, for they were male provinces. Her income did not permit the purchase of entertainment, such as it was for workers. Public transportation from the factory neighborhood to areas of interest in the city was beyond her means.[45] Her illiteracy ruled out the diversion of books and newspapers.[46] It is not surprising, then, that she sought compensation in a pair of new shoes or minimally more comfortable living quarters where she had a shred of privacy unknown to her country cousin. Yet, the filthy and crowded living quarters of the rural factory woman were probably a more companionable environment. The rural factory woman ate with her fellow workers, and she could escape the filth, crowding, and discomfort of her sleeping quarters by joining the other adults who "try to spend their free time in one of the multitudinous teahouses or taverns surrounding the factory settlement."[47]

Only a minority of women factory workers left the factory when they married. With the exception of the highly

44. Robert Johnson, *Peasant and Proletarian* (New Brunswick, N.J., 1979), p. 72; Olga Crisp, "Labour and Industrialization in Russia." In *The Cambridge Economic History of Europe,* vol. 7, part 2 (Cambridge, 1978), pp. 376–378.

45. James Bater, "Spatial Mobility in Moscow and St Petersburg in the Late Imperial Era," passim.

46. Davidovich, pp. 14, 24.

47. Kats, p. 664.

skilled worker in heavy industry, men did not often earn enough to support two adults, let alone children. In the first decade of the twentieth century, roughly 80 percent of factory workers' families depended on the combined earnings of husband and wife.[48]

The factory unwittingly provided a sort of dowry for the "retired" woman worker in the form of stolen cotton stuffing and fabric from which she could sew blankets and bed linen for the family.[49] Subsequently, the male factory worker's wife found other ways to augment the family's coffers. In cities, families with a woman at home frequently rented a separate apartment, not so much to accommodate the larger family as to rent rooms or corners and to realize some small profit from the housewife's services to the boarders: laundering, feeding, baby-minding. Time permitting or need dictating, factory wives did outside laundering and sewing, for even the most affluent of factory families were hard put to survive on the husband's factory earnings alone. In St Petersburg, for example, male factory workers often stole fuel from nearby state-owned forests, or as the workers themselves expressed it, "by day—the factory; by night—to the forest" (*dnem na fabrike, a noch'iu—v les*).[50] In rural factories, if the family was indigenous to the area, the worker's wife contributed to survival by renting rooms or selling eggs.[51]

The retired woman factory worker did not live a discernibly better life than the woman who continued to work in the factory, at least not in quantifiable ways, although she probably ate more nourishing and better-prepared food, since a daily hot meal was a regular feature of life in such families. Her material well-being did not differ appreciably in other

---

48. Davidovich, p. 12; Shaposhnikov, p. 2; N. K. Druzhinin, *Usloviia byta rabochikh v dorevoliutsionnoi Rossii (po dannym biudzhetnykh obsledovannii)* (Moscow, 1958), p. 100.

49. Davidovich, p. 12.

50. Ibid., p. 5. The wife's earnings and the husband's theft combined amounted to only 3 percent of the income of factory workers whose wives stayed at home.

51. Shaposhnikov, p. 13.

ways from that of her erstwhile co-workers who stayed in the factory after marriage, for the higher income of her husband had to be distributed among more people.

The married woman worker was usually older and more experienced than the unmarried and had probably reached the pinnacle of her earning power. But her earnings were not significantly higher. As one worker complained in 1885, "Take my wife, for example. In the last three months she was fined 12 rubles and only earned 20 rubles. She is, after all, an excellent weaver, having worked at it for eighteen years."[52] Her potentially higher income was undermined by domestic obligations and child-rearing, and the working mother was frequently absent from work: "According to one male weaver, in fifteen years of marriage his wife missed an average of three to four days a month and not less than one working month in the year."[53]

The immediate effects of the woman's lower wage on the life of the married woman worker whose income was combined with her husband's are not so clear. Her earnings were, at the very least, allocated in different ways. The male worker's outlay for clothing, for example, did not fluctuate with his marital status; the woman worker's dropped sharply with marriage. New clothing became a memory, for the married woman and her family were more likely to buy clothing from the pawnshop, from the secondhand market, or from vendors of stolen goods.[54] Certain articles of clothing disappeared from her wardrobe: "We should like to point out the complete absence among married women workers of such necessary articles of linen as underpants."[55] Unlike the worker's wife who stayed at home, she did not provide hot meals, for while the family resources may have stretched to provide a better diet, she did not have the time to cook. All observers remarked that the married woman

---

52. *Rab. dvizh.*, t. 3, chast' 2, p. 222. According to Davidovich, the average earnings of the unmarried woman textile worker in St Petersburg was 286.50 rubles per year. The married woman earned 292.20 rubles per year.
53. Davidovich, pp. 5–6.
54. Ibid., p. 12; Shaposhnikov, p. 18; Druzhinin, p. 50.
55. Davidovich, p. 12.

worker allocated less food to herself than to her husband and children.

The worker's marriage was not the idyll described by Frederick Engels. There is no evidence to support his contention that "now that large-scale industry has taken the wife out of the home onto the labour market and into the factory, and made her often the breadwinner of the family, no basis for any kind of male supremacy is left in the proletarian household, except, perhaps, for something of the brutality toward women that has spread since the introduction of monogamy."[56] The lament of a factory woman in 1908—"At the factory we serve the boss and at home the husband is our ruler. Nowhere do they regard the woman as a real person"—better reflects the somewhat altered but not basically transformed status of women as factory workers and wives.[57]

However, the material gains and losses of the married woman worker cannot be assessed in any reasonable way, enmeshed as they are with the subjective rewards of cohabitation in a social milieu that took marriage as the natural state for adult women. Marriage may well have been a welcome alternative to the single woman's drab and isolated life, especially in the cities, compensating for the modicum of independence and privacy that she relinquished when she married.

The substantive change in the factory woman's life, however, occurred not simply with marriage but with the birth of children, for there were few resources to help her cope with the physical and material responsibilities of pregnancy and child-rearing as she simultaneously attempted to continue her working life.

In 1882 P. A. Peskov described the responses of Moscow entrepreneurs to his queries about provisions for pregnant women workers:

56. Frederick Engels, *The Origin of the Family, Private Property and the State* (New York, 1972), p. 135.
57. See n. 40, chap. one.

The question is so unexpected to factory owners and their administrative personnel that they express bewilderment. Then, with complete conviction that there is no need for it, they answer frankly that in their factories there are no provisions for pregnant women except that sometimes they are paid up and released from the factory to the four winds.[58]

The most generous of Moscow factories—three out of the seventy-eight that Peskov studied—made the following concessions to the pregnant worker: at one factory, pregnant workers were not fined for arriving late to work; in a second, pregnant women were taken off the loom and given easier work; and in a third, pregnant women were permitted to take three days off without pay after giving birth. Normally, women not only lost their earnings for the time lost in childbirth, but were fined as well, for this was considered a "major truancy."[59]

The law was oblivious to pregnant workers until 1894. In that year, twelve provinces established local bureaus (*Gubernskie po fabrichnym delam prisutsviia*) to supplement the factory inspectorate. The local bureaus had the power to pass so-called "obligatory resolutions" intended, in these provinces, to have the force of law.[60] Between 1894 and 1899 several resolutions were passed regarding pregnant workers. The St Petersburg bureau resolved that factories employing over a hundred women must hire a full-time midwife. Regulations in the other eleven provinces ranged from forbidding pregnant women to carry weights to the more generous provision of periodic visits by a midwife to factories employing "a significant number of women" and a place in the factory for women to give birth. But the laws were poorly defined, and supervision of their execution was

58. P. A. Peskov, *Sanitarnoe issledovanie fabrik po obrabotke voloknistykh veshchestv v gorode Moskve*, vyp. 2. Trudy komissii, uchrezhdennoi g. moskovskim General-Gubernatorom, kn. V. A. Dolgorukovym, dlia osmotra fabrik i zavodov v Moskve (Moscow, 1882), p. 158.

59. TsGIA, f. 20, op. 13[b], d. 28, l. 24.

60. A. V. Pogozhev, *Obzor mestnykh obiazatel'nykh postanovlenii po fabrichnoi sanitarii v Rossii* (St Petersburg, 1894), p. 5.

entirely lacking. They were merely written testimony to good intentions.[61]

Until 1912 medical care for pregnant women depended on the whim of the individual employer, whose fancy did not voluntarily turn very often to the protection of pregnant workers. As late as 1911 a factory doctor from Kiev testified that "you can count on the fingers of one hand the number of factories who give the subject any thought."[62] Some factory owners avoided the problem by refusing to hire pregnant women or firing them if they became pregnant. Factory doctors perceived this as "a great injustice to the woman because she is deprived of an income over a protracted period of time—precisely when her financial needs are increasing."[63] The main result of this policy was self-inflicted abortion.

In the 1880s women workers did not indulge in futile dreams of time off with pay for pregnancy or childbirth. This had not yet occurred to even the most compassionate and sophisticated proponents of workers' welfare. The idea was first expressed in the 1890s and translated into reality by the Insurance Law of 1912. For the typical factory woman, the loss of a few days' pay was the least of her worries. Mainly, she was concerned about keeping her job. Consequently, women working in the most deleterious industrial tasks worked through pregnancy to the onset of labor, with neither hygienic safeguards nor physical respite. They felt the same pressure to return to work almost immediately after childbirth. A questionnaire circulated among women workers in 1912 revealed that almost 75 percent of women workers worked up to the onset of labor, 18 percent left work two weeks before labor, and 7 percent stopped work two to four weeks before labor.[64]

61. "Odin iz voprosov professional'noi gigieny v sektsii akusherstva i zhenskikh boleznei na predstoiashchem IX Pirogovskom s'ezde vrachei," *Promyshlennost' i Zdorov'e* (1903), no. 8, pp. 147–148; Pogozhev, p. 6.

62. *Trudy vtorogo s'ezda fabrichnykh vrachei i predstavitelei fabrichno-zavodskoi promyshlennosti*, vyp. 1–2 (Moscow, 1911), p. 78.

63. Ibid., p. 79.

64. *Voprosy Strakhovaniia* (1914), no. 8, p. 6.

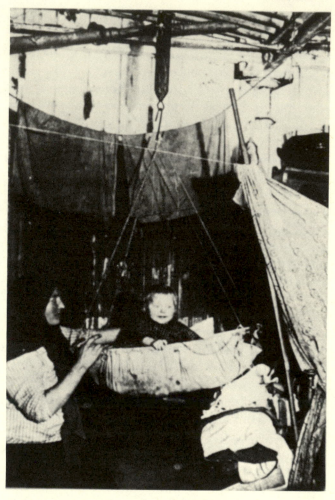

9.   *Quarters for a worker's family in a factory barrack. Moscow.* From Miriam
     Kochan, *The Last Days of Imperial Russia* (London, 1976), p. 67.

If the factory woman survived the hardships of the
prenatal period and successfully bore her child, she was
confronted with new problems as the care of her child was
added to the long hours and exhausting toil of the factory.
The concern of Russian officialdom for the factory woman,
such as it was, centered on her maternal role, and factory

inspectors as well as members of the medical profession frequently exhorted factory owners to provide facilities for the care of infants. Factory owners, indifferent to the plight of the factory mother and her child, were free to disregard pleas and promptings, since they were never translated into effective laws. Of the seventy-one factories that Peskov inspected in Vladimir province in the 1880s, only one had a nursery for the care of children to the age of five.[65]

A partial solution to the care of nursing infants, advocated strenuously by factory doctors and later demanded by striking workers, was for the factory to provide time off and a minimal space for nursing on the factory premises. Even this limited suggestion was rarely heeded by factory owners. In St Petersburg in 1912 only one-fourth of working mothers were permitted to feed their infants at work—"in corridors, on stairways, beside the factory buildings."[66] In typical cases of callous insouciance, several factories in Moscow province evicted workers with babies from the factory barracks. The women were forced to find their own living quarters: "Mothers live only in rented apartments. They have to travel far to feed their infants. This is considered a major truancy [for which women were fined] . . . and it lowers earnings significantly."[67]

In rural factory settlements, factory women who were still part of the peasant household could count on daytime help from women who remained in the peasant hut. This was surely an advantage, economically and psychologically, but one that did not come free:

> Among the women workers are those who simultaneously do field work and factory work . . . [as well as] housework and child-rearing. After a sleepless night they have no time for proper rest. Women workers have told me that during the busy agricultural season they sleep only three hours in twenty-four, and at the factory they have to muster all their strength not to

65. Peskov, *Fabrichnyi byt*, p. 58.
66. TsGIA, f. 767, op. 1, d. 27, l. 142 (*Voprosy Strakhovaniia* [1914], no. 8, p. 6).
67. TsGIA, f. 23, op. 13, l. 120.

doze and therefore be fined. I often saw women workers doz-
ing and half-asleep.[68]

But the majority of factory families were two-generational
and had to find ways to care for children unaided by a circle
of kin.[69] Peskov's observations were characteristic of child-
care arrangements throughout our period:

> At all the other factories there is no trace of facilities for infant
> care during working hours. Usually mothers give their infants
> to women who do not work and who live with the family,
> mainly old women. I often saw such old women caring for
> several infants from many families. Sometimes they charge two
> and a half to three rubles per month . . . , taking many children
> into the family "closet," which is overcrowded with people. But
> the care of children even under these circumstances is not prac-
> ticed everywhere. Normally, the child of parents in the factory
> remains without any care at all. Nursing infants, in the absence
> of mothers, are fed exclusively with a pacifier.[70]

The cost of hiring a nanny was prohibitive, consuming
approximately 15 percent of the urban working family's
budget. It was a luxury few factory families could sustain.[71]
Nor was it the ideal alternative. In the opinion of factory
doctors, the *kukhonnaia matka,* as she was called, was "an old
lady . . . who, with her notoriously filthy pacifier (*zhuika*) . . .
is the cause of colossal infant mortality."[72] Inadequate care
was, of course, only one of many reasons for Russia's infant
mortality rate which, at the turn of the century, was the
highest in Europe.[73] While it was considered a reflection of
the peasantry's low cultural, economic, and educational lev-

68. Katenina, p. 439.
69. Druzhinin, p. 86. The average size of the worker's family was 4.59 persons
in St Petersburg and 4.2 in Moscow and Kostroma provinces.
70. Peskov, *Fabrichnyi byt,* p. 58.
71. Davidovich, p. 8.
72. *Trudy . . . fabrichnykh vrachei,* p. 80.
73. Nancy Frieden, "Child Care: Medical Reform in a Traditionalist Culture,"
in David Ransel, ed., *The Family in Imperial Russia,* (Urbana, Ill., 1978), p. 236. The
author's sources calculated infant mortality for the following countries in 1900:
Russia, 275 per 1,000 live births; Austria, 220; France, 160; England, 140;
Sweden, 90; Norway, 80; and the United States, 162.4.

els, infant mortality may have been even higher in the factory population. In 1907 the infant mortality among workers and among peasants of Vladimir province was compared. One-fourth of peasant children and two-thirds of workers' children died in the first year of life.[74] Other, albeit scanty, data suggest similar comparisons in other provinces as well.[75]

The greatest material deprivation was experienced by what Davidovich called the "incomplete family": the woman worker, abandoned, widowed, married to an unemployed worker, or mother of an illegitimate child, who supported a family solely by means of her own resources. Marital statistics were not sufficiently refined to expose this category of women workers, and led even such assiduous and dedicated students of labor conditions as Erisman to conclude that unmarried women workers and widows "had no family obligations."[76] As one woman worker wrote of her plight: "When I was a girl I always thought, well, I'll work for a while and then I'll get married and my husband will support me. And, look, it all turned out exactly the opposite."[77] She told of the husband's unemployment, followed by his long illness, which culminated in death, leaving her the mother of a three-year-old child and pregnant with another. A study of Kiev workers estimated that 85 percent of women workers were the sole support of their families. This astonishing figure is undoubtedly a reflection of the researcher's atypical sample. However, the woman worker responsible for the economic survival of a family was not exceptional.[78]

Single women who supported families earned less than single women living on their own. The average was brought down by widows: "The [smaller] earnings . . . of widows is [due to] their age. On the average they are forty years old,

74. TsGIA, f. 767, op. 1, d. 27, l. 142.
75. Rashin, *Naselenie*, pp. 205–206.
76. Erisman, *Sbornik*, p. 266.
77. TsGIA, f. 150, op. 1, d. 154, l. 138 (*Stanok Tekstil'shchika* [1908], no. 1, p. 5).
78. See Kats, Druzhinin, Shaposhnikov, and Davidovich.

at which time . . . factory life has already succeeded in aging the woman worker."[79] Predictably, women who supported families spent the highest proportion of all workers on rudimentary necessities. In St Petersburg the female heads of households spent 60 percent of their wages on food, half of it for bread. They were the poorest meat consumers of all categories of workers. The 18 percent of their income which they spent on housing put them at the lowest end of the spectrum of comfort and privacy.[80] While all workers practiced the greatest economy in the purchase of clothing, the female head of household spent far less on her clothing, which was made to stretch "to the very outer boundaries of the possible."[81] Davidovich presented the following illustration: A St Petersburg scutcher who supported herself and two small children on 24 rubles a month spent 1.60 rubles on boots, which she wore for three years, and 1.50 rubles on a cotton dress, worn for five to seven years. She spent an equivalent sum on her children's clothing: "Only by clarifying the length of time that clothing must be worn can a person of another social circle understand how it is possible to survive by spending three rubles on footwear and four on dresses, as we observe in this mother of an incomplete family."[82]

Indebtedness was a chronic feature in the lives of Russian workers. Budget studies could not account strictly for the unexpected in the worker's life or for the periodic accounting with the shopkeeper or factory store which had advanced credit over a long period of time. In the budget of the woman head of household, the deficit was clear with just the simple enumeration of yearly expenditures. She fell into that class of poorest workers who "in fact, could not survive without help from outside": the compassionate neighbor who shared produce brought from the village kin, or donated an old jacket, or the teacher who made a gift of

79. Davidovich, p. 17.
80. Ibid., pp. 18, 26–27.
81. Ibid., p. 12.
82. Ibid., p. 7.

boots to the children.[83] Such episodic benevolence kept the single woman factory worker and her family alive.

The gains and losses of motherhood experienced by the woman worker elude the tools of rational analysis, and to attempt to weigh them would reflect the historian's biases rather than the factory woman's reality. It is certainly unlikely that factory women questioned the importance, indeed the primacy, of motherhood. No one else did. If she derived pleasure as well from her children, it was one of her few pleasures, for her income did not allow for entertainment beyond a barely perceptible amount allocated to religious artifacts. The workers' environment, day in and day out, was conspicuously barren of facilities for entertainment. A St Petersburg worker described a factory ghetto in St Petersburg:

> The entire working-class population of Smolensk tract lived in crowded, filthy, and primitive conditions. . . . Throughout the tract there were innumerable taverns, inns, beer halls and churches. . . . For the sixty thousand inhabitants there were only two shabby theatres.[84]

The "two shabby theatres" rarely saw the woman worker's money.

Alcohol consumption, the male worker's "only available source of entertainment and oblivion from the conditions of his life,"[85] was not part of the female world. Women workers consumed no tobacco and little alcohol. For example, a study of St Petersburg workers in 1898 showed that in the preceding twelve years 15,043 men and 1,799 women had been treated for alcoholism. Of the women workers only 100 were factory workers.[86] The taverns and

83. Ibid.; Shaposhnikov, pp. 23–24.
84. Kanatchikov, p. 79.
85. Shaposhnikov, p. 26.
86. N. I. Grigor'ev, "O p'ianstve sredi masterovykh v S-Peterburge," *Zhurnal Russkogo Obshchestva Okhraneniia Narodnogo Zdraviia,* (1898), no. 12, pp. 859–865. Impressionistic observations as well as more precise investigations agreed that Russian male workers were heavy drinkers and that women workers drank hardly at all. However, they do not agree on whether women workers drank more in city or rural factories. See Shaposhnikov, p. 18; Davidovich, p. 32; Druzhinin, p. 125; Naumov, p. 67.

beer halls were sites not only of drunken brawls and sullen withdrawal, but of conviviality, companionship, and respite from the grind of work and the stultification of crowded and comfortless dwellings. They were the centers of male social life and, as much as the factory floor, were places where workers could reach one another and where the outside world could reach them. The woman worker may have benefited morally, physically, and financially from abstinence, but she was also deprived of the only available social arena. Thus, the celebration of family and religious rituals had an important niche in the lives of factory women who stayed close to home and to unmarried women workers who could afford to return home periodically: "On the eve of St Peter's day each woman worker rushed off to the country without even waiting to be paid off."[87] Her haste is quite comprehensible.

* * *

The urban factory woman had one narrow egress from her impoverished social and intellectual condition. In the cities there were certain opportunities to acquire literacy, sometimes even education. These opportunities were thoroughly inadequate to affect seriously the great majority of workers, but they added a significant dimension to the lives of the city workers whom they reached.

State provision for the education of Russia's lower classes consisted of one-, two-, and three-year elementary schools; they were neither compulsory nor numerous, as is obvious from the figures on illiteracy. A heterogeneous array of people from among Russia's educated and monied strata attempted to fill in the near vacuum of government concern with privately sponsored schools dedicated variously to the spread of basic literacy, to general education of a slightly more advanced nature, or to vocational training. Some organizations whose members presumably knew a lot about workers expressed attitudes toward educating women workers which were not much advanced over peasant atti-

87. Romashova, p. 154 (see n. 12 above).

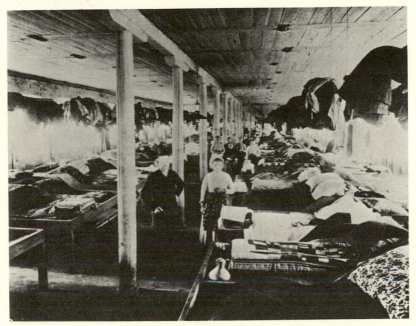

10. *Women workers' dormitory, Giraud silk factory. Moscow, 1891.* From Kiril
Fitzlyon and Tatiana Browning, *Before the Revolution* (London,
1978), p. 133.

tudes, avowing that "a woman's calling is the family. She
needs information, general education, or skill [only] as part
of the family and for the sake of the family."[88] Even the
most enlightened efforts to educate women workers were
frustrated by bureaucratic indifference and unofficial hostility. Schools for women workers were "neither necessary
nor desirable," responded factory owners to a questionnaire
circulated by the Moscow provincial school board in 1906,
since "[schooling] only distracts the workers" from their
place in life.[89]

In 1898 in the Russian Empire there were 48 vocational

88. S'ezd russkikh deiatelei po tekhnicheskomu i professional'nomu obrazovaniiu. *Trudy IV otdeleniia* (1890), p. 16. Cited in N. M. Kuz'min, *Nizshee i srednee
spetsial'noe obrazovanie v dorevoliutsionnoi Rossii* (Cheliabinsk, 1971), p. 258.
89. TsGIA, f. 741, op. 8, d. 43, l. 109.

schools for women, 30 special classes attached to regional primary schools, 3 schools of cooking and housekeeping, and 165 courses in general education, which included instruction in needlework.[90] They accommodated very few students. For example, one of the first vocational schools for women was founded in Orenburg in 1885. By 1902 it had taught only ninety-two pupils.[91] In about 1904 there was an eruption of interest in vocational training for girls and women—at least by comparison with the previous level of interest—on the part of local school boards, private individuals and organizations, and finally, the Ministry of Education, which acknowledged that "while the vocational needs of the male population are answered [a gross overstatement] . . . almost nothing has been done to cater to women's vocational needs."[92] The ministry sponsored its first vocational school for women that year in St Petersburg and subsequently several more in other parts of Russia. It was a haphazard venture with neither statutes nor a common plan of instruction, and simply imitated earlier and equally haphazard private schools. In 1913 the ministry concocted a proper legislative act, also a variation on earlier private attempts, but with the virtue of better funding and wider regional distribution. It was never implemented.[93] The founders of the vocational schools intended to help "the children of poor parents . . . to attain some vocational training,"[94] but they were equally guided—or misguided— by the notion that poor women really needed to be schooled "in domestic work which [a woman] . . . must know in any family."[95] The curricula consisted of instruction in hat-making, elegant embroidery, artificial-flower making, knitting, crocheting, and tailoring, occupations already overrun with

90. Kuz'min, p. 263.
91. TsGIA, f. 741, op. 5-zh, d. 1, l. 3–4, 13, 88; TsGIA, f. 741, op. 5-zh, d. 8-1904, l. 67.
92. TsGIA, f. 741, op. 5-zh, d. 2-1905, l. 3; TsGIA, f. 741, op. 5-zh, d. 3-1905, l. 131.
93. Kuz'min, p. 268.
94. TsGIA, f. 741, op. 5-zh, d. 12, l. 2.
95. TsGIA, f. 741, op. 5-zh, d. 4-1904, l. 13.

unemployed or underemployed women. While the schools' resources were never sufficient to accommodate the great demand, only a sprinkling of girls from the factory milieu attended. These schools appealed mainly to the children of a more urbanized segment of the lower classes: cab drivers, police, soldiers, tailors.[96] Factory women and their children did not share the regret expressed by the director of the vocational school in Tula that the vocational classes in his city did not include cooking instruction.[97]

Factory women were far more interested in basic literacy and the academic subjects that were often taught along with crafts in the vocational schools, but the conditions of entrance were prohibitive. Most of the schools were forced to charge tuition, since private funding was lethargic and inadequate. Frequent appeals to the Ministry of Education were met with indifference and claims of the ministry's scanty funds. Indeed, in 1904 the Ministry of Education allocated only 23,000 rubles a year to women's vocational training.[98] Further, most vocational schools either refused to train girls over the age of fifteen or limited enrollment to students who were already literate.[99]

In addition to devising curricula that were irrelevant to the needs and interests of factory women, and to charging tuition and demanding prior literacy, the vocational schools required full-time attendance. In other words, they catered to segments of the urban poor whose resources were beyond those of the factory women.

Far more successful in both concept and accessibility were the free Sunday schools for the urban poor, which held classes on Sundays and evenings. The so-called Sunday-school movement was born in the flush of heightened social

96. TsGIA, f. 741, op. 5-zh, d. 12, l. 2; TsGIA, f. 741, op. 5-zh, d. 8, l. 7; TsGIA, f. 741, op. 5-zh, d. 1, l. 13; TsGIA, f. 741, op. 5-zh, d. 12, l. 55; TsGIA, f. 741, op. 5-zh, d. 13, l. 184; TsGIA, f. 741, op. 5-zh, d. 1, l. 186; TsGIA, f. 741, op. 5-zh, d. 2, l. 136.

97. TsGIA, f. 741, op. 5-zh, d. 12-1904, l. 3.

98. TsGIA, f. 741, op. 5-zh, d. 12-1904, l. 13; TsGIA, f. 741, op. 5-zh, d. 8-1904, l. 10–12.

99. TsGIA, f. 741, op. 5-zh, d. 4-1904, l. 13–14.

consciousness which accompanied the end of the Crimean
War and the preparations for the emancipation of the serfs.
The founders and teachers in the schools shared a sympathy for the urban poor, which was channeled into the
desire to spread literacy among them, and to this end in
1859 they began to organize free schools outside the state
school system but with the approval of the government. A
combination of waning enthusiasm on the part of teachers
and the government's disenchantment with the venture—
the schools were soon perceived as breeding places for revolutionary ferment—brought the experiment to an end in
1862.[100] In the middle of the 1880s the Sunday schools were
revived in a more tentative and piecemeal way than their
predecessors; however, over a twenty-year period they
mushroomed and expanded to include classes designated
for women workers. By 1899 there were 147 women's
schools in about fifteen cities, as well as forty-one schools
that women workers attended with men.[101]

It is impossible to estimate with any pretension to accu-
racy how many women passed through the Sunday schools.
The St Petersburg schools taught roughly seven thousand
women between 1884 and 1898, but St Petersburg had
more and larger schools than other cities.[102] Nor were all
the pupils from the factory. Some Sunday schools were intended specifically for factory workers, but did not exclude
other kinds of working women.[103]

One of the largest and most successful women's Sunday
schools was the Smolensk Women's Evening and Sunday
Classes located in St Petersburg on the Shlissel'burg high-
way, a huge factory district stretching through almost the

100. Reginald E. Zelnik, *Labor and Society in Tsarist Russia* (Stanford, 1971), pp.
174–199; idem, "The Sunday School Movement in Russia, 1859–1862," *Journal of
Modern History* 27 (1965), June, no. 2.
101. Ia. V. Abramov, *Nashi voskrenyia shkoly* (St Petersburg, 1900), p. 283.
102. Ibid., p. 103.
103. Khar'kov, for example, boasted a vigorous and popular Sunday school
which attracted mainly seamstresses. But Khar'kov's level of industrialization was
relatively low. Factory women were 18 percent of the enrollment, probably in
proportion to the number of factory women workers among the female working
population. See Abramov, pp. 103, 139.

entire southern part of the city. Between 1893 and 1903 over three thousand women attended, although as the director pointed out, the women's classes "were by no means as intensive as the development of the men's classes, since in the working class women's education is considered far less important than men's education. However, women workers' demand for education has grown consistently—not only for more classes but for a higher quality of education as well."[104] Indeed, the initiative often came from women, although they were far more enthusiastic about classes specifically for women than they were for mixed classes.[105]

Roughly 50 percent of the women students were between the ages of fifteen and nineteen and unmarried, for "the [married] woman worker has much more to do than the men, who have more free time."[106] On Sundays, when the classes were held, married factory women "were busy with cleaning and preparing food."[107] Sheer lack of time was reinforced by powerful antagonism toward education for women:

> [Within the working class] there is still the opinion that school is serious business for men, whereas for women it is only "indulgence" [*balovstvo*]. There seems to be agreement that women's schools should be for everyone, but only until the woman has achieved minimal literacy. Arithmetic is considered superfluous. It is not surprising, therefore, that without a clear idea of the goal of their studies, women pupils find it difficult to stay in school for the entire year.[108]

Women of the older generation often felt that "school for women is not only useless but a threat,"[109] because when a

104. Leningradskii Gosudarstvennyi Istoricheskii Arkhiv (hereafter, LGIA), f. 997, op. 1, d. 16, l. 2.
105. Abramov, pp. 243–248; *Prechistenskie rabochie kursy. Pervyi rabochii universitet v Moskve* (Moscow, 1948), p. 39.
106. LGIA, f. 997, op. 1, d. 16, l. 19. Only a smattering of the pupils were under the age of fifteen. A somewhat larger but still small group was over twenty-five.
107. Abramov, p. 134. LGIA, f. 997, op. 1, d. 16, l. 19.
108. LGIA, f. 997, op. 1, d. 16, l. 10.
109. LGIA, f. 997, op. 1, d. 16, l. 21.

younger woman in the family went to school, part of her
domestic obligations fell to the mother. The director of the
Smolensk school described a typical example of the struggle
between generations: A girl registered for the school surreptitiously. When the mother found out, she forbade the
girl to go out on the streets at night and attempted to discredit the school among the girl's friends, claiming that the
women were taught only to strike and to shirk work. For a
month the girl persevered, circumventing the mother by
going to school directly from the factory and foregoing her
supper. Ultimately, the mother's will prevailed and the girl
dropped out.[110]

Married women, free of parental control, still had to contend with the opposition of the husband "who sees no sense
in school for his wife."[111] The factory woman who could
"tolerate the contempt and scorn" of her elders and
peers,[112] and was able to endure the added physical strain of
school in the precious few hours of free time available to
her, had still to acknowledge that simple literacy had little
practical value in her life. As we have seen, it was not a
ticket to more interesting or more remunerative jobs. Why,
in the face of formidable obstacles, physical and emotional,
did women workers come to the Sunday schools?

Many women workers attended Sunday schools as much
for the companionship and conviviality as for the studies.
They attended more regularly and persevered longer if their
groups remained stable. They formed fierce attachments to
a teacher and were known to repeat a class voluntarily to
remain with a familiar cohesive group and a beloved
teacher.[113] The rapid turnover of teachers was a constant
problem. The director of the Smolensk school noted that
"people were far more reluctant to teach in the women's
schools than the men's," partly because women students were

110. LGIA, f. 997, op. 1, d. 16, l. 22.
111. Abramov, p. 134.
112. Ibid., p. 137.
113. LGIA, f. 997, op. 1, d. 16, l. 21–23.

more passive.[114] To overcome the diffidence and trepidation of the majority of women students required experience and dedication from the teacher. There were many who had one or both of these qualities, but more who did not or, worse, some who regarded the women workers as "coarse savages."[115]

The women who were mainly impelled by the desire to learn were often inspired by male workers who attended classes. The women expressed discomfort at not being able to follow the discussions of their male friends.[116] But the great majority of women students were satisfied with the acquisition of simple literacy, with the ability to read "some kind of a book," write a letter, work an abacus, and write numbers.[117] The greater sacrifices necessary to attend classes after a year or two were enough to undermine any enthusiasm they might have felt for continuing.

Yet a small but growing number of women who had attended the first year or two of the Smolensk Sunday school were eager to continue. On the initiative of one group of students special advanced classes were added to the school in 1896 despite the skepticism of the school's founders, who feared it might turn out to be an unjustified expense.[118] Quite the contrary, attendance increased over the next seven years, although the proportion of nonfactory to factory women increased, for

> the obstacles that interfere with the attendance of women workers to the school in general become almost insurmountable when it comes to the special classes. The special classes meet [every night except Saturday] for three years. So first the woman worker has to find the time. Her social environment is not yet even receptive to the idea of literacy for women, and in the special classes she studies real subjects which, however, have

---

114. LGIA, f. 997, op. 1, d. 16, l. 43.

115. *Godovoi otchet o deiatel'nosti zhenskikh vechernikh klassov v Nezhine za 1897–1898 g.* (Chernigov, 1899), p. 2.

116. LGIA, f. 997, op. 1, d. 16, l. 30.

117. TsGIA, f. 91, op. 1, d. 575, l. 9.

118. LGIA, f. 997, op. 1, d. 16, l. 25.

absolutely no practical application to her life. . . . It is not surprising that only exceptional women attend these classes, women who . . . are prepared to make sacrifices for it.[119]

The special classes consisted of a three-year program, which met for ten evening hours a week and five to six hours on Sunday. They offered classes in religion, Russian language and history, geography, arithmetic, geometry, physics, and drawing. The explicit goal of the school's administration was to raise the cultural level of the women worker-students in the hope that they would in turn influence other women workers. But the school's director commented sadly that the effect of the special classes was to make the woman worker "too dissatisfied with her workers' environment."[120] Of the thirteen factory women who completed the first graduating class "five abandoned their previous social surroundings."[121] One registered in a more advanced state school; another entered midwives' school; a third enrolled in a teacher's seminary; a fourth passed the examination to become a village teacher; and the last entered the gymnasium.

It is likely that some combination of the influence of education and the original motivation, however vague, for pursuing education drew these women out of the factory. Side by side with the sentiments expressed by one woman worker—"I feel the uncontainable striving for knowledge quite apart from any rewards of job or good income"[122]— were requests for more concrete education as a preparation for a life outside the factory.[123] A study of eleven thousand workers in Moscow province concluded that among women workers over the age of twenty-five there was a "[clearer] aspiration to abandon the factory" than among men.[124] For

119. LGIA, f. 997, op. 1, d. 16, l. 28.
120. LGIA, f. 997, op. 1, d. 16, l. 32.
121. Ibid.
122. LGIA, f. 997, op. 1, d. 16, l. 30.
123. LGIA, f. 997, op. 1, d. 16, l. 29; TsGIA, f. 91, op. 1, d. 575, l. 9.
124. "Vliianie fabrichnoi raboty na rasprostranenie gramotnosti sredi naseleniia v serpukhovskom uezde moskovskoi gubernii," *Promyshlennost' i Zdorov'e* (1904), kn. 2, p. 46.

most workers, of course, there was "no place to go,"[125] but when opportunity smiled upon the exceptionally energetic and motivated woman worker, she took it. She paid for it, often, with the loss of family ties, the contempt of her peers, and the sacrifice of her little free time. Her personal success may indeed have been a deprivation for the working class. From among this already small segment of factory women, an even smaller group was politicized, which, as we shall see, did in fact dedicate itself to the enlightenment of other factory women.

In 1903 the director of the Smolensk school, glancing back over the school's eight-year existence, observed that "there is at present an energetic struggle between the old and young generations which does not always end in victory for the former." She saw this as a portent for the future: "Perhaps the day is not far off when contempt for women's education among the working class will disappear without a trace . . . and will be relegated to an unpleasant memory."[126]

* * *

The distinctions among factory women that influenced the quality of their lives outside the factory walls were annulled at the workplace. Age, marital status, living conditions, literacy, whether they were childless or mothers— none of these features were of consequence to the machine and the organization of work. But the factory administration was not blind to gender and subjected women workers to specific kinds of abuse as well as specific kinds of neglect and indifference.

The factory woman's day began and ended with humiliation. The routine search of workers, profoundly resented by all, was experienced by women workers as a symbol of their general abasement, because the searches of women workers were conducted by male supervisory personnel. A woman worker described them:

125. Ibid.
126. LGIA, f. 997, op. 1, d. 16, l. 29, 22.

The searches were disgraceful. Often they took place in the presence of the shop stewards and other [male] administrative personnel. Of course, it is clear why they all gathered by the women's exit of the factory. During the search . . . they would toss out remarks of such a content that I cannot bring myself to repeat them. . . . When I worked in the factory I recall leaving work after a fourteen-hour day of whirling around the machine, unable to see straight, as they say, from fatigue, and on top of that to submit to this vulgar humiliation of my person.[127]

The distance between factory owner and worker was never expressed better than in a factory owner's contention that "there [is] nothing immoral about women being searched by men: women workers [are] accustomed to it and see it as quite an ordinary thing."[128]

On the shop floor abuse and sexual harassment were commonplace in the woman worker's experience. In a rare complaint to a St Petersburg factory inspector in 1901, a factory woman described a day in her life:

I have been working three years at Stal' [a large cotton-spinning factory] and I am struck by the disgraceful things that go on, the beastly system, which goes unpunished at this factory. . . . When you come to work you hear only curses and swearing from [the foreman]. . . . He does not permit us to go to the toilet. If he sees you going, he puts his hand in your way, pulls your hair, fines you, and threatens to fire you. If a woman worker pleases him, he calls her to his office and is not shy about making the most foul propositions. If she refuses she is subjected to pressure, oppression, and even firing. Once a girl ran out of his office screaming, and the very next day she was fired. We are supposed to take breakfast while we work. But the machines do not stop, and if you sit down for a moment to drink tea, the foreman turns up, pulls your hair, and breaks the dishes which we have bought with our pittance. We are not allowed into the factory in street clothes, and they force us to change clothes almost on the street in the cold corridor. You

127. V. Karelina, "Rabotnitsy v gaponovskikh obshchestvakh," In P. F. Kudelli, *Rabotnitsa v 1905 g. v S-Peterburge* (Leningrad, 1926), pp. 18–19.
128. I. Kh. Ozerov, *Politika po rabochemu voprosu v Rossii za poslednie gody (po neizdannym dokumentam)* (Moscow, 1906), pp. 255–256.

leave work sweaty and feverish, so you get a cold. The boss pays no attention to our complaints. He only knows how to swear and set fines. As for the foremen, there is nothing to say except that they do not give out [our tools] until they get a bribe. Imitating the boss, they pull such tricks that it makes me ashamed to speak of them. There is no way to avoid it. We are miserable, but there is no one to complain to [*tiazhelo nam—a zhalovat'sia nekomu*].[129]

Thus, widespread sexual molestation was only the most extreme form of abuse and contempt endured by women workers.[130] As another woman worker related to a Tver' court: "Piskunov [the foreman] is merciless, especially with us, the women. He is afraid to fight with the men workers, but he beats us, the women, ruthlessly when we turn to him with our requests."[131] When a workers' press emerged after 1905, women workers complained above all about this kind of treatment.

The disregard for hygienic safeguards in Russian factories not only had ruinous physical consequences for workers, but was an affront to the woman worker's dignity. For example, in the extreme heat and poor ventilation characteristic of factories of every description, "women, suppressing their natural modesty, in the majority of cases work only in their underwear."[132] The factory inspector who reported that "in the extreme heat all the women workers must work half naked" and then accused the women workers of immorality was not aware of the paradox in his judgment.[133]

Women workers were vulnerable to the demands of factory administration that they play out their domestic role in the workplace as well, and especially in small rural factories, they were coerced into performing unpaid personal domes-

129. LGIA, f. 1229, op. 1, d. 146, l. 3.
130. *Rab. dvizh.*, t. 4, chast' 2, p. 89; TsGIA, f. 23, op. 30, d. 2, l. 32, 240.
131. *Rab. dvizh.*, t. 3, chast' 1, p. 327. See also t. 1, chast' 3, pp. 394–395, 369; Katenina, p. 447; TsGIA, f. 23, op. 30, d. 26, l. 108; and f. 23, op. 20, d. 43, l. 75.
132. Katenina, p. 440.
133. TsGIA, f. 20, d. 188[2a], l. 133, 123.

tic services for stewards and owners, like doing their laundry and cleaning their houses.[134]

The specific degradation was in addition to the features of factory work which women workers shared with men: the long hours of work without adequate rest periods, the deleterious effects on their health of filthy, poorly ventilated factories where regard for the worker's health and safety took a back seat to profit, or simply fell into that great vacuum of indifference toward the welfare of all workers. Each industry was accompanied by its own set of health hazards. The shop floor of the textile factory was dangerously crowded with machinery whose constant din impaired the hearing. In tobacco and match factories the dust and noxious fumes eroded the lungs and produced chronic nausea, vomiting, and diarrhea. In all industries long, uninterrupted hours of standing at the machine led to varicose veins in women, especially in mothers: "They reach enormous proportions, covering not only both legs from top to bottom but also the pubic area and the lips of the vagina."[135] Delicate work requiring constant vigilance and attention played havoc with the eyesight and the entire nervous system.

In 1913 the *zemstvo* of Kostroma province commissioned a group of women doctors to investigate the effects of factory work on the health of women workers. The study concentrated on four textile factories employing nine thousand women workers. The senior doctor, L. Katenina, was sensitive not only to the women's physical condition but to their psychological responses as well. Women doctors understood from experience that unless the women workers overcame their suspicion of official and semiofficial persons they would not answer questions truthfully. Dr. Katenina noted that at first the women workers appeared to be indifferent: "The women workers came in groups without protest, submissively undressed, dressed again and obediently answered our questions. . . . This is because women workers were ac-

134. *Rab. dvizh.*, t. 3, chast' 2, pp. 527–528; *Pravda* (1912), no. 200, p. 4.
135. M. K. Valitskaia, *Issledovaniia zdorov'ia rabochikh na tabachnykh fabrikakh* (St Petersburg, 1889), pp. 14–15.

customed to fulfilling all the administration's demands without a murmur." Slowly the women began to respond with interest and curiosity: "They often expressed their surprise at our [the doctors'] respectful treatment of them. Truly the woman worker of Sereda has not been pampered by respectful treatment!"[136] Katenina concluded her report with the following description:

> One cannot help but note the premature decrepitude of the factory woman. A woman worker of fifty who has worked at the factory thirty or more years frequently looks ancient; she sees and hears poorly, her head trembles, her shoulders are sharply hunched over. She looks about seventy years old. It is obvious that only dire need keeps her at the factory, forcing her to work beyond her strength. . . . While in the West, elderly workers have pensions, our women workers, having given decades to the factory so that they are prematurely enfeebled, can expect nothing better than to live out their last days as latrine attendants.[137]

* * *

"There is a Hell more terrible than Dante's ninth circle. It is female labor," wrote a Russian church dignitary of women factory workers in 1906.[138] Yet the woman worker in Russia had few champions. Until the turn of the century most of society barely noted, much less lamented, her plight, a subject we will discuss in subsequent chapters. Of course, government and industrialists, as partners in industrialization, could not help but be aware of the growing presence of women in the factory. But they could ignore it, and until 1885 they did. They simply regarded women as a subspecies of worker, and the abuses of the factory system were distributed equally among men and women without regard to gender. If government and industry were insensitive to the needs of women workers as mothers or indifferent to the difficulties of women's survival on lower earnings,

136. Katenina, p. 445.
137. Ibid., p. 447.
138. A[rkhimandrit] Mikhail, *Zhenshchina-rabotnitsa* (St Petersburg, 1906).

and if they ignored the humiliation of sexual harassment that women workers endured, it was not from a conscious desire to discriminate against them. Rather, these attitudes were reflections of attitudes toward women which were imbedded in the entire social fabric.

To the extent that industrialists distinguished women workers from men, it was to value them as cheaper labor. As we have seen, the increasing use of female labor was determined by the dictates of maximizing profit. The demand for jobs was such that the factory owner did not have to ease the factory woman's burden in order to attract her to the factory. The government's position was more complicated. Anxious to promote and defend industry, it nonetheless felt some obligation to protect workers from excessive exploitation—in part to insure public order and in part out of jealous regard for its role as sole arbiter of justice. The woman worker, as an object of concern, slipped in through the back door, as it were, in the early 1880s and, as a by-product of other concerns, became one of the central issues in a dialogue between government and industrialists.

At that time Russia was suffering from an economic crisis of serious proportions. In response to a drop in consumer demand for textiles, factories had been lowering piece rates and wages and releasing workers. As the crisis gathered momentum the textile industry was threatened with the closure of entire factories, and the large industrial areas, especially St Petersburg, with the social consequences of large numbers of unemployed workers. In 1885 the government invited Russia's textile manufacturers to propose legislation that would alleviate the crisis.

The St Petersburg industrialists blamed the crisis on overproduction. They proposed to avoid mass layoffs that would follow decreased production by abolishing night work for women and adolescents. The industrialists of the Central Industrial Region (CIR) protested adamantly. The CIR included the provinces of Moscow, Vladimir, Riazan', Tula, Kostroma, Tver', and Nizhnii-Novgorod. Of these,

Moscow and Vladimir were by far the most highly industrialized. The disagreement between Russia's two major textile-producing areas was based on long-standing competition between them. Textile factories in St Petersburg had easier access to raw materials from abroad, were more highly mechanized, and boasted higher labor productivity than factories in the CIR. Therefore, night work was already nearly obsolete in St Petersburg. Industrialists of the CIR, more dependent on labor-intensive production, felt that without the night work of women and adolescents they could not compete with St Petersburg.

In the ensuing debate each side masked its economic interests with the rhetoric of morality and professions of compassion for women workers. St Petersburg claimed that night work was physically excessive and morally harmful for women and adolescents. Eliminating night work, they predicted, would "raise the morals of factory women and children, which have fallen to intolerable depths in areas where night work has become the norm."[139] The CIR industrialists retorted, "It can scarcely be proven that night work is more detrimental for [women and adolescents] than the places they spend their [evening] hours—the barracks, the drinking establishments, and other places that promote debauchery and from which it is impossible to keep the workers."[140] Further, they asserted that women's night work was necessary for the integrity of the workers' families: "Only by working nights can women combine industrial work with keeping house and caring for children."[141] They were clearly not much concerned about when women workers might sleep.

Three agencies of the government were empowered to sift the evidence and draft the legislation. The Ministry of Finance agreed unconditionally with the St Petersburg manufacturers that "night work destroys the fabric of hu-

139. TsGIA, f. 1152, op. X, d. 286, l. 24.
140. Ibid., l. 26.
141. Ibid., l. 2.

man life and is, in general, not normal. As experience has shown, it is harmful to workers, especially to women and adolescents."[142] The Ministry of Internal Affairs agreed with the Ministry of Finance in principle, but wished to accommodate factories in the CIR which could not survive without women's night work. The Department of Economics (an organ of the State Council) was the least inclined to consider the welfare of women workers: "To proceed hastily to the irrevocable prohibition of night work for women and adolescents . . . is hardly reasonable, keeping in mind that the crisis is temporary. Once it passes, factories will again have a great need for working hands."[143] Finally, a few of the major CIR manufacturers who could afford to dispense with night work, who would indeed benefit from eliminating competition from smaller factories in their own region, agreed to the prohibition of night work. The balance was thus tipped in favor of the St Petersburg solution, and the new law prohibited night work for adolescents to age seventeen and for all women in the cotton, linen, and wool industries. As a concession to its opponents, the law was formulated as an experiment to be reevaluated in three years time.

In the original draft, night work was defined as work from 9 P.M. to 5 A.M. Between the time the law was promulgated in June of 1885 and the time of its projected application, October 1885, workers of Vladimir province protested the law with massive strikes. The Vladimir industrialists quickly conveyed the news to their St Petersburg opponents. As a result, two hours were added to the workday, and night work was redefined to include the hours between 10 P.M. and 4 A.M.[144]

The efficacy of the law was undermined by two serious omissions. It neither stated how failure to comply was to be punished nor gave responsibility for its supervision to a

142. TsGIA, f. 1149, op. XI-1890, d. 7, l. 41.
143. Ibid., l. 42.
144. A. N. Bykov, *Fabrichnoe zakonodatel'stvo i razvitie ego v Rossii* (St Petersburg, 1909), p. 156.

specific administrative organ. De facto supervision fell to the Factory Inspectorate, whose only weapon was a vague article limiting fines for any offense to 50 rubles.[145]

When the law was reviewed in 1890 it took away with one hand what it had given with the other. Although the revised law specified that violations could be punished by a fine of one hundred rubles or one month in jail,[146] it assumed the "obligation to protect the moral foundations of family life." The Ministry of Finance stated:

> If one of the grounds for prohibition of night work [for women and adolescents] . . . was that night work has a pernicious influence on workers' morals, then it must be conceded that the unconditional prohibition of night work is just as ruinous when it [forces] members of the same family to work at different times.[147]

Thus, the revised law stated that night work for women and adolescents was permissible when it secured the rights of "husbands and parents to have constant supervision over their wives and children."[148]

The government was torn in its desire to protect both industry and workers—to reconcile the irreconcilable. Official solicitude for women workers was sincere, but by no means decisive. Its overriding concern was to promote the health of Russian industry. In an addendum to the law of 1885, factory owners were given the right to hire women without the permission of their husbands.[149] However, greater freedom and independence for women was not the issue. Like the law prohibiting night work, the needs of

---

145. A. A. Mikulin, *Fabrichnaia inspektsiia v Rossii, 1882–1902* (Kiev, 1906), p. 47.

146. Ibid., p. 47.

147. TsGIA, f. 1149, op. XI-1890, d. 7, l. 43.

148. Ibid.

149. *Rab. dvizh.*, t. 3, chast' 2, p. 758. In 1835 when the factory population was made up in large measure of peasant serfs, the government forbade factories to hire a wife without the consent of her husband. Undoubtedly more honored in the breach, the 1885 law removed that obstacle to hiring women workers. See also Litvinov-Filanskii, *Fabrichnoe zakonodatel'stvo i fabrichnaia inspektsiia v Rossii* (St Petersburg, 1900), p. 65.

women workers were instrumental, a means to meet the
needs of industry. So much the better if women's needs and
family integrity could be supported as well.

Slipshod and ambiguous as the laws were, night work for
women gradually diminished over the decades. The prohibition was extended to all areas of textiles as well as to other
light industries that employed female labor. Factories that
wished to take advantage of the legal exceptions were en-
cumbered by having to make special application to local
administrative bureaus and the Factory Inspectorate.
Gradually, then, many factories created new shifts that
maximized the use of female labor within the limits of the
law. For example, some industrialists discovered that two
nine-hour shifts were more economical than twenty-four-
hour production. There was less outlay for heat, light, and
administrative personnel and less spoilage and waste of
material.[150] Larger economic trends contributed to the decline of night work as well. As CIR manufacturers began to
acquire cotton from Russian Central Asia, their competitive
disadvantage with St Petersburg—and their reliance on
female and adolescent night work—diminished. Smaller
factories dependent on women's night work could not survive the competition with the increasing numbers of larger,
more mechanized factories.[151] Hence, by the early years of
the twentieth century, night work, especially in textiles, was
the exception.

The law of 1885 (and its subsequent amendments) was
the last legislation to include specific provisions for women
workers until the Insurance Law of 1913. However, provincial bureaus for factory affairs, established in 1886 and expanded in 1893, were empowered to pass local, binding
rules, and these local bureaus were sometimes responsive to
a wide variety of women workers' needs. Rulings were
passed, for example, on factory provision for women
workers' medical care, on questions of work safety for

150. Bykov, p. 158.
151. Ibid., p. 154.

women, on provision of separate toilets and dressing rooms for women in the factory and separate sleeping quarters in the barracks. In 1890 the St Petersburg bureau passed the first and only rule that women workers be searched by women instead of men.[152] Unfortunately, the sensitivity of the local bureaus was not matched by the zeal, nor indeed the power, to enforce the rulings. The abuses they were intended to correct pervaded factory life to the end of our period.

Between profit-seeking industrialists and the government, with its more complex goal of protecting both industry and workers, stood a group of semiofficial persons whose knowledge of and concern for factory workers was unsurpassed in Russia. They did their field work assiduously as factory inspectors, *zemstvo* researchers, or factory doctors, exploring the noxious workshops and crowded factory barracks, serving as mediators in strikes, compiling industrial statistics. For the most part, these well-trained, sophisticated, and learned specialists—some with estimable reputations in the West—applauded Russia's industrialization. But they lamented the price paid by workers, especially women, for the benefits that allegedly accrued to the society as a whole.

Their attitude toward women in the factory was a fascinating blend of pragmatism, compassion, and traditional prejudices. In the words of I. I. Ianzhul,

> If industry has such a ruinous effect on male workers, as we can see from the data . . . then obviously the effects on women are far more pernicious. In general women have more delicate, sensitive constitutions and are less resistant to illness than men. Therefore, all the harmful conditions of factory life are worse for women than for men.[153]

However, the alleged delicacy of women's constitutions (here the specialists were in general but not universal agree-

---

152. TsGIA, f. 20, op. 13, d. 192, l. 55, 58, 75; f. 20, op. 13[b], d. 24, l. 9. A. V. Pogozhev, *Obzor mestnykh obiazatel'nykh postanovlenii po fabrichnoi sanitarii v Rossii*, p. 11–28.

153. Ianzhul, *Ocherki i issledovaniia*, p. 381; Litvinov-Filanskii, p. 178.

ment) was no reason to keep them from factory work. The specialists did not propose to send the woman worker back to some mythical rural bliss, for they understood that peasant women did hard physical labor as well.[154] Women's work in the factory, the specialists agreed, was necessary for the survival of the factory family, for the success of industry, and for the well-being of the entire nation. To be sure, the woman's primary duties were "the fulfillment of her maternal functions dictated by nature" and responsibility for the health of the "entire future generation of the working class."[155] But "normal pregnancy should not be cause for dismissal if only the slightest concern is shown for the pregnant worker."[156] Indeed, the economic realities made the woman's factory work all the more important when she faced maternal responsibilities. It was not the factory work as such, but the conditions of factory labor, that made all workers' lives a misery and women's more so. The specialists sought then to ameliorate and humanize those conditions.

The specialists had no illusions that industrialists would initiate changes in factory conditions. As Peskov noted in an admirable understatement, "From experience we know how the factory administration's accounts [of conditions] can differ from reality."[157] Instead, they looked to the government to legislate the health, safety, and general well-being of women workers and their offspring. They envisioned laws to end night work for factory women, to sanction a shorter workday, to prohibit women from working in dangerous industries, to make medical facilities available to factory women, especially mothers. They kept up a constant pressure for child-care facilities in the factory. And, until the middle of the 1890s, they were optimistic. As Erisman wrote in 1890: "Between the factory owners, following their own interests [cheap labor], and the government, which is morally

154. Sviatlovskii, *Fabrichnyi rabochii*, p. 12.
155. Ianzhul, *Ocherki*, pp. 381, 393.
156. S. V. Petrykovskii, "Polozhenie beremennykh rabotnits na zavodakh," *Trudy vtorogo vserossiiskogo s'ezda fabrichnykh vrachei*, vyp. 1 (Moscow, 1911), p. 79.
157. Peskov, *Trudy komissii*, vyp. 1, p. 166.

obligated to protect the weak and defenseless, there will be a new struggle like the contemporary struggle over child labor; but it will be played out in another equally important arena—over the protection of women workers."[158]

In the 1880s and early 1890s there was reason for optimism. The law of 1885, however inadequate, officially acknowledged the need to legislate for women workers. The establishment of the Factory Inspectorate allowed the specialists to implement their goals in practical ways. Although the government's instructions to the inspectors emphasized that "attention to factory conditions was only . . . a secondary or even tertiary task," the inspectors themselves saw the Inspectorate as "an organ . . . devoted to defending the workers, considering that the interests of captial and labor were not the same and could be reconciled only by deliberately introducing new legislative norms."[159] They reported on factory conditions in great detail, barely troubling to disguise their compassion for the workers and their disgust with the industrialists. But the government was acutely uncomfortable with public exposure of factory conditions, and factory inspectors' reports of 1885 were the last to be published until 1900. The inspectors continued to report on conditions in the factory in unpublished reports to the government and to plead for improvement. But their initial optimism was based on their humanitarian compassion and sense of justice rather than on a realistic estimate of the forces ranged against the promulgation of truly effective legislation. The anticipated battle for the protection of women in the factory never came to pass.

In 1894 the Factory Inspectorate was reorganized, and the first generation of inspectors—doctors, economists, lawyers, and scientists—was replaced primarily by technocrats. The inspectors were now instructed to aid industrial development with their technical expertise and to keep a sharp eye out for potential industrial conflict.[160] The new generation of inspec-

158. Erisman, p. 209.
159. Sviatlovskii, *Fabrichnyi rabochii*, p. 3; Mikulin, p. 101.
160. Mikulin, p. 173.

tors was, by and large, indifferent to factory conditions and more sympathetic to industrialists. By 1900, Vladimir Litvi-nov-Filanskii, one of the most articulate of the second generation, proclaimed that the conflict between labor and capital was already resolved in the best interests of both. As for women workers specifically, they (along with their children) were the beneficiaries of the government's high moral obligation to protect them from the "selfish exploitation by [both] husbands and employers."[161] Not one of the first factory inspectors would have uttered such nonsense.

A few of the older type of inspector remained among the engineers and technicians and used their limited influence to prevent industrialists from violating the prohibition against night work. Others, with their like-minded colleagues in other capacities, continued to do research in the *zemstvos,* as factory doctors and publicists. But their optimism was justifiably diminished, for, in the words of a factory doctor from Kiev, their work had become "archive dust and food for rats."[162]

These dedicated, knowledgeable, and compassionate men were, of course, concerned with male workers as well, but on the basis of their broad expertise, were convinced that women workers needed greater legal protection. Yet, if they believed that the woman worker should have more in one sense, they agreed that she deserved less in another. The specialists did not question the woman worker's lower wages. Even as the numbers and proportions of women in the factory increased, even as women were absorbed, albeit slowly, into male industries, the specialists did not perceive the woman's lower wages either as a cause of her dismal condition or as an injustice. Although they had a better command of facts and figures than any other group in society and were better equipped to understand the factory woman's life from personal observation, they assumed either that married factory women were provided for by

161. Litvinov-Filanskii, p. 178.
162. Petrykovskii, p. 80.

working husbands or that unmarried women "had no family obligations."[163] The very existence of factory women, married or single, who were responsible for the support of a family assumed vague outlines only in the early years of the twentieth century as budget studies were conducted and as women doctors entered the ranks of the specialists. Even then these perceptions were not absorbed into social expectations. The relationship of women's wages to men's seemed, as it were, invulnerable to human intervention.

163. See fn. 76, above.

5
THE NATURE OF FEMALE PROTEST
(to 1905)

It is a commonly accepted and valid generalization that the most exploited, deprived, and hopeless elements of the working class are the least likely to protest against their condition. Women workers were indisputably among these elements. As we have seen, by the turn of the century factory owners began to hire women in preference to men because women were the "calmer, steadier, less-demanding element" in the labor force. Above all, this meant that women accepted lower wages than men: that women were less inclined to react to lower wages or poor working conditions with petitions, work stoppages, or violence, and when they did react they were more easily pacified or coerced into withdrawing their demands. Women workers were indeed relatively quiescent. But relatively does not mean invariably, and the generalization, unassailable in its broadest sense, eclipses a rich diversity of behavior. Moreover, passivity as well as activism is a statement: about how women perceived their relationship to work, to their fellow workers, and to their masters; about how women workers perceived themselves; and about what they expected of life. This chapter and the next will explore the nature of women's protest as well as the reasons for their passivity when they did not protest. We will begin with a rough typology of the forms and substance of women's protest, which, in certain important ways, did not change over time and ran like a leitmotif through the vicissitudes of our period.[1] There were, of course, important developments between the 1880s and 1914, changes within the working class and between workers and society which influenced women workers—some women workers—to respond in new ways. The most important of these developments occurred in 1905 and subsequent years. We will, therefore, divide the study of women's protest at the Revolution of 1905, concentrating in this chapter on the patterns and events of the period preceding the revolution.

* * *

Most strikes in factories that employed both men and women were initiated by men. Even when women workers stood to gain as much—indeed, more—than men from a successful strike, they were frequently reluctant to join their male co-workers. Typically, women stopped working only when men coerced them. Take, for example, a strike in Tver' province in 1892. Five hundred male workers struck over fines and high prices in factory shops. Although these features of factory life were harder on women, because of their lower wages, than on men, the women participated only when the men threatened to beat them.[2] The more violent the strike, the more likely it was that male workers would carry out their threat, as in the 1896 strike at St Petersburg's enormous Samsonievskaia cotton-spinning factory. Workers broke windows and "beat up the women [workers] without mercy."[3] In 1896, 675 male workers in a textile factory in Vladimir province demanded a shorter day before holidays and the firing of a brutal factory manager: "There were those who wanted to return to work,

1. The historical record does not provide the kind of evidence necessary to make quantitative assessments of women's participation in strikes. Most sources simply refer to striking workers as *rabochie* (workers), which is both a masculine and a collective plural. The word offers no clue to the sex of strikers. Whether or not women workers participated in strikes cannot be assumed, let alone demonstrated, from strike reports that do not make gender distinctions. My sample consists of 91 strike reports (1880–1904) that specify female participation.

2. *Rabochee dvizhenie v Rossii v XIX veke*, t. 3, chast' 2 (Moscow, 1952), pp. 142–144.

3. Ibid., t. 4, chast' 1 (1961), pp. 416–418.

especially the women, who were equal in numbers to the men. But, as usual, the [more militant] terrorized the rest. As a result no one turned up to work," reported the factory inspector.[4]

Factory authorities were quick to use women workers' reluctance as leverage in breaking strikes. In an 1898 strike in Vladimir province the factory inspector called in police to prevent the men from restraining the women. The women workers returned to work, and the strike was defeated.[5] To be sure, this tactic was not always effective. In 1889 all two thousand workers struck the Vysokovskaia textile factory in Moscow province. The vice-governor, called in to quell the protest, divided the men from the women and tried to negotiate with each group separately. When the male workers refused to return to work, he approached the women.

> From the women's side [of the factory yard] came such an incoherent shriek that it was impossible to understand what was being said. As soon as the vice-governor moved away, the men and women were united again into one crowd.[6]

It took a vicious cossack assault to break them apart and defeat the strike. However, such cohesion was exceptional. Separate appeals to men and women worked frequently enough that factory inspectors routinely advised factory managements to ignore strike demands when the women workers participated unwillingly. They assumed, correctly, that women would respond sooner to persuasion or coercion than men.[7]

Women workers' reluctance to strike did not always mean indifference to the issues or greater submissiveness. The issue of night work is an example of how women's passivity could be a way of protecting their immediate self-interest. When the government prohibited night work for women and adolescents in 1885, many workers shared with their

---

4. TsGIA, f. 23, op. 30, d. 18, l. 1–2.
5. *Rab. dvizh.*, t. 4, chast' 2, p. 263.
6. Ibid., t. 3, chast' 1, p. 550.
7. Ibid., t. 3, chast' 1, pp. 110, 666–667; chast' 2, p. 93.

employers a certain antipathy to the new law. As a factory inspector reported to the government:

> Such apparent solidarity between employer and worker is actually easily explained. The majority of the workers are excessively dependent on the factory (especially those, albeit a minority, who have no ties with the land). Their entire survival depends on factory earnings. For such workers, apparently, it was disadvantageous to forbid women to work nights and to limit child labor. Previously, the burden of maintaining the family was shared. Now the adult men must carry the responsibility with insignificant support from female labor.[8]

Indeed, all the male weavers in Ivanovo-Voznesensk went on strike to protest the prohibition of night work for women.[9] But their objections to the law were not purely economic:

> The men, especially the weavers, announced that they are parted from their wives and must sleep separately from them, and that for them the law is not advantageous, since each member of the family must keep house for himself.[10]

Once again, in 1897, the male weavers at several factories in Vladimir province struck because the factories decided to abolish night work entirely. The wages of the male workers were to be reduced on the grounds that day work was less arduous than night work. The striking male weavers complained that they were "made equal to the women . . . who were laughing at them because before they [the men] were worth more than the women." The male weavers were "ashamed to show their faces before the women," but the women expressed their pleasure that their wages would be equal to the men's.[11]

It is unlikely that the women's wages were actually made equal to men's. This would have been an unprecedented

---

8. Ibid., t. 3, chast' 1, p. 717. In 1885 women were only 25 percent of textile workers.

9. TsGIA, f. 1149, op. XI (1890a), d. 7, l. 3.

10. *Rab. dvizh.*, t. 3, chast' 1, p. 400. See also t. 3, chast' 1, p. 631.

11. Ibid., t. 4, chast' 1, pp. 666–667.

deviation from the normal state of affairs. The point is that men objected to the elimination of night work not only because they feared the effect on the family economy. Despite the universally acknowledged hardship of night work, they preferred it to a system that threatened their wage superiority over women and the traditional allocation of domestic duties. Women workers never willingly joined men to protest against the prohibition of night work. They defended themselves against night work with passivity. On the other hand, women sometimes initiated strikes to protest the illegal imposition of night work. For example, in 1893 two thousand women workers struck when the Egorov factory in Riazan' province tried to force them to work nights, "against the law . . . and against the workers' wishes."[12]

At times male assertiveness encouraged women workers to strike on their own behalf. In 1886 three hundred male weavers struck a cotton-weaving factory in Moscow province and received a rise in wages. Some days later five hundred women weavers struck as well. As the factory inspector commented, "Although the men weavers did not leave work [to support the striking women], they nonetheless influenced the women to stay on strike."[13] Now and then this kind of moral support was translated into mild assistance. In 1898 a St Petersburg textile factory devised an original system of wage payment. The output of each machine was to be calculated at the end of each twenty-four-hour period, and the wages were to be divided between the woman who operated the machine during the day and the man who worked it on the night shift. At the same time, the night shift was reduced from eleven and a half to ten hours. Three hundred and forty women weavers struck for a similar reduction in the day shift on grounds that they produced more on their longer shift than the men. The factory manager refused to equalize the shifts, so the women demanded that their out-

---

12. TsGIA, f. 23, op. 30, d. 2, l. 27–31. See also, f. 20, op. 16, d. 3, l. 64.
13. *Rab. dvizh.*, t. 3, chast' 1, p. 491; TsGIA, f. 23, op. 30, d. 10, l. 93.

put be calculated separately and paid accordingly. The factory owner agreed to calculate output separately, but lowered day wages and raised night wages each by 10 percent. In a rare expression of sensitivity the male weavers left their machines for one and a half hours to support the striking women, explaining that "the men are getting paid extra for the work of the women," a double injustice because the women were "burdened with children and housework as well."[14]

But men rarely supported women's strikes at all, let alone with enthusiasm, and women rarely attempted to enlist their support. Only one extant strike report speaks of the reversal of the more common pattern. In 1897 at the Krengol'm factory in Narva fifteen hundred striking women weavers forced the male workers to leave work, with a show of violence. The women beat one male worker so badly that he required hospitalization.[15]

When women initiated strikes, the battle for support was not between women and men, but between militant and passive women. On the sixth day of a strike of four hundred women spinners in St Petersburg in 1898, twelve women returned to their machines. But they came many hours late because, in an effort to keep the returning women on strike, "the older, more experienced women workers told them that work did not begin until 10 A.M."[16] More typically, striking women used the tactics of violence to coerce the recalcitrant. For example, in Moscow province in 1899, eight hundred women struck for higher piecework rates. The striking women "beat the women fly-frame tenters and ring-frame spinners who had remained at work. In the ensuing fight windows and electric lamps were broken."[17] Striking women were also quick to use force on women scabs.[18]

14. TsGIA, f. 23, op. 30, d. 26, l. 4.
15. *Rab. dvizh.*, t. 4, chast' 1, pp. 793–795.
16. TsGIA, f. 23, op. 30, d. 26, l. 26.
17. Ibid., d. 11, l. 216. See also "Stachka tkachei Ivanovo-Voznesenskoi Manufaktury v 1895," *Krasnyi Arkhiv* (1955), 5 (72), p. 118.
18. *Rab. dvizh.*, t. 4, chast' 2, p. 377.

Women workers in the tobacco industry were remarkably volatile, militant, and tenacious, compared with women in other industries. The first recorded tobacco strike took place in two St Petersburg factories in 1878, which Georgii Plekhanov, reporting in the populist *Zemlia i Volia,* noted "was all the more interesting because it occurred in an exclusively female setting."[19] Some three hundred women workers attempted to negotiate with the management over lowered piecework rates. When the management answered with curses and threats, the women returned to the factories and threw everything, machines and furniture, out of the window. The management acceded to their demands.

We next hear from the tobacco workers in a series of strikes in the mid-1890s, a period of generally heightened labor protest. In 1895 a strike of thirteen hundred "cigarette girls" took place at the Laferm factory in St Petersburg. The strike became a legend and was used over and over again by radical intelligentsia to encourage strikes in other factories.[20] The factory had introduced machines of a new type and assigned forty workers to operate them at lower wages. One-half of the remaining workers were to be fired. Thirteen hundred striking women announced that "they and the cigarette girls of all the St Petersburg factories would not tolerate the new machines—neither at Laferm nor in the other St Petersburg factories." To emphasize their point, they broke windows and threw machines into the street. The factory management argued that the women would earn more on the new machines when they had learned to use them. For the women workers, this was beside the point: "We do not want and will not permit the machines, since they leave one-half the workers without bread." When the factory manager's assistant slipped out to get armed help from the municipal governor, the workers broke yet another window and threw out all the tobacco. It

19. *Zemlia i Volia* (1879), no. 3, cited in V. Iakovlev, ed., *Revoliutsionnaia zhurnalistika 70-kh godov* (Paris, 1905), pp. 296–298.
20. *Rab. dvizh.,* t. 4, chast' 1, pp. 42–45, 271, 195–197; *Zhizn' Tabachnika* (1907), no. 1, p. 4.

took a hundred armed police and two fire brigades to quell the protest.[21]

Three years later, in 1898, four hundred women workers at another St Petersburg tobacco factory broke fifty-six hanging lamps and several windows and stools and destroyed the tobacco and the cigarette paper. The local police, called in to restrain the women, were showered with tobacco. The grievance here was similar to the one at the Laferm factory. Twenty-eight older women workers were informed that they could either start work on a high quality tobacco for higher wages or continue working the lower quality tobacco at reduced wages. The older women refused both alternatives. In the words of the younger spokes-women, "They cannot change to work with the higher sort because after long years of work they have lost much of their vision. They wish to stay at the old job for the previous wages," for even with an increase in wages on the better tobacco they could not make enough to earn a living wage.[22]

In these strikes the women struck out of what appears to be conservatism and fear of change—animosity to machinery or irrational reluctance to do new work despite alleged economic benefit. It would be a mistake, however, to view their actions as simply conservative or irrational. Like the machine breakers of early nineteenth-century England, the women tobacco workers of St Petersburg were not responding to the introduction of new machines and techniques out of primitive animosity to innovation. They were protesting the effects of innovation on their livelihood with the only weapon at their disposal—violence. As two hundred striking tobacco women declared in 1898, "With the high cost of living in St Petersburg, even on the old wages [we] can barely make ends meet. With a decrease in wages [due to new techniques] earnings will drop to an impossible minimum."[23] Promises of higher earnings on new machines smacked of pie-in-the-sky to them and were, of course, ir-

21. *Rab. dvizh.*, t. 4, chast' 1, pp. 18–21.
22. TsGIA, f. 23, op. 30, d. 26, l. 18.
23. Ibid., d. 36, l. 139.

relevant to those who were displaced by innovation. Indeed, the most remarkable feature of these strikes was the way women unaffected by the proposed changes supported their threatened co-workers. This was unusual foresight and solidarity, masked, perhaps, by the old-fashioned *form* of their protests. Nor was solidarity and foresight expressed only by St Petersburg workers. In a 1903 tobacco strike in the province of Kiev the women workers collected strike funds to permit them to survive weeks of anticipated unemployment—farsighted behavior unusual in any strike of this period.[24]

What accounts for the militancy and solidarity of tobacco women, so rare among women workers in other industries? From the beginning of our period the industry employed a high and growing proportion of women. By 1895 women were 87 percent of the St Petersburg tobacco workers.[25] Although most tobacco factories in the provinces were small, in Moscow and St Petersburg there were several that employed one thousand or more workers. The Laferm factory was among the largest, with twenty-five hundred workers by 1890.[26] The technology of tobacco production was primitive, and handwork predominated well into the twentieth century.[27] As in all low-skilled female-dominated occupations, wages were notoriously low. However, compared with women in other industries, a much larger proportion of tobacco workers were urban-born.[28] They also were more literate than other women workers. Three Kiev tobacco factories reported literacy rates of 84, 54, and 42

24. Ibid., op. 20, d. 43, l. 88. See also f. 23, op. 3, d. 3, l. 65; "Materialy dlia istorii rabochego dvizheniia," *Krasnaia Letopis* (1923), no. 7, pp. 222–223.

25. *Otchet byvshego departamenta neokladnykh sborov, a nyne Glavnogo upravleniia neokladnykh sborov i kazennoi prodazhi pitei za 1895* (St Petersburg, 1897), pp. 125–126.

26. James H. Bater, *St. Petersburg: Industrialization and Change* (Montreal, 1976), pp. 126–127.

27. M. V. Dzhervis, *Russkaia tabachnaia fabrika v XVIII i XIX vekakh* (Leningrad, 1933), pp. 17–19.

28. *Perepis' Moskvy 1902 goda,* pp. 95–97. Women tobacco workers—21.3 percent were born in Moscow. Women textile workers—2.6 percent were born in Moscow. See also M. K. Valitskaia, *Issledovanie zdorov'ia rabochikh na tabachnykh fabrikakh* (St Petersburg, 1889), pp. 2–3.

percent, respectively.[29] In St Petersburg women tobacco-factory workers were significantly older than women workers in other industries, which may signify a longer work life.[30] We can only speculate about the relative weight of each of these characteristics in eliciting greater militance, tenacity, and solidarity. It was most likely some combination of greater urban experience and literacy, longer work life, and the predominance of women under one roof. Numerical preponderance was a contributing factor in the sporadic militancy of women in other industries as well. The majority of reported strikes in the textile industry, in which women were either the initiators or the most tenacious or violent strikers, took place in factories employing a large majority of women.[31]

Until the late 1890s women struck mainly over grievances that they shared with men: wages, hours, fines, the length of the working day, the unjust firing of fellow workers. They seldom challenged the factory on the abuses and hardships to which they alone were vulnerable. Most unusual was a strike demand in 1880 at the Krengol'm factory that nursing mothers be allowed to nurse their infants twice a day for nine months instead of six.[32] (Most factories, of course, did not permit time off for nursing mothers.) Conditions relating to their maternal obligations or to their health as mothers took a back seat to more basic survival. That is to say, women were more likely to strike *in opposition* to special treatment—such as release from work for some period before and after childbirth—because they paid for it

29. E. I. Bulgakova, *Stranichka iz zhizni kievskikh rabotnits* (Kiev, 1906), p. 13.
30. *S-Peterburg po perepisi 15 dekabria 1900 goda*, vyp. 2 (St Petersburg, 1903), pp. 38–93.

Women Textile Workers (%)	*Ages*	*Women Tobacco Workers (%)*
6	−16	2.98
22	16–20	11.36
56.9	21–40	62.59
13.3	41–60	21.78
0.8	+60	2.98

31. *Rab. dvizh.*, t. 2, chast' 2, p. 425; t. 3, chast' 1, p. 637; t. 3, chast' 2, pp. 305–310; t. 4, chast' 1, pp. 105–112; t. 4, chast' 2, pp. 280–283, 401.
32. Ibid., t. 2, chast' 2, p. 471.

with loss of wages at best and more commonly with loss of job.[33]

Women workers' resentment of sexual molestation, physical bullying, and verbal insults was an incessant hum in the background, an undertone that aggravated other kinds of grievances, but that was voiced only under extreme pressure.[34] Even in the 1890s, when workers in general were growing more openly indignant over disrespectful treatment from supervisory personnel, women only rarely protested openly and collectively. The profundity of their indignation, however rarely it was expressed, can be gauged from the following strike: In May 1893 seventeen hundred weavers, "mainly women and adolescents," began a rowdy strike at the Egorov factory in Riazan' province. Crowds of striking workers roamed the factory premises. They invaded the factory office, where "they [women workers] broke up the furniture, destroyed the record books, broke the iron door leading to the cashier." They then moved on to the company food store, which they looted and destroyed. They invaded the weaving department and wrecked the looms. Finally, they went in search of the factory director and, not finding him on the factory premises, went to his house with the intention of killing him. On the eighth day of the strike the workers were pacified by the blandishments of the factory inspector, reinforced by a battalion of soldiers. The factory inspector, reciting the litany of the workers' complaints, concluded that

> Above all, the workers were upset that Howard [the steward of the weaving section] used his unlimited power to seduce and rape attractive girls and married women . . . who had the misfortune of appealing to him. If one refused to submit to his bestial desires, she would be unceremoniously fired. And not

33. Ibid., t. 3, chast' 2, pp. 611–612; t. 4, chast' 1, pp. 143–146.
34. Ibid., t. 3, chast' 1, p. 327; t. 4, chast' 3, pp. 369, 394–395; TsGIA, f. 23, op. 20, d. 43, l. 75; op. 30, d. 2, l. 240; op. 30, d. 26, l. 108; f. 1229, op. 1, d. 146, l. 3; *Robochee dvizhenie vo vladimirskoi gubernii, 1910–1914* (Vladimir, 1957), p. 118. As we shall see, in 1904 the humiliation of being searched by men was the most effective issue around which to organize women workers. Yet, to that moment, only one open protest was reported. See TsGIA, f. 23, op. 30, d. 38, l. 6.

just she, but her entire family would be kicked out of the factory.[35]

The most palpable symptom of women workers' reluctance to stress their specific grievances was their silence on the one injustice that affected them universally. Not all women workers were mothers for whom maternity benefits would have meant an unequivocal improvement in their lives. Not all women were the victims of lust and brutality. But all women earned less than men for comparable or equal work, and all women were systematically excluded from the skilled occupations. The single surviving record of a dispute over unequal wages is particularly instructive. In 1901 the women fly-frame tenters at a Moscow textile factory complained that they earned less than the women ring-frame spinners even though the work was the same.[36] In other words, they perceived their right to equal wages with other women who did equal work, but never with men. To be sure, women workers were very pleased when Providence handed them near equality in wages, as we saw in the strike over night work. But if they doubted that their lower wages were part of a natural order, they were unwilling to translate their doubts into action. Nor is this surprising. When women struck over grievances that they shared with men, they confronted the common enemy—the factory authorities, the factory inspector, the law. To demand equality with male workers would have antagonized their fathers, brothers, sons, and husbands, the entire patriarchy, which their male kin and co-workers not only accepted but fervently supported.

* * *

These patterns of protest persisted throughout our period. Despite the important degrees and nuances of submission, the consistent exceptions to it, and despite the alterations—demographic, economic, intellectual, and political—

35. TsGIA, f. 23, op. 30, d. 2, l. 32, 240.
36. TsGIA, f. 23, op. 30, d. 13, l. 57.

in Russia's industrial labor force, women workers as a group remained more submissive than men. There were, however, seeds of something qualitatively different buried in this substratum of submission, which were nourished by the emergence of an interaction between Russia's radical intelligentsia and workers.

In the mid-1870s, bitterly disappointed with the results of the emancipation of the serfs, Russia's radical opposition began to search for new solutions to Russia's backwardness, poverty, and oppression. The Populists, as they were called, adapted the principles of socialism to Russian conditions. They believed that Russia, a nation of peasants, had little to gain from the Western type of industrialization which had spawned socialism. Industrialization would only make an oppressed worker of an oppressed peasant. Instead, they envisioned a revolution that would allow Russia to bypass capitalist industrialization and achieve socialism by building on the peasant commune writ large. The Populists believed that peasants, not workers, were the potential revolutionary army and the main beneficiaries of a new socialist order. While factory workers were numbered among the victims of tsarism, Russian workers were a potential revolutionary force, not as workers, but as peasants who happened to work in the factory and could, therefore, serve as conduits of revolutionary ideas back to the countryside. The goal of the Populists was to enlighten and inspire the peasants, whether they worked the land or the lathe, to create a mass movement that would confront and ultimately defeat the autocracy.

The Populist movement contained an extraordinary number of intelligentsia women (*intelligentki*). They had come to Populism by way of an earlier involvement in the movement for women's emancipation, a major concern of men as well in the 1860s. It is not surprising, then, that the Populist circles were uniquely egalitarian. Women went to the countryside to educate and propagandize among the peasantry. They executed spectacular feats of terrorism against tsarist officials and worked equally with men in the less dramatic but dangerous day-to-day work of under-ground activity.[37] But Populist women had little interest in the women among the peasants and peasant-workers in whose name they struggled. True, a few Populist women, posing as factory workers, made desultory attempts to reach women workers. Even before mass arrests ended this phase of Populist activity, most Populists questioned the wisdom of sending women "who had never experienced factory conditions into such difficult circumstances."[38] Ex-perience justified their apprehensions. As a male Populist recounted:

> I remember the Sunday night in 1874 when Gravchevskii and I surrendered Betia Kaminskaia to the Moiseev factory. . . . It seemed to me as if we were leading this girl to some kind of terrible execution. Subbotina wept as if foreseeing disaster.[39]

A week later Kaminskaia returned to her comrades in a cab. "We greeted Kaminskaia as if we had literally not seen her for years. And, in fact, she had changed markedly, as if years had passed. Before, she was rosy-cheeked and fresh. Now she looked pale, thin, and exhausted."[40]

Populist women did not survive long in the factory. A few were forced to leave because factory officials became suspi-cious of them, others because they could not physically en-dure factory life.[41] Still others were discouraged by "the diffi-cult working conditions, but still more, by the hostility of the women workers."[42] Women Populists, meeting with "only ob-tuse indifference, incomprehension, and even derision" from women workers, more often than not abandoned the

---

37. The best and most complete discussion of Populist women is to be found in Richard Stites, *The Women's Liberation Movement in Russia* (Princeton, 1978).

38. I. S. Dzhabadari, "Protsess piatidesiati (Vserossiiskaia Revoliutsionnaia Or-ganizatsiia 1874–1877)," *Byloe* (1907), no. 22 (10), p. 169.

39. Ibid., p. 170.

40. Ibid., p. 171.

41. S. O. Tsederbaum, *Zhenshchina v russkom revoliutsionnom dvizhenii, 1870–1905* (Leningrad, 1927), pp. 24, 57, 127; "Nekrologi: M. D. Subbotina i B. Kamin-skaia," *Obshchina* (1878), no. 6–7, p. 1; V. M. Sablin, ed., *Protsess 193-kh* (Moscow, 1906), p. 797.

42. Tsederbaum, p. 53.

attempt to enlighten women workers, to work instead with more responsive men workers.[43]

Populist women of the 1870s were passionately devoted to the cause of revolution. They relinquished the comforts and security of their social origins for the rewards of dedication to the revolutionary cause, among which were arrest, exile, and sometimes death. But nothing in their background or mentality prepared them to share the life of factory women. Nor did Populism provide them with a theoretical rationale for the rewards of attending to women. They were easily discouraged. However, the egalitarian spirit that guided the relations among the intelligentsia in populist circles provided an important model for their successors, the radical circles of the 1890s.

After the assassination of Alexander II in 1881 by the terrorist wing of the Populist movement, the government moved quickly and efficiently to undermine the movement by arresting, imprisoning, and executing its leadership. The remnants of the radical opposition to the tsarist order were forced to reassess its theoretical formulations and tactics. Looking at the failure of Populism either to radicalize peasants or to topple the government by means of terrorism, young radicals of the 1880s and 1890s grew more hospitable to Western socialist thinkers, especially Marx. In the Social Democratic analysis, industrialization was an inevitable and positive development in Russia. The worker was not simply a peasant in worker's garb, but a member of a distinct social class, a proletarian, and the harbinger of a new social order. And such workers actually materialized. In these decades small groups of workers, among them women, began to grope for a clarification of a misty vision of personal improvement entwined with the general improvement of the factory worker's lot. The radical intelligentsia and politicized workers made common cause in loose clandestine circles. Their goal was to generate a stratum of enlightened, educated workers who, aided but not

43. Ibid., p. 22.

manipulated by the intelligentsia, would shape their own future.[44]

Given the enormous risks of unofficial political activity in tsarist Russia, workers were recruited to the circles of the 1890s with great discretion. Usually a radical *intelligent* or worker made overtures to workers who seemed promising by giving them books to read. The workers who seemed eager to engage in discussion, to read and learn, would be invited to the outer rim of the circles to discuss nonpolitical topics that interested them, often, in the case of women, religion. Then, gently and cautiously, the leaders of the circle discussions would introduce other topics and other readings: belle lettres, natural science, history, and of course, factory conditions. Finally, workers who passed through a period of observation and education were invited into the political core, where difficult and more pointedly political readings were discussed and from which the workers were encouraged to recruit other workers.

The initial contacts were usually made by men, but women radicals took an active part in the educational work of the circles. They, like the men, represented a hodge-podge of ideologies—Populism, Marxism, and even religious sectarianism—but they were less reluctant to reach out to women workers than their predecessors of the 1860s and 1870s. After all, enlightening women workers in the circles was less demanding and more gratifying than trying to reach them in the factories. The women workers who came to the circles, like their male comrades, were usually at least partly literate, eager to learn, and receptive to ideas and activities that offered a hope for egress from their dismal life situations. They were not the "obtuse and hostile" mass in the factory, but self-selected and responsive.

Semen Kanatchikov, one of the most active and articulate of the skilled workers in the circles of the 1890s and subse-

---

44. See Allan K. Wildman, *The Making of a Workers' Revolution: Russian Social Democracy, 1891–1903* (Chicago, 1967).

quent revolutionary organizations, recalled his impressions of the first women workers in the circles:

> In our workers' environment previously, as of old, we saw the woman worker as a creature of a lower order. She was not interested in higher things, she was incapable of fighting for ideals and was only a drag and a burden on the life of a conscious worker. Great was my astonishment and admiration when for the first time I met two conscious women workers who reasoned and argued as we did.[45]

It would be surprising indeed if women workers had been accepted into the workers' circles automatically and graciously, considering the place of women in the peasant universe from which nearly all workers came. Although a new kind of social relationship between men and women was forged in the circles, it was an ongoing struggle. Ivan Babushkin, a worker who cut his political teeth in the circles, described the reactions of male workers four years after women's circles were already an accepted phenomenon:

> At that time [1894] one girl and one of the worker's wives wanted to attend our lessons or the readings which were led by the intelligentsia. . . . I brought up the question whether the presence of beings of the fair sex would have an undesirable effect on the circle. Certain fears were expressed, and one member of the circle even said that he could not be responsible for his behavior if they were to attend. . . . Therefore, it was decided to exclude creatures of the female sex from the readings, although once in a while they visited anyway.[46]

Further, the politicized worker's antagonism to women was reinforced in a recurrent family conflict. Kanatchikov observed (and his observations were not unique):

> If the [conscious] worker was older and married, a conflict immediately arose in the family, mainly with the wife, who was

---

45. S. Kanatchikov, *Iz istorii moego bytiia* (Moscow and Leningrad, 1929), p. 78.
46. I. V. Babushkin, *Vospominaniia Ivana Vasil'evicha Babushkina, 1893–1900* (Moscow, 1955), pp. 59–60. See also, S. I. Muralova, "Iz proshlogo," in S. I. Mitskevich, ed., *Na zare rabochego dvizheniia v Moskve* (Moscow, 1932), p. 154.

almost always backward and uncultured. She did not understand his spiritual needs, she did not share his ideals. She feared and hated his friends, nagged him, and cursed his unproductive expenditures on books and other cultural and revolutionary things. But mainly she feared the loss of a provider. . . . For this reason, conscious workers had a negative attitude toward family, marriage, and even toward women. They looked upon all contact with girls as the suffocation of personal freedom leading to the loss of their comrades in the revolutionary cause.[47]

In spite of the hostility of many male workers, women workers were members of circles all over Russia—in St Petersburg, Moscow, Ivanovo-Voznesensk, Tula, Odessa, Rostov, Tver', and Kostroma.[48] One of the most active and cohesive groups of circles, the so-called Brusnev organization in St Petersburg, included two outstanding women workers, Vera Karelina and Anna Boldyreva. They subsequently recounted their experiences in brief autobiographies; together with those of their male comrades these accounts provide valuable insights into the experience of women workers.[49]

Vera Karelina was an illegitimate child abandoned to the care of the St Petersburg charity home for foundlings shortly after her birth in 1870. The home farmed her out to a penurious peasant widow not far from St Petersburg, who had three foster children as well as three children of her own. Karelina's good fortune was to spend the first fourteen years of her life with this illiterate but "exceptionally intelligent and serious woman," who, among other things,

47. Kanatchikov, p. 86. See also, K. Norinskii, "Moi vospominaniia" in *Ot gruppy Blagoeva k "Soiuz Bor'by" 1886–1894* (1921), p. 13–14.

48. Mitskevich, *Na zare*, passim; and *Revoliutsionnaia Moskva, 1888–1905* (Moscow, 1940), pp. 173–174; E. A. Korol'chuk, ed., *V nachale puti. Vospominaniia peterburgskikh rabochikh 1872–1897* (Leningrad, 1975), pp. 121, 125; Ts.S. Bobrovskaia, *Zapiski riadovogo podpol'shchika*, chast' 1 (1922), p. 1; "Iz vospominaniia S. V. Perazicha," *Krasnaia Letopis'* (1923), no. 7, p. 250; L. P. Menshchikov, *Okhrana i revoliutsiia*, t. 1 (Moscow, 1925), pp. 157, 244, 257; O. A. Varentsova, *Severnyi rabochii soiuz i severnyi komitet RSDRP* (Ivanovo, 1948), p. 5.

49. V. M. Karelina, "Na zare rabochego dvizheniia v S-Peterburge," *Krasnaia Letopis'* (1922), no. 4, pp. 12–20, and "Vospominaniia o podpol'nykh rabochikh kruzhkakh brusnevskoi organizatsii," in Korol'chuk, *V nachale puti*, pp. 269–291; A. G. Boldyreva, "Minuvshie gody," in Korol' chuk, *V nachale puti*, pp. 249–268.

encouraged her to attend the village school and to read. In the long winter evenings neighboring peasant women would gather in Karelina's foster home with their spinning and mending to listen to her read religious works and folk tales:

> They gathered in our house because there were no men present; the rural woman was happy to feel a bit freer in her women's circle; speaking with her women friends of her sorrows and humiliations made the drudgery of her life seem easier to endure.[50]

When her foster mother died, the foundling home found work for Karelina in a maternity hospital in St Petersburg. The foundlings who worked in the hospital were brutally exploited. They worked long hours—sometimes around the clock—were beaten regularly and subjected to a prison-like regimen of supervision. The hospital administration forbade Karelina to read, but, encouraged by young students of midwifery, she read surreptitiously. By the time she was nineteen years old Karelina was very skilled in the various duties at the hospital. The administration was anxious to keep her on as a paid worker and therefore allowed her more freedom to go out in the evenings. She began to visit with young men whom she had known from the foundling home, by now (1889) all workers at a nearby cotton-spinning factory. In their company she met radical workers who slowly drew her into Brusnev circle.

After passing through the initiatory discussions on religious questions, "especially important to the beginning girls,"[51] Karelina and her fellow novices read fiction and poetry, history and the natural sciences, and finally settled on readings with political content. Karelina, like the other workers in the circles, devoted evening hours and Sundays to the circles after working fourteen to sixteen hours a day

50. Karelina, "Vospominaniia, p. 270.
51. Ibid., p. 275.

under the most trying conditions. Little wonder that despite her literacy she found the studies difficult:

> It was not always easy, especially in those first years, to make head or tail of Pisarev, the economic articles of Chernyshevskii, and many other writers. I would read perhaps four pages and grow weary from the strain. Our studies in the circles were very serious. We would read an article, tell about it, and be expected to explain our own conclusions.... They [the intelligentsia teachers] forced the workers to analyze the readings deeply.... We did not begrudge the time, whether it was two–three hours or five–six hours—just to be able to learn![52]

In 1890 two of her colleagues in the circle helped Karelina to get work at the Novyi cotton-spinning factory. One of them was Anna Boldyreva, who became her close friend and associate in circle work and later in other kinds of revolutionary activity.

Boldyreva was born a peasant in 1870 in Tver' province. When she was seven the family began to take seasonal work in St Petersburg textile factories. Two years later they settled permanently in the city, and Boldyreva, at the age of nine, was put to work in the same textile factory as many of her relatives and fellow villagers. She and the other children and adolescents worked nights so that mothers with nursing infants could work the day shift. In 1882, when she was twelve, she was considered old enough to find work for herself. She became a weaver at the Pal' cotton-weaving factory, where the workers existed, as she put it, in a "state of half-starvation."[53] Boldyreva recalled how most workers looked for succor to discussions with religious sectarians and orthodox priests: "Driven into the blind alley of factory bondage and oppressed by need, the ignorant working folk sought a way out in the search for 'God's Truth.' "[54] But a small minority, she among them, was diverted from the promise of heavenly rewards to a dream of human well-

52. Ibid., pp. 275–276.
53. Boldyreva, p. 258.
54. Ibid., p. 257.

being on earth. Boldyreva attributed her first awakening to episodic lectures on natural science held in workers' apartments in the 1880s (subsequently banned by the government), which, in turn, inspired her to attend a workers' Sunday school. Here, in the manner described above, she met conscious male workers and was singled out for initiation into circle work.

Karelina and Boldyreva were taken into the highest level of the Brusnev organization, the organizing circle. Together they formed a special circle for women workers consisting of about twelve women workers within the larger organization.[55] Several of the women had been Karelina's friends in the foundling home and now worked in textile and rubber factories. Another worked in a typography shop, and two were seamstresses. Karelina and Boldyreva lived communally with some of the women and men in the circles, moving from apartment to apartment as each one fell under the scrutiny of the police. One of the conspiratorial apartments was in a building occupied by a brothel. At first appalled at the prospect of sharing premises with prostitutes and their customers, the circle members came to regard it as a good joke and, more important, as an excellent cover. The police regarded the frequent comings and goings of men and women into the building as unexceptional: "From an impure house there came workers who were pure and devoted to the struggle."[56]

Despite—perhaps because of—the constant danger of underground work, the conspiratorial apartments were havens of emotional and intellectual sustenance for the men and women of the circles. Here the women's circle met, the *intelligenty* came to hold discussions and readings, the weekly recruiting meeting took place. The atmosphere was intimate and familial.[57] Karelina recalled:

55. Boldyreva, p. 260; Karelina, "Na zare," p. 13; "Vospominaniia," p. 286.
56. Karelina, "Na zare," p. 15.
57. See M. I. Brusnev, "Vozniknovenie pervykh sotsial-demokraticheskikh organizatsii," *Proletarskaia Revoliutsiia* (1923), no. 2 (14), p. 20.

The form our lives took [in the apartments] flowed simply and naturally from our needs. . . . We lived together naturally as in a commune: put our money in a common treasury, bought and prepared food together, had a common laundry and library. Everyone participated in doing the housework, and there were no arguments or quarrels among us about it.[58]

Thus, traditional sex roles were consciously eschewed for a new kind of equality and comradeship:

What comradeship and purity there was between us! The men treated us girls with consideration and courtesy, and we, in turn, tried to be worthy of their treatment. Among us there were no stupid jokes or coquetry. There was only purity of relations; nor could it have been otherwise. After all, we women had a heavy responsibility. Our behavior had to be an example for newcomers to our ranks as well as for all the other women members of our circles.[59]

The circle members frowned upon sexual promiscuity. Exploitation of women by men in the group was simply not tolerated. Karelina describes an incident of potential sexual exploitation and how it was resolved:

I recall how we judged Mikhail Kniazev, who seduced a girl and then refused to marry her, claiming that he did not have enough money to support two. We pooled our money and made him a wedding.[60]

But her frequent use of the word "purity" to describe the relations between the sexes did not represent a puritanical attitude toward fun and entertainment.

The girls played an important role in the organization. We were young, healthy, gay, and we attracted young working men. Like the others, I loved to dance and sing. "Vera wants to dance," they often said, and we would arrange a party. From courtship came good revolutionary activity.[61]

58. Karelina, "Na zare," p. 18.
59. Karelina, "Vospominaniia," p. 289. See also A. Fisher, *V Rossii i v Anglii* (Moscow, 1922), p. 21.
60. Karelina, "Na zare," p. 15.
61. Ibid., p. 18.

And from "good revolutionary activity" came marriage. Almost all the women workers in the Brusnev circle married young men from the circle. Given the difficulties of marriage for the conscious male worker, marriage between comrades in the circles was regarded as a most felicitous arrangement. As one worker, K. Norinskii, who had been involved in the circles since the mid 1880s, avowed:

> The women, our new comrades, brought a new, living force [into the movement]. These women exuded energy and, simultaneously, hate for their enemies, the possessing class, for all they personally and their mothers had had to endure. . . . They became the mothers of a new generation of workers. And most important of all, they were able to ease family life in difficult moments. The burden that usually fell on one pair of shoulders could now be shared by them as well.[62]

The women workers in the circles were well aware of the problems that Kanatchikov described in marriages between conscious workers and women who were "not interested in higher matters." But their compassion lay equally with the wives:

> At that time there were few enough conscious male workers. As for women, the workers' wives, there is nothing to say. The majority were illiterate. The wives were desperately afraid for their families: the husband could be arrested, and then he would fall and with him the whole family. And further, we girls were in the circles, and [the wives] were jealous. Jealousy is a worse enemy than the police. The husband spent every free minute either reading a book or trying to get out of the house, especially on holidays. He comes home late, not drunk but taciturn. He hardly speaks to his wife, does not tell her where he has been and what he has been doing. Naturally, the simple woman becomes suspicious.[63]

Karelina considered it part of her radical obligation to allay the wives' suspicions with patience, tact, and compas-

---

62. Norinskii, p. 18.
63. Karelina, "Vospominaniia," p. 283.

sion, and even, on occasion, to teach them to read and write.[64]

Even though Karelina acknowledged how difficult life was for the wives of politicized workers, she felt they gained something from their husbands' involvement as well. In her recollections conscious workers gave up drink and behaved with a new tenderness toward their wives.[65] On this issue, as well as others, Karelina seems to err on the side of generosity. The memoirs of male workers suggest that their comrades did not so easily divest themselves of old patterns of behavior. Kanatchikov, for example, reproached one of his comrades in the following way:

> The one thing I did not like about Vasilii Alekseevich was that when he got drunk on payday he would grow jealous for no reason at all and beat his wife. She was a thin woman, worn out by domestic cares and children.[66]

Women workers in the early revolutionary circles found it difficult to recall the blemishes on the halcyon days of the early 1890s. They were too exhilarated by acceptance into a milieu that uplifted them, took them seriously, provided them with hope for a future they could help to mold. The circles inherited the spirit of sexual egalitarianism that had been so appealing to the women Populists of the 1870s. The circles of the 1890s simply expanded egalitarianism to embrace the women workers whom the Populists had ignored. Neither the *intelligenty* nor politicized male workers of the early 1890s were discouraged by women's "backwardness." On the contrary, they made special efforts to attract women workers by adapting the readings of the preparatory circles to the women's religious interests. The intimacy of the circle movement and the high regard for the women in it were not to be sustained in subsequent years as political tactics veered away from circle work.

The women workers, as well as most of the male workers

---

64. Ibid., p. 284.
65. Ibid., p. 283.
66. Kanatchikov, p. 657. See also Norinskii, p. 26.

in the circles, were not committed to specific ideologies, although many subsequently became Marxists. They read illegal oppositional literature without regard to its precise ideological sources. The women, Karelina and Boldyreva recalled, treasured portraits of Zheliabov and Sofia Perovskaia, two outstanding Populists of the 1870s. They were thrilled with the news that a feminist writer, Maria Tsebrikova, had written an inflammatory letter to the tsar excoriating the entire social order. They worked closely with a woman Populist, Elizaveta Aleksandrova. And they read Marxist literature. The workers were privy to increasingly heated debates between Populist and Social Democratic *intelligenty* but took their stand with the latter only in 1892 as the circles were breaking up.[67] As Boldyreva described the nature of their political formulations:

> Were we socialists at that time? The revolutionary "contagion" had infected each one of us, and if, perhaps, we had not yet assimilated for ourselves the theory and methods of class struggle, we were at least distinctly aware of who was the enemy of the working class.[68]

In the summer of 1892 the police obliterated the Brusnev circles in a wave of arrests. Karelina, Boldyreva, and the other women spent the next three years in prison and exile. Some who had escaped arrest and others who returned from jail, often to places of exile, continued to engage in some form of underground activity. But the circles as instruments of enlightenment and politicization were losing their importance in the revolutionary movement. In 1893 and 1894 the Marxist intelligentsia all over Russia, in part stimulated by a rising wave of strikes, began to reassess the efficacy of the circle movement. They concluded that circle work could only create a tiny worker intelligentsia that would forever float on the surface of the mass of workers, which could not be reached by the necessarily slow and

---

67. Karelina, "Na zare," pp. 16–18; "Vospominaniia," p. 286; Boldyreva, p. 263.

68. Boldyreva, p. 259.

The Nature of Female Protest (to 1905)   181

cautious methods of recruitment. To awaken the masses it
was necessary to reach them at their own level, to use their
daily struggles on the factory floor as a means of politicization. If workers could be encouraged to confront the authorities in strikes over immediate issues, they would realize
far sooner that the authorities' resistance to the slightest
modification of exploitation and injustice required a more
radical stance. In short, the task of Social Democrats was to
direct their efforts to agitation among the many rather than
to political and cultural elevation of the few.[69]

Many workers in the circles, and women workers in particular, were dismayed at the prospect of switching from
circle work to mass agitation. Iulii Martov, Lenin's colleague
in the Marxist center, described the response:

> As soon as we acquainted the workers' circles with our plan, we
> met with powerful opposition from a significant majority. . . .
> Especially the women workers rebelled (*buntovali*). They were
> less taken up by the strike movement as a corrective to the circle
> psychology than were the men. After all, our circles opened up a
> new world of spiritual experience for these poor milliners, stock-
> ing knitters, box makers, and fine seamstresses. . . . For them,
> self-education . . . was the alpha and omega of the socialist
> movement. It was intolerable for them to give up their incessant
> endeavors to make of themselves "critically thinking personali-
> ties" for the sake of agitation.[70]

The circle remained the primary building block of the
emerging Marxist edifice, called the Union of Struggle for
the Liberation of the Working Class (*Soiuz bor'by za osvobozhdenie rabochego klassa*). But circle members no longer spent
their time patiently recruiting and enlightening new members. Now they printed and circulated agitational literature
designed to prod workers into direct confrontation with the

69. See Wildman, chap. 2.
70. L. Martov, *Zapiski sotsial-demokrata*, kn. 1 (Berlin, 1922), pp. 227–228. See
also Babushkin, p. 76. There is more than a touch of condescension in Martov's
description. As we know, in St Petersburg the women in the circles were mainly
factory workers. The artisanal trades that Martov attributes to women in the circles
were assumed by Marxists to breed the most "backward" mentality.

authorities. They tried to take leadership in spontaneous strikes and encouraged strikes in factories where workers were known to be extremely dissatisfied.

The change in tactics from circle work to mass agitation was bound to affect the gender composition of the circles, and from 1895 separate women's circles all but disappeared.[71] With the shift to mass agitation and the relegation of education and enlightenment to a position of secondary importance, the qualities formerly valued in workers were replaced by new criteria for membership. It was no longer enough to be eager to learn and receptive to new ideas about the nature of society. As a woman Marxist described her experiences in Moscow circles in 1895:

> At this time our work was in full swing. . . . A workers' union was formed, but women were not permitted to join because of lack of preparation. The union consisted of fully conscious workers who had already conducted [political] work among their comrades.[72]

Thus, the worker accepted into Social Democratic circles had to be already fully "conscious" and willing to take the risks of agitating in the factory. These were not characteristics of the great majority of women workers. The women workers from the Brusnev circles accepted the change to agitational work and remained politically active. But they were already an aristocracy of consciousness among women workers which was no longer to be cultivated.

The consequences of indifference to recruiting women workers to the movement were soon apparent. In St Petersburg between 1895 and 1897 the Union of Liberation distributed fifty-nine leaflets to factory workers. Only five were addressed to women workers.[73] However, the 1895 strike of women workers at the Laferm tobacco factory was

71. Muralova, p. 155; *Rab. dvizh.*, t. 4, chast' 1, p. 678; t. 4, chast' 2, pp. 505–513; Perazich, "Iz vospominaniia," p. 249–250.

72. Muralova, p. 155.

73. S. N. Valk and I. Tovstukha, *Listovki peterburgskogo "Soiuz bor'by za osvobozhdenie rabochego klass," 1895–1897* (Moscow, 1934), passim.

noted with some excitement, and the Union tried to infiltrate the factory. Because no women workers had been recruited since the days of the Brusnev circles, and those were in jail or exile, the Union was unable to make direct contact with the striking tobacco workers.[74] The lesson was lost on the Union and would not be heeded either by its successor, the Russian Social Democratic Workers Party.

* * *

One of the major determinants of the decision to shift to mass agitation was the greater frequency and tenacity of strikes from the mid-1890s. This trend was carefully noted by the government as well. The potential consequences of a strike movement infiltrated and influenced by revolutionaries were sufficiently ominous to provoke an unprecedented turn in tsarist labor policy. In 1901 the government tentatively departed from its age-old prohibition of workers' associations and permitted a government agent, Sergei Zubatov, to form a number of workers' organizations designed to channel workers' discontent from the nascent revolutionary movement to narrow economic improvement. Industrialists deplored the experiment for its possible adverse influence on their control over workers. Radicals and politicized workers scorned the Zubatov organization as a police-manipulated hoax; they dubbed it "police socialism." But rank-and-file workers flocked to it in Moscow and several other cities. By 1903 the government itself had become frightened of its creation, and Zubatov was dismissed. Subsequently, the experiment was repeated in St Petersburg under the leadership of a priest, Father Gapon, who overcame workers' suspicions with his charisma and sincere compassion and satisfied the government with his apolitical, religious, and moral goals.[75]

74. Tsederbaum, pp. 167–168.
75. For studies of "police socialism," see J. Schneiderman, *Sergei Zubatov and Revolutionary Marxism* (Ithaca, N.Y., 1976); W. Sablinsky, *The Road to Bloody Sunday* (Princeton, 1976); G. Surh, "Petersburg Workers in 1905: Strikes, Workplace Democracy and the Revolution" (Ph.D. diss., University of California, Berkeley, 1979), and "Petersburg's First Mass Labor Organization: The Assembly of Russian Workers and Father Gapon," *Russian Review*, 40 (1981), nos. 3 and 4.

The Zubatov and Gapon organizations admitted women workers as "active members." But both stated explicitly in their rules that "persons of the female sex may not be chosen as members of the administration."[76] Since the rules were in neither case devised by workers or their representatives, we may take this to be the government's attitude toward women workers. However, many male workers also "viewed their [women's] presence negatively."[77] Or, in the more graphic description of Vera Karelina:

> The mass of male workers felt that social activity was not a woman's affair. She had her business—in the factory, the machine; at home, the children, diapers, and pots. I recall what I had to contend with when the question of female membership in the Assembly was discussed. There was not even a mention of the woman worker, as if she were entirely nonexistent, as if in industry she was some kind of appendage—despite the fact that there were industries with an exclusively female work force.[78]

Thanks to Karelina, women workers found a niche in Gapon's Assembly of Russian Factory Workers. Karelina (with her husband, a comrade from Brusnev days) was a vigorous and influential participant in the Assembly and was co-opted to the governing board despite the explicit exclusion of women.[79] Dismayed at the workers' hostility to women, she decided to form separate women's sections. In October 1904 Gapon agreed to request official permission for the women's section, although he despaired of "uplifting this mass [of woman workers] . . . with their worn faces and poor clothing . . . in the near future."[80] Karelina was, of course, marvelously well suited to understand the trepidation, anxiety, and wariness of women workers. She sought

76. A. Kats and Iu. Milonov, *1905: Materialy i dokumenty* (Moscow and Leningrad, 1926), pp. 88–89, 92–94.

77. V. Sviatlovskii, *Professional'noe dvizhenie v Rossii* (St Petersburg, 1907), p. 82.

78. V. M. Karelina, "Rabotnitsy v gaponovskikh obshchestvakh," in P. F. Kudelli, *Rabotnitsa v 1905 g. v S-Peterburge* (Leningrad, 1926), p. 14.

79. Sablinsky, p. 106.

80. Sviatlovskii, p. 82.

an approach that would attract them to the women's sections, put them at ease, and encourage them to speak out. She found it in a story, published in *Russkoe Bogatstvo*, called "In the Courtyard," that touched on "the most painful aspect of the woman's lot"—the degradation of the daily search.[81]

The story is set in a tobacco factory. The factory administrator is notorious for the sadistic pleasure he derives from inflicting the search on workers and, in particular, for his lecherous behavior toward the women workers. He pursues a young woman who is extremely popular among all the workers for her natural dignity and sweet character. To punish her for her indifference to his sexual advances, he accuses her of stealing from the factory and orders a special search in full view of the entire factory:

> Two guards fulfilled the command. One fumbled in her sleeves, unbuttoned her dress, and exposed her breasts. . . . The other emptied her pockets, searched the pleats of her skirt, and groped in her stockings.[82]

No stolen property is found, of course, but the search serves its purpose. The girl walks away in a state of shock, dazed and humiliated. The other women try to comfort her:

> "Don't cry, darling," said one of the women workers, solicitously righting her clothing. "They have only insulted you. They shame our sisters everywhere—at the weaving factories, at the spinning factories. It's the same everywhere. . . . They should shame the boss's daughter that way, then they'd understand." The women workers discussed the event under their voices. "She is weeping. . . . It was a terrible humiliation. . . . Wonder what her fiancé will say. . . . How is *she* guilty? . . . Ah, my dear, not everyone understands that. They will say that she is shamed and that's all."[83]

---

81. Karelina, "Rabotnitsy," p. 19.
82. V. Temnykh, "V prokhodnoi. Ocherk iz fabrichnoi zhizni," *Russkoe Bogatstvo* (1903), no. 3, p. 78.
83. Ibid.

The format Karelina developed was to read this story aloud at the beginning of the meetings. It was enormously successful, and the women's sections flourished. The weekly meetings soon attracted two hundred to five hundred women, workers and wives of workers, in each of five major working-class boroughs of St Petersburg. By the end of 1904 roughly a thousand women were regular members.[84] The women began to speak out, to elect their own officials, and to formulate their own agendas. Many male workers in the Assembly were curious about the women's meetings and tried to edge their way in. The women stoutly resisted male intrusion:

> The women themselves decided that not a single man should be present at their meetings. They said, "If they come to listen and something is not right, they will spread it all around the factory or at their meeting and condemn us. It is better if none of them come and mess around in our souls. Our sister workers will not judge us."[85]

Slowly, women were admitted to certain positions within the larger organization: as monitors at concerts and dance evenings, in the planning sections of the library and lecture bureau. They cautiously began to express themselves in the general meetings. But the Gapon Assembly, like the Zubatov organization, was not destined for a long life. In a curious interplay between Gapon's aspirations for the workers and their influence on him, a peaceful demonstration of workers and their families was arranged for Sunday, January 9, 1905, to petition the tsar for redress of their grievances. The petition was supplicating in tone but, in the eyes of the autocracy, audacious in content, for it requested what amounted to a fundamental alteration of society and the workers' place in it: basic civil rights, a constitutional government, legal trade unions.[86] Nicholas II's troops opened fire on the enormous unarmed assemblage, killing and

---

84. Sablinsky, p. 106.
85. Karelina, "Rabotnitsy," pp. 24–25.
86. Sablinsky, pp. 344–349.

wounding hundreds. The event has gone down in history as Bloody Sunday.

An eye-witness report of the mood among women workers and wives of male workers on the eve of Bloody Sunday beautifully illustrates the influence on women of participation in the Gapon Assembly:

> The approaching storm was felt in the air. There was great excitement throughout the Shlissel'burg tract. Workers, passing one another, spoke encouraging words, sometimes with humor. Their wives, with baskets in their hands, quickly went to the factory shop to take the most essential foodstuffs on credit. Their faces expressed inner turmoil—"something will happen tomorrow"—but they voiced no complaints; not one reproached her husband for preparing to strike. The mood of the workers' wives . . . can . . . be explained by the fact that women workers had participated in the Nevskii section of the Gapon Assembly, as well as in other neighborhood sections.[87]

A male participant in the Gapon Assembly summarized the achievements of women workers in the following way:

> Despite all this, the ultimate bias against women was not obliterated, and each time the question of chosing a woman for a position of leadership was raised, the great mass of men stood against it. The most that was attained was that women could occupy an elected position provided that it was not visible. For example, women were allowed to be secretaries, but never under any circumstances to be seen as chairwomen.[88]

One would not expect the "ultimate bias" against women to collapse in the two months of the life of the women's sections. Even in the highly selective and carefully nurtured circles of the 1890s, women workers had to wage a continuous battle for recognition and equality. That it was overcome more completely in the circles than in the Gapon Assembly is not surprising. Both men and women workers in the circles were exceptional among workers. They num-

87. N. P. Paialin, *Zavod imeni Lenina, 1857–1918* (Moscow, 1933), pp. 111–112.
88. Sviatlovskii, p. 83.

bered in the hundreds. The Gapon Assembly attracted the great masses of workers numbering in the thousands. But even here illiterate, frightened, and timid women began to break out of the stranglehold of fear and passivity, and male workers began a no less arduous process of shedding the indifference and scorn they had for women workers.

6

FEMALE PROTEST (1905–1914): REVOLUTION AND WORKERS' ORGANIZATIONS

The government's first attempt to mollify the workers' outraged response to Bloody Sunday was establishment of a commission to study the reasons for their discontent. The Shidlovskii Commission, like police socialism, was an experiment, a reluctant departure from the government's tradition of legislating for workers without their participation: unlike all previous efforts to cope with labor unrest, the commission was to include workers' elected representatives.[1] Presented with this singular opportunity to speak for themselves, St Petersburg workers immediately began to hold elections to the commission. The Shidlovskii Commission permitted factories with a hundred or more workers to choose representatives. Male and female workers over the age of eighteen could vote, but only men could be chosen as representatives.[2] However, the prohibition against women was not made clear, and two large textile factories and an enormous rubber factory elected a total of five women.[3] When Shidlovskii informed the factories that women could not serve, women workers from several factories submitted to him the following petition:

1. For the Shidlovskii Commission, see S. Schwarz, *The Russian Revolution of 1905* (Chicago, 1967), and G. Surh, "Petersburg Workers in 1905: Strikes, Workplace Democracy and the Revolution," Ph.D. diss., University of California, Berkeley, 1979.
2. A. N. Kats, and Iu. Milonov, *1905: Materialy i dokumenty* (Moscow and Leningrad, 1926), p. 129.
3. Schwarz, p. 94; M. Kniazeva and M. Inozemtsev, "K istorii rabochikh vyborov v komissiiu Shidlovskogo," *Istoriia Proletariata SSSR* (1935), sbornik 2, p. 163.

Women workers are not permitted to be deputies to the commission under your leadership. This decision is unjust. Women workers predominate in many of St Petersburg's factories. In the spinning and weaving departments the number of women increases every year because men are going to the factories where the wages are higher. We women workers carry a heavier and heavier burden of work. Taking advantage of our helplessness and lack of rights, our own male comrades oppress us, and we are paid less. When the formation of your commission was announced our heartbeats quickened with hope; finally the time has come, we thought, when the St Petersburg woman worker can loudly proclaim—throughout Russia and in the name of all her sister workers—the oppression and humiliation that no male worker can possibly understand. And then, after we had already chosen representatives, we are told that only men can be deputies. But we hope that this decision is not final. The government's decree must not separate the woman worker from the entire working class.[4]

Shidlovskii ignored the petition. Male workers and Social Democrats ignored it as well. Workers' enthusiasm for the commission waned as the limitations on their autonomy became apparent, but none of their objections included a word about the prohibition against women.[5] In any case, the Shidlovskii Commission died *in utero.* Just as Bloody Sunday undermined the workers' faith in police socialism, the Shidlovskii Commission shook their illusions of genuine succor from the autocracy. The strike emerged again as the predominant form of protest. The year 1905 was one of massive strikes, escalating demands, of economic and political disorder that, by the year's end, embraced virtually the entire society.

Before 1905, in periods of sweeping upheaval, women workers, like the normally frightened and passive segments of the male work force, were released from their inhibitions and intoxicated by the general enthusiasm. In 1895, for example, there had been a notable strike of five thousand

4. "K istorii rabochikh vyborov v Komissiiu Shidlovskogo," p. 195.
5. Kats and Milonov, pp. 129–180.

workers at the Morozov textile factory in Vladimir province. One of the male strike leaders described the response of women workers:

> [The strike demands] were read in the barracks, and I called out to the women to support the men, to make clear how their own suffering and grief made this necessary. Everywhere I heard the unanimous cry that they too would strike. . . . From the women's exit [of the workshops] they yelled, "*Muzhiki*, leave off work." . . . I saw how all the women changed clothes and turned off the machines.[6]

So it was, on a much grander scale, in 1905. "I never once heard that it was necessary to force a woman to strike," reported Karelina, and indeed, few strike reports suggest that women workers had to be persuaded or forced to strike.[7] Although there was an ebb and flow of strike activity throughout the year, early in October the movement gathered momentum in St Petersburg. It then spread to the railroad workers in many of Russia's major cities and, by October 12–15, burst through the confines of class. Many layers of society, long chafing under the constraints and oppression of the old order, found patches of common ground with workers. Teachers, doctors, pharmacists, artists, bankers, clerical workers—even industrialists—joined workers in a brief, spectacular protest that surpassed the scope of all previous strikes not only in Russia but in Europe to that point. "When the October general strike began," rejoiced Karelina, "the women workers at the Laferm tobacco factory . . . were the first on the streets. [I saw this happen] at the Shtiglits thread factory . . . the Kirkhner bindery and the Vol'f topography [as well]."[8] In November women devised a unique expression of female solidarity with the strike movement. On November 6 a huge demonstration by women took place on Vasilev Island. The women, workers and wives of

6. *Rabochee dvizhenie v Rossii v XIX veke*, t. 3, chast' 1, (Moscow and Leningrad, 1952), pp. 163, 212–213.
7. V. Karelina, "Rabotnitsa posle 9ogo ianvaria," in Kudelli, *Rabotnitsa v 1905*, p. 64.
8. Ibid., p. 67.

workers, demanded that the taverns that served hard liquor, wine, and beer be closed to remove all temptations from the striking workers and to stifle rumors that strikers were a drunken mob.[9]

The great strikes of 1905 generated a sense of power and optimism among workers. Even before October new notions of what was legitimate and possible for workers to strive for surfaced in unprecedented political and economic demands. The consistent participation of women workers led to equally consistent demands for the protection of women, most prominantly involving the protection of women workers as mothers. The strike demands from most factories employing women included some variation of paid leave before and after childbirth.[10] There were many demands for factory-sponsored nurseries and crèches, with time off for nursing mothers. Taking this a step farther, workers at the gigantic Savva Morozov textile factory requested the dubious right of an extra half-day off for women to do the family laundry.[11] Undoubtedly, the influence of Social Democrats as well as liberals was important in phrasing these demands. Maternity-related benefits had long been included in platforms of all groups concerned with the plight of women workers.

However, demands for the improvement of the woman worker's life as *worker,* rather than as mother or housekeeper, were not so consistent or so clear-cut. The demand of equal pay for equal work was conspicuously absent. The demand for a *minimum* wage equal for all adult workers regardless of sex was common. But this was neither in concept nor in practice the same as equal pay for equal work.[12] Most common of all was the demand for a minimum wage lower

9. V. P. Obninskii, *Polgoda russkoi revoliutsii* (Moscow, 1906), p. 13.

10. L. M. Ivanov, *Vserossiiskaia politicheskaia stachka v oktiabre 1905.* chast' 1 (Moscow and Leningrad, 1955), pp. 35–36, 43–44, 77–78, 395–396, 428–429; A. M. Pankratova, ed., *1905. Stachechnoe dvizhenie* (Moscow and Leningrad, 1925), p. 164; *Istoriia odnogo soiuza* (Moscow, 1907), p. 90.

11. M. Zaiats, *Tekstili v gody pervoi revoliutsii, 1905–1907* (Moscow, 1925), p. 186.

12. Ibid., p. 255; *Istoriia odnogo soiuza,* p. vii.

for women workers than for men.[13] Demands regarding the actual working conditions of women workers were few and far between. The Moscow tea-packers asked that women not be forced to carry heavy boxes, that there be a sufficient number of workers at each workbench, that women be given the right to leave the factory barracks at will, and so forth.[14] Finally, while overt expressions of hostility to women were rare, occasionally they cropped up in demands that women be forbidden to do "men's" work or that men be hired in preference to women.[15]

The October general strike was more than a strike of greater magnitude and class diversity than the countless strikes that had preceded it throughout 1905. It was also an expression of class solidarity within the working class, of the workers' desire to organize independently and to take for themselves what government and society would not give them. On October 17, out of the year's imbroglio, the St Petersburg Soviet of Workers' Deputies emerged. Followed by similar soviets in forty to fifty cities throughout Russia, the St Petersburg Soviet was, and remained, the core of the revolutionary upsurge until its destruction by the government in early December. It undertook not only to coordinate strikes aimed at improving workers' conditions but to modify the existing political and social relations between workers and government, between workers and society. Consisting of workers' representatives from factories and unions, of representatives from the three revolutionary organizations, Bolshevik, Menshevik, and Socialist Revolutionaries, the Soviet was an organ of workers' self-government.

The composition of the Soviet and its Executive Committee fluctuated. At certain fixed points, however, it is possible to attach names to the representatives and ascertain their occupational or social status. Thus, by mid-November

---

13. Ivanov, pp. 77–78, 428–429; TsGIA, f. 23, op. 4, d. 30, l. 20–22; *1905 g. v Ivanovo–Voznesenskom raione* (Ivanovo-Voznesensk, 1905), p. 2.

14. *Istoriia odnogo soiuza*, p. 90. See also N. S. Trusova, ed., *Nachalo pervoi russkoi revoliutsii. Ianvar'-mart 1905 goda* (Moscow, 1955), pp. 182–184.

15. Ivanov, pp. 565–567, 428–429; TsGIA, f. 23, op. 30, d. 23, l. 87.

the Soviet consisted of 562 deputies—among them seven women—from 147 factories, 34 shops, and 16 trade unions.[16] Karelina described how she was chosen:

> I myself was a deputy. For me, as for many others, it was necessary to do this illegally. Many women workers knew me from union meetings, factory meetings, and underground circles. The women workers from Laferm put me up for election, but I could not be chosen, because I was not [actually] working there. The rule was that the factory had to vouch for the workers' actual employment there. So a woman worker, Anna Afanas'eva, was chosen, and she gave her credentials to me.[17]

Of course, Karelina, whether or not she was employed at the time of the elections to the Soviet, was in fact a worker, as were Boldyreva, Anna Barkova, and Tatiana Razueva, the latter a "graduate" of the Brusnev circle. Of the remaining three women delegates, information exists only on Valentina Bagrova, a Bolshevik *intelligentka* of gentry origin.[18]

Boldyreva was a delegate to the Soviet from the Maxwell textile factory. She was indefatigable, giving speeches at sessions of the Soviet and at individual factories, rousing workers to greater commitment to the Soviet's policies.[19] A worker from the Siemens-Halske electromechanical plant recalled Boldyreva's exhortations to workers to support the Soviet's demand for an eight-hour day:

> Since the deputies from the Putilov spoke categorically against the possibility of establishing the eight-hour day, Boldyreva attacked them sharply. After her speech we all joked that we should divorce our wives and marry women workers from the Maxwell factory.[20]

16. Surh, p. 423; Kudelli, pp. 11–12.

17. Karelina, "Rabotnitsa posle 9ogo ianvaria," p. 67.

18. Kudelli, *Rabotnitsa v 1905*, pp. 11–12; N. I. Sidorov, ed., *1905 god v Peterburge.* Vyp. 2. Soviet rabochikh deputatov. Sbornik materialov (1925), p. 279; P. F. Kudelli, *Vospominaniia chlenov sovieta rabochikh deputatov Peterburga 1905* (Leningrad, 1926), p. 18.

19. Sidorov, passim.

20. Ibid., p. 183.

Karelina does not appear as frequently in the accounts of the Soviet's struggles, but she too was known to her constituency as an ardent supporter. As an account of the debates during the Soviet's waning days attests:

> Some of [the orators] were decisively in favor of continuing the struggle no matter what. Two women delegates spoke especially passionately in this vein, one from Laferm [Karelina] and one from a weaving factory [Boldyreva].[21]

On December 3, 1906, a large fraction of the Soviet and the whole of its Executive Committee were arrested. By then the 230 representatives to the Soviet included eighteen women, and the thirty-seven members of the Executive Committee included three women. Of these twenty-one women in the Soviet and its Executive Committee, thirteen were *intelligentki,* seven were of unknown origins, and only one, Barkova, was a worker.[22]

The numbers of women in the Soviet was at once very small and very great. Although all the women workers in the Soviet were elected from factories where female labor predominated, the great majority of factories with predominantly or large female contingents chose male representatives. That there were, at the very least, even seven women workers willing to take their place in this most original and audacious workers' organization speaks for an important if modest development in the confidence of women workers. Four of the seven women workers in the first Soviet descended from the Brusnev circles of the 1890s, a point of great significance to which we shall return subsequently. Of the women who passed in and out of the Executive Committee, only one—Boldyreva—was a worker. The others were *intelligentki* of the educated strata of society who had allied themselves with the Bolsheviks or the Mensheviks. The proportions of women among the Social Democrats was impressive, but few were workers.

---

21. Ibid., p. 59.
22. Ibid., pp. 136, 151–152.

The possibility of root-and-branch change in the relations between workers and society was buried, at least temporarily, with the St Petersburg Soviet's demise. But the combined events of 1905 left in their wake two institutions that altered Russia in significant ways. The brief alliance of many components of society in the October general strike was sufficiently powerful to wrench from the reluctant autocracy the Duma, an elected legislature, the first in Russia's history. Further, and again reluctantly, the autocracy acknowledged the legitimacy of workers' autonomous associations, and the first legal unions were born.

For reasons beyond the scope of this study, Russian workers in general did not embrace the union movement with anything like the fervor of many of their European counterparts.[23] What is most striking in our context is that the meager successes of the union movement were achieved with minimal female participation. The quantitative data, sparse and not always reliable, show nonetheless clearly that female membership in unions was far lower than male membership and, more significant, far below the proportions of women in the industrial labor force. In Moscow city in 1907 where women were roughly 30 percent of the factory work force, they constituted only 4.4 percent of union membership.[24] An incomplete survey of 1907–1908 estimated that for the parts of the Empire that reported, women were 10.8 percent of total union membership.[25] Even the tobacco workers, so militant, so quick to initiate strikes when threatened, so eager to join in the general strike of 1905, avoided the union in St Petersburg. The tobacco union journal, *Golos Tabachnika,* lamented in 1907,

23. Not the least of these reasons was severe and continuous government harassment of unions. For an excellent discussion of the union movement, see Victoria Bonnell, *Roots of Rebellion: Workers' Politics and Organizations in St Petersburg and Moscow, 1900–1914* (Berkeley, 1983), and "Radical Politics and Organized Labor in Prerevolutionary Moscow, 1905–1914," *Journal of Social History* (1979), March.

24. Iu. Milonov, *Moskovskoe professional'noe dvizhenie v gody pervoi revoliutsii,* p. 408.

25. *Svod otchetov professional'nykh obshchestv za 1906–1907* (St Petersburg, 1911), p. 3.

"In particular we have had almost no success among women workers. They are afraid not only to join the union, but even to buy the [union] newspaper."[26]

True, there were occasional exceptions. In Kostroma province three factories reported female representation in the textile union of 22 percent, 25.8 percent, and 28 percent, respectively. Women were 44 percent of the Moscow tobacco workers' union in 1907.[27] In a few cases, low female membership was balanced by outstanding activism. The St Petersburg textile union, for example, recruited only 10 percent of its membership from among women, but, as a participant recounted, "There was not a single [union] administration that did not have several women. The women not only did technical work, but gave reports at general meetings. To do so meant a grasp of the issues, and, given the presence of the police, courage as well."[28] Yet again we meet Boldyreva among the most diligent of the women workers in this union.[29] Further, we know that a so-called Central Committee of a Women Workers' Union was formed in St Petersburg. It issued a bold invitation to women workers and promised that in "fraternal [?] union you will be victorious in the struggle for a better future."[30] Delegates were dispatched to other cities, and in May 1906 another meeting of women workers was held in St Petersburg.[31] But no further evidence of these attempts to build exclusively women's unions has survived.

The few exceptions scarcely make a dent in the overall picture of women's reluctance to join unions. Why were women workers unable to translate into union activism the élan which brought them into the strike movement? The

26. *Golos Tabachnika* (1907), no. 2, p. 8.
27. Zaiats, p. 99; Milonov, *Moskovskoe professional'noe dvizhenie*, p. 408.
28. Milonov, p. 12. See also T. Shatilova, *Ocherk Leningradskogo soiuza khimikov (1905–1918)* (Leningrad, 1927), pp. 10, 16.
29. V. Perazich, "Iz materialov po istorii klassovoi bor'by tekstil'shchikov Leningrada," in *Materialy po istorii professional'nogo dvizheniia v Peterburge za 1905–1907* (Leningrad, 1926), pp. 96, 101.
30. *Professional'nyi Soiuz*, 1905, no. 1, p. 14.
31. *Materialy po istorii professional'nogo dvizheniia v Peterburge za 1905–1907*, p. 220. See also *Zhenskoe dvizhenie poslednikh dnei* (Odessa, 1905).

answer lies tangled in the interaction between the physical and psychological conditions of women's lives and the attitudes of male toward female workers.

To begin, unions were created on the initiative of male workers. Only two, the Union of Tavern Workers and Waiters and the Union of Precious Metal Workers, wrote the exclusion of women into their statutes.[32] Most unions included women as a matter of course, incorporating into union goals the ubiquitous strike demand for maternity benefits: paid release of women from work before and after childbirth with retention of wages and construction of nurseries for infants and young children.[33] The goal of equal pay for equal work was extremely rare, demanded only by the printers union, the tea-packers in Moscow, and one local union from among the textile workers.[34] Most textile unions set the more modest goal of a minimum wage.[35] Only in 1912 did the St Petersburg textile union belatedly assert:

> It is necessary to come closer to our female comrades, who make up two-thirds [of our industry]. Few of them are organized. . . . We must speak out for equal wages for men and women, and equal hours as well. Slogan: equal work, equal time, equal pay.[36]

A few unions made a point of demonstratively welcoming women workers: The All-Russian Union of printers spoke out clearly in support of equal rights for women workers: "Acknowledging that in all areas of printing, female labor can exist equally with male labor, this conference considers it obligatory that under no circumstances should women's earnings be lower."[37] In February 1906 the leaders of the

32. Kats and Milonov, p. 47; K. Dmitriev, *Iz praktiki professional'nogo dvizheniia v Rossii* (Odessa, 1907), p. 32; K. Dmitriev, *Professional'noe dvizhenie i soiuzy v Rossii* (St Petersburg, 1909), pp. 61–62.
33. Zaiats, p. 186.
34. Ibid., p. 255; *Istoriia odnogo soiuza*, p. viii.
35. Zaiats, p. 186.
36. *Zvezda* (1912), no. 17 (53), p. 19.
37. Dmitriev, *Iz praktiki*, p. 32.

Bolshevik-dominated Moscow textile unions noted the daily increase of women workers in the textile industry. Given that "women, because of their economic and domestic situation, are much less able to defend themselves against the bondage and exploitation of capital," the conference urged that "all measures be taken to attract women on an equal basis with men into unions and all other workers' organizations."[38]

One union in particular advanced far beyond words of welcome. In 1902 the stocking knitters of St Petersburg had formed an illegal union. Machine knitting was a tiny but skilled industry in St Petersburg with some three hundred workers distributed among small workshops. The union was the inspiration of several Jewish knitters who had come to St Petersburg from the western regions, where illegal organizations had existed from the early 1890s. Although there were four women among the eleven migrant knitters who started the union, the first executive committee was all male. In the spring of 1903 another woman knitter, Elena Isakovna Gasul', with several years of Bund membership behind her, came to St Petersburg. She became a member of the executive committee and soon after was joined by other women. Within the year the tiny, precarious organization began to recruit women hatmakers and seamstresses. From the outset the union stated explicitly that one of its most important goals was to break down the barriers of sex within the union. At the beginning of 1906 when the question of becoming a legal association arose, one of the most important issues under discussion was whether to sanction female labor on the large machines. A majority resolved that women should work on the large machines "on the condition that the bosses paid women the same wage as men." The unique stance of stocking-knitters left few traces, for, unable to survive on their own, they were soon incorporated into the larger textile union.[39]

From 1912 a few more unions discussed or actually imple-

38. Zaiats, p. 255.

39. V. Perazich, "Soiuz viazal'shchikov," in *Materialy po istorii professional'nogo dvizhenia v Peterburge za 1905–1907*, pp. 179–185.

mented measures to attract women workers. In 1912 the textile unions initiated a discussion of the need for child-care for workers' children and proposed that the unions take the initiative in actually creating such institutions. They were supported by a union of sales employees (in enterprises selling household goods) and by the metal workers' union.[40] The project was not realized. In 1913 at a meeting of the metal workers' union in St Petersburg, in spite of a letter written to the union from "some stupid comrades on Vyborg side" urging the union to "shake loose from [women workers]," two women workers were chosen for the board of directors "without a single protest and to friendly applause."[41] A year later the metal workers' union took up the question of lowering union dues for women workers. Some male workers argued against giving women "special privileges," but the proposal won the day. Similarly, the Metal Workers Union in Tula ruled that women could pay one-third of men's union dues, rejecting a demand from some male workers that, therefore, the women should get only one-half the benefits. These were the only concessions among unions to the universally acknowledged fact that "with earnings of seventy to ninety kopeks a day even conscious women workers often cannot afford to join our union."[42]

But the principle of women's equality with men in unions was sometimes violated in practice. In 1912 the Moscow tea-packers' union permitted men but not women to take over-time work, accusing women workers of competing unfairly with men.[43] St Petersburg weavers refused to take on women apprentices, equating them with scabs.[44] The printers union, despite its welcoming fanfare to women in 1905 and its repeated promise to "accept persons of the female sex for ap-

40. *Pravda* (1912), Nov. 21, no. 174, p. 4; Dec. 7, no. 187, p. 3; *Za Pravdu* (1913), Nov. 24, no. 43, p. 4.
41. *Severnaia Pravda* (1913), Aug. 23, no. 18, p. 1.
42. *Put' Pravdy* (1914), Jan. 23, no. 2, p. 4.
43. *Pravda* (1912), Oct. 4, no. 134, p. 4.
44. *Tkach* (1906), no. 6, p. 7.

prenticeship in typesetting,"[45] consistently sought to limit the number of women workers. While printers, fearing the threat to their status as skilled workers, were attempting to limit the influx of apprentices in general, women apprentices were special targets.[46] As an irate woman typesetter remonstrated, "The question of women typesetters and their apprenticeships has never appeared on the program [of the union shop sections]. Are the women typesetters not workers just like the male typesetters? . . . No one is concerned with [women workers] anymore. Everyone, from the factory management to the workers is concerned only to mock them."[47] An equally irate male typesetter retorted in no uncertain terms that women's needs were secondary to more important problems and added, inappropriately, that "it is time for women typesetters to speak for themselves [which is precisely what they were doing] instead of having someone speak for them . . . and constantly looking to someone for help, evoking pity for their helplessness."[48]

Unions found other ways to exclude women workers as well. In 1914 a group of women typesetters angrily denied the accusation that they were strike breakers and described how they were "completely uninformed about preparations for the strike. Our male comrades . . . never even thought to invite us to discuss and work out demands and in general ignore us as if we were not comrades." When one male worker pointed out that this would put the women typesetters in the position of being involuntary strike breakers, the other male typesetters answered, "We have no interest in them [*Oni k nam ne otnosiatsia*]." How can you call us strike breakers, the women demanded, when "we were isolated by the prejudiced and uncomradely behavior of the male typesetters. . . . We cannot accept the terrible accusation of

45. Dmitriev, *Iz praktiki*, p. 33. N. S. Trusova, *Vtoroi period revoliutsii: 1906–1907 gody* (Moscow, 1963), pp. 26–27.

46. Dmitriev, *Iz praktiki*, pp. 61–62.

47. *Golos Pechatnika* (1906), no. 11, p. 67.

48. Ibid., no. 12, pp. 9–10.

strike breaking . . . and we request that the Printers' Union
investigate this incident."[49]

A woman textile worker succinctly summarized the relationship between men and women in the unions:

> I can point to several women who are union members in good
> standing . . . [who] are the first to extend a hand to a comrade,
> the first to pay their dues. The twenty women ring-frame spin-
> ners all used to pay their dues promptly. Now only ten do. Why?
> The foreman began to bother them, to give them bad cotton,
> imposed a speed-up. . . . They finally mustered up the courage
> to complain to their boss. And they turned to the male mule-
> spinners [fellow union members] for support. But the mule-
> spinners refused and even had the nerve to lecture them. "What
> do you want anyway? Be satisfied with your eighty kopeks." . . .
> This is how our gentlemen mule-spinners behaved. . . . They
> hide.[50]

Thus, in exceptional cases male workers went out of their
way to exclude women from unions and in others to accommodate women. By and large, the unions simply ignored
women. As one male activist acknowledged sorrowfully,
"Even sadder . . . is the fact that in union affairs very little
actual energy was directed toward the organization and enlightenment of women workers."[51] The nature of the energy expended on convincing women to join the unions was
mainly rhetorical, appearing as exhortations in the pages of
union journals. Sometimes men were called upon to make
greater efforts to attract women, as in the following typical
article:

> Growing up in need and darkness, she [the woman worker]
> is . . . afraid of everyone . . . not only of every authority,
> but . . . her father and husband as well. . . . Her husband beats
> and curses her, her father punishes her, and then her grown
> children order her about. And this being, timid and deprived
> of all rights, is the most desirable "merchandise" for the

49. *Put' Pravdy* (1914), Feb. 23, no. 20, p. 5.
50. TsGIA, f. 150, op. 1, d. 154, l. 97 (*Stanok* [1908], no. 4, p. 10).
51. Dmitriev, *Prof. dvizh.*, p. 62.

bosses. They can pay her less and she will work more. . . . For her to understand all these things [how union membership can improve her condition], it is necessary for the male worker to enlighten her, to call her to his unions, to make her a comrade.[52]

Pleas were also directed to women, sometimes emphasizing past glories. A letter signed simply "A Worker" recalled to women workers the 1895 strike at the Laferm tobacco factory:

> Even though this strike was not organized, even though that was not the way to act, i.e., destruction and violence, still the women tobacco workers defended themselves . . . and they won. The boss, after this strike, did not lower the pay nor kick them out of the factory. Now our women workers are silent about everything: fines and every other oppression. They are afraid to defend their most vital interests.[53]

Some of the letters, articles, and reports in union publications acknowledged that it was difficult for women to join unions because "not only the bosses view women as the lowest kind of being; male workers do as well."[54] This compassion existed in an uncomfortable balance with a great sense of irritation with "the backwardness of women [which] is a brake on the entire workers' movement."[55] Men accused women workers of cowardice and chicanery. A male worker from the huge Shtiglitz textile factory wrote acerbically about the goings-on in the spinning department, "where all the women workers hysterically bribed the shop steward for better work." (This was common practice for male workers as well.) He recounted also that one morning the male workers went for tea and discovered there was no water. "It turned out that the faucet was stuffed with some kind of rag. We pulled it out—a woman's blouse. . . . Ah, comrade women workers! If you paid as much into our fraternal

52. L-a, Ia, "Zhenshchina rabotnitsa," *Rabochii Soiuz* (1906), no. 2, pp. 5–7.
53. *Zhizn' Tabachnika* (1907), no. 1, p. 4.
54. TsGIA, f. 154, op. 1, d. 154, l. 187 (*Fabrichnaia Zhizn'* [1910], no. 3, p. 1).
55. *Golos Zhizni* (1910), no. 1, p. 6.

union treasury as you spend bribing these upstarts [the shop stewards], we would not have to drink tea with boiled blouses."[56] Further, women workers were accused of frivolity and myopia. "But you, women workers, think more about smart clothes and parties than about uniting with your comrades. Which one of you thinks about the future, of how you will live when there is no money for bread?"[57]

Finally, and more seriously, women workers were blamed for taking the bread out of the mouths of male workers:

> Factory owners often throw your fathers, brothers, and husbands out on the streets and replace them with you, women workers. Do you know why factory owners so willingly take you on? . . . Because you, women workers, cost them less. . . . Step by step, you make your position worse.[58]

The irony of berating women workers for accepting lower wages escaped the author, a male worker, of this letter.

Why is it that the unions, both leadership and rank-and-file, did not welcome women workers? The explanation for union apathy at best and hostility at worst toward women lies far deeper than any simple discussion of events can reveal. The union was not a thing apart from the workers who composed it. Whatever impelled a male worker to take the risks of union involvement, to develop a political and class consciousness, did not necessarily include a transformation of attitudes toward his female comrades. The underlying conviction that women were a lower order of being, as Kanatchikov put it, made of the woman an unnatural comrade.

This was well understood by women workers.After 1905, with the emergence of a workers' press through which women could confront not only management and society but male comrades as well, women workers complained above all about the male hostility that began on the shop floor and persisted through all levels of interaction between men and women. Women workers dependent on men to keep their machines in repair were especially vulnerable.

---

56. TsGIA, f. 150, op. 1, d. 154, l. 151 (*Stanok* [1908], no. 1, pp. 11–12).
57. Ibid., l. 15 (*Stanok Tekstil'shchika* [1909], no. 2).
58. *Golos Zhizni*, Prilozhenie k no. 5 (1911).

Listen to the complaint of a woman in a factory where the entire work force consisted of women workers and a few male machinists whose job it was to repair the women's machines:

> If a woman worker's appearance does not please the machinist, she . . . can just sit and wait until he comes to fix her machine, and if she complains, then—even worse—he will dismantle the machine and give the parts to the workshop or keep them at his bench. The woman worker remains without work. . . . It is not unusual for the machinist to make obscene propositions. In most cases the woman submits to them because she is afraid that he will not repair her machine. . . . This, despite the fact that [the machinists] sell their labor as we do.[59]

A woman worker in a carton factory complained that "the men [workers] treat the women workers and apprentices as if they were street prostitutes. All the time one hears from them [nothing but] insults and obscene propositions." She described how one male worker exhibited his genitals to mock the women and how another raped a young woman worker in an out-of-the-way corner of the factory. On another occasion a worker deliberately broke a woman worker's cup. When the woman asked why he had broken it, he answered, "It doesn't matter, dearie. Tonight you'll go to the restaurant and earn yourself five kopeks. Then you can buy several cups." The writer concludes, "Truly, the woman worker's burden is heavy. If this had been said by an overfed boss or a tyrannical foreman, one would not be surprised. But this is how people who are themselves oppressed by capital speak to us."[60]

Male workers who were not inclined to insult or assault women nonetheless refused to disassociate themselves from their more aggressive comrades. A woman worker in a wood-processing factory wrote of an incident of attempted rape. Two male workers followed a woman worker to an isolated part of the factory. When she fought off their attempts to rape her, one of the men held her down while the

59. *Pravda* (1912), June 9, no. 35, p. 4.
60. *Za Pravdu* (1913), Oct. 19, no. 14, p. 4.

other smeared "the lower part of her torso with black grease." The factory manager refused to hear her complaints. Far worse, in the woman worker's opinion: "What did our comrade workers do? Nothing! They turned away and began to laugh in an unwholesome way [*zasmeialis' nekhoroshim smekhom*]."[61]

There were, of course, male workers who condemned this kind of behavior. In a unique display of solidarity and compassion, representatives from fifteen factories in St Petersburg in 1913 reprimanded the male workers at Novyi Bessner for standing at the women workers' exits and hurling "curses and obscenities at them [women workers]," threatening to make the offenders' names public if they did not stop.[62] Very rarely, men as well as women used the workers' press to condemn their fellow workers' mistreatment of women. In 1913 there was a prolonged strike at the Novyi Aivaz metal-working plant and a great deal of animosity toward the women workers who responded to the administration's blandishments, some returning to work and others only reluctantly continuing to strike. In a letter to *Pravda*, the Bolshevik newspaper, a male worker blamed male workers for the women's attitude toward the strike. Let us look, he admonished, at how male workers treat their comrade women workers. They insult them, mock them, make disgusting propositions, and beat them up for no reason "but to have fun." But, he added, "We, a group of conscious workers ... protest this kind of behavior. ... We highly value the worth of the woman and respect her sufferings when she bears our children." Workers should not beat and humiliate her, but help her, he advised, because "we workers only hurt ourselves when we belittle women. She could be a life companion, and if, as such, she is oppressed, beaten down, and crippled, she cannot beautify a man's life."[63]

61. *Put' Pravdy* (1913), March 9, no. 32, p. 3.
62. *Put' Pravdy* (1913), March 15, no. 35, p. 3.
63. *Rabochaia Pravda* (1913), July 19, no. 2, p. 4. Actually, in all of *Pravda*, 1912–1914, there were two letters from male workers corroborating women's complaints.

Preferable as this attitude was to the one it opposed, it missed the point, as a woman worker from the Novyi Aivaz plant argued a year later. In an open letter to her comrades she told how some of her male comrades demanded that she give up her job because her husband worked at the plant as well; she, therefore, was not among the neediest of the women workers:

> Thanks to the fact that I have a husband, my comrade workers want me to step off the path of labor on which I embarked twelve years ago (in the textile industry). I have lived as a worker this entire time, having worked consistently in factories and participated in the textile union; now I am expected to tear myself away from the workers' environment. How painful to hear such things from male workers . . . especially at a time when women workers are rising in defense of their [previously] trampled rights. I ask you, all my comrade male workers: What do you want from us women? A wife—a brood-mare and slave to your basest instincts—or a free woman, a comrade? If you want the latter, then don't drive us from our environment to the kitchen pots and don't say that an unmarried girl can work in the industry, but a married woman must be domestic and worry about cooking well for her husband. . . . I, as a member of the metal workers' union, have decided to turn to the union to investigate this issue.[64]

The consequences of this strained relationship between men and women workers were clearly articulated by a woman typesetter who, after describing a "scandal" at a union meeting between the men and women workers, declared:

> Comrades, it is time to cast off your weaknesses, to attend with a sober mind to the important business of uniting and, with all your strength, to try to eliminate such conflicts between women and men workers. . . . The woman worker suffers from the very start from the administration, which sees her not as a worker, but as a woman. But why speak of the administration? . . . Walk through the typesetting room and you will see a drunken worker

64. *Put' Pravdy* (1914), March 9, no. 32, p. 3.

molesting almost every woman. And listen to what he's saying! You will hear nothing but the most vulgar and disgusting words. . . . Comrades! When will you understand that you are working not with a woman but with a person just like your-self? . . . That is why men and women workers frequently come from different sides. One thing really astounds us women type-setters. The comrades are always demanding that the adminis-tration treat us with respect, but they have not the slightest interest in demanding that of themselves. That is why women are often strike breakers. That is why instead of unity we have disorganization. Only when you learn to see that the woman is the same kind of worker as yourself will you really be able to organize.[65]

* * *

The workers' thirst for autonomous association was not assuaged by the unions. In the heady days of strikes and union formation workers also formed clubs in many cities of the Empire. The clubs were granted limited official sanction in mid-1906 and survived amidst the subsequent shambles of the revolutionary movement because they were less politi-cally threatening than unions. Indeed, to survive they had to emphasize cultural activities at the expense of political. They survived also because they provided a way for workers, men and women, to satisfy their yearnings for self-education, for culture, and for comradeship.

The clubs were grass-roots associations, organized some-times by workers from many factories living in the same neighborhood, sometimes by workers from a given factory. They offered lectures on a wide variety of topics in the natural and social sciences, history, and literature.[66] To at-tract women, lectures were given on prostitution, the family, women's education, and on general women's history. Most clubs had libraries, a few had inexpensive cafeterias, and many had evenings of music and dance. Dances, which

65. Ibid.
66. The information on clubs is taken from I. D. Levin, "Rabochie kluby v Peterburge (1907–1914)," *Materialy po istorii professional'nogo dvizheniia v Rossii*, vols. 3 and 4 (Moscow, 1925).

the more ascetic clubs eschewed, were regarded as a good way to attract women, for often women who came simply to enjoy themselves in dance were inspired to attend lectures and use the libraries. Most significantly, many clubs lowered dues especially for women.[67] In St Petersburg there were ten workers' clubs at the end of 1905 and twenty between 1907 and 1914. By the end of 1913 women constituted between 15 and 20 percent of the 37,000 worker members.

The deterrents to club and union membership for women were similar. A contemporary who studied the clubs attributed the low female membership to the "double burden of work and family" and to male hostility:

> Workers, to a man, do not give credence to women's competence. . . . I often asked [workers] why their wives did not come to the club and very often got the following answer—"What business is it of theirs?"[68]

Yet, women who had to extricate themselves from the double burden to find time for any activity away from home and workplace—and to face male hostility when they did so—were more likely to choose clubs than unions. Only 30 percent of the women workers who joined clubs were union members as well, while 70 percent of male clubs members belonged to unions. In other words, for men union and club memberships were more likely to be simultaneous forms of activism, while women were more likely to choose between them and more likely to choose clubs over unions. Nor is this surprising. Club leadership made a more conscious and persistent effort to attract women, not only by offering events of special interest to them, but by lowering dues as well. Further, the union required consistent and dependable service and the risk of confrontation with factory authorities. The demands of the union were great, the

67. O. D. Dubrovina, "Rabochie Obshchestva samoobrazovaniia v SPb-e," in *Trudy pervogo vserossiiskogo zhenskogo s'ezda, 10–16 dekabria,* (St Petersburg, 1909), p. 579.
68. Levin, Ocherk pervyi, p. 99.

rewards distant and, it must have seemed, theoretical. In clubs the risk was small, the rewards immediate.

* * *

By 1907 Nicholas II's government, guided by the forceful and competent Minister of the Interior, Peter Stolypin, had regained much of the confidence that the events of 1905 had so shaken. In large and small ways the autocracy eviscerated the gains of the revolution and resumed its repressive role with impunity. The great coalition of opposition to the older order splintered, and each fragment pursued its own course in isolation from the others. Stolypin's electoral law of 1906 drastically curtailed the suffrage, undermining the liberal majority of the first two Dumas. To keep the truncated semiconstitutional order alive, most liberals decided on compromise with the autocracy, losing interest in the workers' cause and turning to narrower parliamentary politics. The radical parties were hounded almost out of existence, and in their weakened state reduced their support of unions. A stratum of worker activists struggled tenaciously to keep the workers' movement and the unions alive, but the rank and file, lacking a tradition of militant association, crushed by official opprobrium and enduring economic hardship, lost its élan. The strike movement abated and the unions withered.

In 1910 industry began to revive from the slump following the Russo-Japanese War and the revolution of 1905. Factory labor slowly began to grow in size, discontent, and militancy. In 1912 a shocking massacre of striking workers at the Lena goldfields in Siberia awakened workers from their torpor, and the strike movement picked up a momentum that did not subside until the outbreak of World War I. The union movement too revived, although it never approached the gains of the immediate post-1905 period.[69]

The basic pattern of women's participation in strikes did

---

69. A. Zvanov, "Iz praktiki professional'nogo dvizheniia v Peterburge," *Prosveshchenie* (1913), no. 11, p. 83. See also Bonnell, *Roots of Rebellion*.

not change in the period 1912–1914. We find the same complaints about women's passivity juxtaposed with examples of tenacity, initiative, and even leadership in strikes, with the greater weight, as it had been before 1905, on the side of the former. Yet, woven into this pattern are strands of evidence that the revolution of 1905 and its aftermath had left an imprint on the behavior of women workers.

The union press, for example, reported novel boldness on the shop floor. Let us contrast a woman worker's testimony from 1885 with the description of an incident on the shop floor in 1908. In 1885 a woman weaver in Tver' province complained to her foreman about a hole in the ceiling above her machine from which dirty water repeatedly dripped on her material. She was fined for spoilage:

> On January 16 I tried to tell [the foreman]. He paid no attention to me. I thought he had not heard me, so I followed him to the door and told him again. [He] then grabbed me by the hand and flung me from the door. I hit my head on the door . . . and clutched at my eyes because the blow produced sparks in my head. I went back to my machine, crying and holding my eyes. . . . My eye swelled up, and now two weeks later there is still a yellow mark on my neck and under my eye. . . . [The other workers] advised me to complain. I didn't want to. I was afraid to fall into the black book.[70]

In 1908, at a St Petersburg textile factory, a woman worker on a ribbon machine asked the assistant foreman to repair her machine. He worked on the machine for awhile, but was unable to fix it. The woman worker, returning to find the machine still defective, complained again. When the assistant foreman insisted that he had repaired the machine, she took him to it to demonstrate that it did not work.

> He got furious and yelled, "Every pig wants to humiliate the assistant foreman." Then he slapped her face so hard that blood flowed. But this time the assistant foreman paid for his hooligan behavior. The woman worker grabbed him, threw

70. *Rab. dvizh.*, t. 3, chast' 1, pp. 327–328.

him into a box and rained blows all over his body. Everyone
[the other women workers] laughed heartily.[71]

Women tobacco workers were exceptionally assertive in
the period 1912–1914. They organized strikes all over Russia, and as before, the women at Laferm in St Petersburg
stood at the forefront.[72] In the summer of 1913, thirty
women in the shredding department initiated a strike in
defense of 170 women who had been fired. They demanded that their comrades be rehired and their wages
raised. When male workers acted as strike breakers, the
women forcibly denied them access to the shop, made their
names public, and finally sent out a request to all workers in
St Petersburg to boycott Laferm's tobacco products.[73] A
month later the Laferm women supported the strikers at
the Gavanera tobacco factory with money donations.[74] In
September of 1913 the women workers at Laferm organized a strike of an explicitly political nature: they struck to
protest against the government's arrest of politically active
workers in Moscow and against the arrest of Mendel
Beiliss.[75]

Women workers in other industries also manifested signs
of a new boldness during these years. In October 1913 the
women workers at the Kersten textile factory initiated a
strike of several months duration. The notable change from
the past in this strike was that a majority of the women
workers at the Kersten factory were married heads of households and therefore had "no one to fall back on." The administration's attempts to persuade older women workers to
scab were unsuccessful. It had always been assumed, cor-

    71. TsGIA, f. 150, op. 1, d. 154, l. 3 (*Stanok* [1908], no. 3). See also, l. 5.
    72. *Pravda Truda* (1913), Sept. 4, no. 12, p. 4; *Za Pravdu* (1913), Nov. 20, no.
12, p. 4. See also, A. B-skii, "Pervoe maia 1906 v Peterburge i okrestnosti," *Krasnaia Letopis'* 1926, 2(17).
    73. *Pravda* (1913), July 2, no. 149, p. 3.
    74. *Pravda Truda* (1913), Sept. 18, no. 7, p. 3.
    75. *Pravda Truda*, (1913), Sept. 27, no. 15, p. 3. Mendel Beiliss, a Jewish factory
worker in Kiev, was falsely accused of the ritual murder of a Christian. His case
became a world-wide *cause célèbre*. Russian workers as well as Russian and Western
luminaries openly protested against this example of semiofficial antisemitism.

rectly, that both these categories of women—for obvious reasons—were the most timid and passive.[76] In December 1913 the workers at the Kirkhner bindery in St Petersburg agreed to withhold overtime labor. On the third day of this partial strike the men went back to overtime work while the women stood firm. "Shame on you, comrades," remonstrated a woman worker. "You are always scornful of the comrade women workers for not marching side by side with the men. True, they do not. They march ahead of the men."[77]

A series of spectacular strikes in which women were the major participants took place in St Petersburg in 1914. The Russo-American Rubber Factory, "Treugol'nik," employed 11,500 workers of whom over 6,000 were women engaged primarily in a procedure that required them to handle noxious solutions in open containers.[78] For years the workers' press had grumbled about the Treugol'nik workers: "Nowhere are there such downtrodden, exhausted and ignorant workers as in our rubber factory."[79] Also frequent were the observations that these backward, overworked, and poorly remunerated workers, especially the women, were exceptionally submissive to rude, even malicious, treatment from their supervisors. In the first week of March, 520 women were poisoned, 70 seriously. Four thousand workers gathered on March 14 to protest, and by March 17 the strike swelled to include 27,000 workers from sixteen factories. The next day reports of more poisonings brought 11,000 women workers out in a separate protest.[80]

In these last years before World War I the government made another belated and inadequate attempt to restrain

76. *Za Pravdu* (1913), Oct. 29, no. 22, p. 4.

77. *Proletarskaia Pravda* (1913), Dec. 17, no. 7, p. 2. See also Trusova, *Vtoroi period*, p. 183; TsGIA, f. 23, op. 30, d. 5, l. 42.

78. *Ekonomicheskoe polozhenie Rossii nakanune velikoi oktiabr'skoi sotsialisticheskoi revoliutsii. Dokumenty i materialy.* Chast' pervyi (Moscow and Leningrad, 1957), p. 41.

79. *Put' Pravdy* (1912), Feb. 23, no. 20, p. 4.

80. *Rabochee dvizhenie v Petrograde v 1912–1917 g. Dokumenty i materialy* (Leningrad, 1958), pp. 164–170.

workers' militance with palliative measures. It offered a
health insurance plan whose benefits were not generous but
whose organization was innovative. Factories were obliged
to establish joint committees of factory management and
the elected representatives of the workers to determine
joint financial responsibility and to allocate the compensa-
tory funds for illness and accidents. The insurance law included two provisions of great significance for women
workers. It provided some payment for childbirth and allowed women to serve as representatives on the workers'
insurance committees as well as to vote for them. The
leadership of the union movement and parties of the left
welcomed the insurance campaign as a means to encourage
worker activism and made a plea for unity between men
and women workers, urging men to

> let her stand beside you so that she cannot shoot you in the
> back. This is not in the interests of justice but in the interest of
> the workers' movement; not courtly attention to ladies, but the
> fate of the workers' organization and the success of the struggle
> for the demands of the working class.[81]

But rank-and-file hostility to women was not so easily overcome: "In the newspapers one reads of how derisively and
scornfully some comrades greet the candidacy of women
for the insurance committees."[82] In addition to accusations
against women familiar to us from the unions, male workers
perceived the election of women as a plot on the part of
factory management to manipulate the committees and undermine their effectiveness: "The women in our factory are
almost completely illiterate, but this is precisely what the
factory administration wants, because they can push their
own line with them better."[83]

Nonetheless, women workers took advantage of legally
sanctioned participation to circumvent the hostility of their
male co-workers. From many factories came reports of

81. *Strakhovanie Rabochikh* (1914), no. 3, p. 1.
82. Ibid.
83. *Voprosy Strakhovaniia* (1914), no. 8, p. 11; no. 26, p. 13.

women elected to serve on the insurance committees, some-times in greater numbers than men.[84] The stocking knitters in Vilna "put together an insurance committee so compe-tently that men [workers] could well take a lesson from them."[85]

Once men and women sat together on the insurance com-mittees, the same antagonisms that bedeviled their relation-ships in the unions emerged. A letter signed "A Woman Worker" told of the conflict over maternity pensions: "The women workers suggested giving out two-thirds of a woman's earnings as her childbirth payment, and the men, one-half. Since men were in the majority, they voted for one-half, as if a new baby costs nothing."[86] In some cases, however, men found verification of their opinion that women workers were their own worst enemies. Such were the cases where young unmarried women workers or women beyond childbearing age balked at funds for maternity bene-fits because "we are not planning to have babies."[87]

The insurance law, which labor activists had hoped would inject new life into the labor movement, met with the suspi-cion and indifference of most workers. After all, the insur-ance law was limited. It did not affect the hours they worked, their meager wages, their insecurity in old age, or, indeed, most features of their difficult and cheerless lives. The re-wards were not commensurate with active participation.

* * *

The submissiveness that characterized women workers was an undeniable but relative truth. Most women were less demanding and, as the political left put it, more back-ward than most men. Although many protested episodi-cally, few women workers engaged in sustained activism. Why was this so?

84. Ibid. (1914), no. 6, p. 12; no. 8, p. 13; no. 14–15, p. 17; no. 11, p. 8; no. 26, p. 13.
85. Ibid. (1913), no. 4, p. 9.
86. Ibid. (1914), no. 2, p. 7.
87. Ibid. (1914), no. 8, p. 12; no. 15, p. 5.

Russian peasant women came to the factory with a legacy
of subordination and submission to male authority, bringing
with them neither the habits nor the expectations of responsibility and initiative. In these critical respects their lives
changed but little in the factory. Occupational segregation
ensured that women did "women's" work in the factory. The
universe of the skilled worker who was master of his craft,
who had control over the work process and the level of productivity, who was proud of his skills and mastery and was
respected by both management and other workers—that
universe was decidedly closed to women. To be sure, the
majority of male workers were excluded from that world as
well. But that small segment of male workers who achieved
pride and self-esteem, who were accustomed to responsibility
and initiative, and who often took the lead in workers' protest had no counterpart among women workers. Further, in
the factory, women functioned in a largely female environment. But every figure of authority and power was male: the
workers on whom women depended to repair their machines, the foremen, the factory managers, the factory inspectors, the judges, and the police.

The peasant legacy combined with occupational segregation and the double burden of work and domestic obligations are of obvious and enormous importance in explaining the behavior of women workers. They were reinforced
by the persistent relationship between men and women on
the shop floor and in their organizations.

Before 1905 women almost invariably struck for goals
they shared with men. Male workers often welcomed
women's participation and, indeed, sometimes forced it. But
they did not invariably seek it. Men rarely obstructed strikes
that women initiated, but, as a rule, neither did they support them. For women to have struck for goals that were
not shared by men—maternity benefits, access to skilled occupations, equal pay—or even to protest sexual abuse,
would have meant to antagonize men and to risk obstruction or even open hostility. The issue of women's lower
wages embraces the entire paradox of their relationship to

male workers. The woman worker's lower pay was a great obstacle to raising her standard of living, to her independence and dignity. With its twin, submissiveness, it was also her greatest asset in getting work. This was no secret to anyone. Men deplored the passivity that hindered women from striking and that led them to accept lower wages. But they could not accept women as full partners in the struggle, because they believed that women were meant to be submissive and to accept lower wages. Women's lower wages, their submissiveness, their vulnerability to sexual harassment and physical abuse were part of a harmony that male workers were no less likely to accept than were the factory authorities. Small wonder that women, reluctant enough to strike with their male co-workers over common issues, were mute on issues that would have incurred the hostility of men.

In 1905 women workers were beneficiaries of, as well as contributors to, a great leap forward in the aspirations of the working classes. It was then that they acquired a vocabulary to articulate their specific grievances, a vocabulary that male workers, too, absorbed into their lexicon. The variety of improvements for which men and women struggled together after 1905 routinely included amelioration of women's maternal burdens. But in the absence of concomitant demands for equal pay, for access to skilled occupations that brought higher earnings and dignity, the demand for maternity benefits reflected the definition of the woman worker as mother rather than worker.

After 1905 women were far more likely to strike than to join unions or any other form of workers' organization. Domestic burdens in addition to long hours of factory work were a greater deterrent to union membership than to strike participation. The constant harassment of union members by the authorities throughout the short history of Russia's unions added risks that the woman worker, with her lower earnings and domestic responsibilities, could bear even less than men. Women lacked the self-confidence and initiative required for union membership which skill and habits of responsibility at the workplace provided: "I would join the union, but I am afraid to be chosen for some kind of responsible position," a woman worker confessed in 1907.[88]

The experience of the workers' circles in the 1890s and Karelina's success with women workers in the Gapon Assembly suggest that women were potentially more receptive to active solidarity with male workers than was normally acknowledged. It reveals that women workers required special nurturance and attention that went beyond rhetorical appeals, that men consciously eschew condescension and indifference to women. But the call to women workers from organized labor, from political groups and parties dedicated to workers, was a whisper when it should have been a shout.

That women's "backwardness" was not sufficient justification for excluding them from the struggle was acknowledged only on rare occasion:

> They [women] are less cultured in the social sense—this is true. But does not one find a great difference in class consciousness between the unskilled day laborer and the Putilov lathe operator? Do not the Chinese coolies, brought in droves to Europe as cheap labor, stand incomparably farther behind the European proletariat than the woman worker from her male comrade? Do you really find it useful to prevent the Chinese coolie from joining workers' organizations?

Entreating male workers not to use the "backwardness" of women workers as an excuse to exclude them from workers' organizations, this writer, who regrettably does not sign his name, promises that mutual struggle of men and women workers "will provide the world with a free, whole, beautiful *human* personality—not a male or female personality."[89] Unfortunately, this vision was not shared by many.

88. *Zhizn' Tabachnika* (1907), no. 2, p. 3.
89. *Strakhovanie Rabochikh* (1913), no. 3, p. 1.

7

WOMEN WORKERS AND SOCIETY: THE EMERGENCE OF THE WOMAN QUESTION

Women workers had, as it were, dual citizenship. The context of their lives was provided by class. As workers their lives were shaped by the determinants of class that affected male workers as well. But, when we examine those aspects of women's experience as workers that distinguished them from male workers, it is clear that within the context of class their position was determined by the assumptions that Russian society and culture held about women of all classes. If, for example, industrialists expected women to work at unskilled jobs and to accept lower wages than men when they performed the same tasks, it was because of convictions about the nature of all women. When factory inspectors sought to ameliorate factory conditions for women, their approach was based on assumptions about women workers not only as workers but as mothers. We need not belabor the issue with more examples. The point is that most of the society perceived women workers as a particular kind of worker. Another perspective emerged, however, which viewed the woman worker as a particular kind of woman and which addressed the problems of women workers as one manifestation of the attitudes that locked women in a fixed and lower position relative to men within all strata of society.

The woman question in Russia surfaced as it had elsewhere in nineteenth-century Europe, as a concern for the liberation of the woman's heart. In the 1830s the Russian intelligentsia, then almost exclusively male, was smitten by the writings of George Sand, and awoke to the inequities that women suffered in sexual and emotional choices. The intelligentsia, therefore, undertook (on paper) to liberate women from the shackles of loveless marriages arranged to satisfy parents, tradition, and society—everyone but the woman herself. While free choice in love and marriage was denied to Russian women of all strata—peasant women no less than upper-class women—the gentry intelligentsia could not surmount the barriers that separated it from the peasantry: the sexual and emotional liberation of women was a concern of the gentry and for the gentry.[1]

In the late 1850s the woman question was drawn into a maelstrom of more inclusive social issues. As the anticipated emancipation of the serfs stimulated the educated public to consider its own emancipation from the constraints of tradition, the definition of the woman question was greatly amplified. It became clear that the woman's heart could not be liberated in a vacuum, that emotional liberation required a multitude of related freedoms. From the pens of publicists, belle-lettrists, and ideologues came, helter-skelter, a veritable flood of ideas about women's right to take their place with men in Russia's social and economic life. Ultimately, the right to economic independence came to be seen as a prerequisite of all other aspects of liberation.

This is not to say that the woman question began with the liberation of the heart and traversed a straight path to economic independence. In the 1860s and 1870s the intelligentsia explored all the byways of biology and tradition, of law, psychology, and religion as it sought to explain and redress women's inequality with and subjugation to men. The terms of the debate paralleled and recapitulated the discourse familiar to us from the history of women in the West. Whatever the emphasis at any given moment, the debate was circumscribed by the social origins of its participants. By the 1860s the educated public was no longer ex-

---

1. See Martin Malia, *Alexander Herzen and the Birth of Russian Socialism* (Cambridge, Mass., 1961); R. Stites, *The Women's Liberation Movement in Russia*, chap. 1 and 2.

clusively gentry, and now drew from children of the clergy, of non-noble state servants, of the embryonic professional strata. But the lower strata—peasants, artisans, urban lower classes, factory workers—did not, and could not, take part in the discourse. However, the increasing focus on work began to bring women of the lower strata into view.

Two perspectives on women's emancipation through work emerged in the 1860s. The first was best articulated in 1862 by Maria Vernadskaia, a writer and publicist well versed in and committed to liberal economics. She wrote that the most demeaning aspect of the woman's condition was the complete lack of freedom to choose the way she spent her life. The few roles that tradition forced upon her—the obedient daughter, the submissive wife, the housekeeper and child rearer—might not be either to her liking or commensurate with her talents. Still worse, the economic dependence that followed from these roles forced her into loveless marriage. However, said Vernadskaia, shifting her ground from social determinants to individual responsibility, women must share the blame for their pitiful lot. Now that civilization no longer relied on the superior physical strength of men, there were abundant opportunities for women to earn money and become independent. If they had capital, what could stop them from becoming factory owners or merchants? If they did not possess capital, they could be doctors, teachers, artists, and writers. As for women whose education did not permit them to engage in intellectual and professional activities: "Their situation is the saddest, but it is partly their own fault. Almost all crafts are open to them. Why can they not be flower makers, tailors; in other words, why avoid all those honorable trades which would not only earn them bread, but often are respectable occupations for women who are not of noble birth." The trick was for women to take work as seriously as men did, because "in the end, any occupation, even the most humble is far more worthy of respect than living off someone else."[2]

2. M. N. Vernadskaia, *Sobranie sochinenii* (St Petersburg, 1862), pp. 105–106.

Nikolai Chernyshevskii, one of the most influential radicals of the 1860s, worked out a powerful elaboration of Vernadskaia's thesis in his novel *What Is to Be Done*.[3] The novel served as a manual for the radical intelligentsia of the 1860s and endured as a classical statement for radicals of subsequent decades as well. The heroine of the novel, Vera Pavlovna, is a young woman of the urban middle stratum who escapes a repellent marriage to a man of her parents' choice by making a marriage of convenience with a young man who shares her goals of female emancipation and sexual equality. With his emotional (and financial) support she strikes off toward personal fulfillment. She establishes a sewing collective that allows her to exercise her administrative skills and altruistic inclinations; the collective attracts poor women normally exploited in workshops or pushed into prostitution. Vera Pavlovna teaches them how to manage their business collectively, how to market their wares and to share instead of exploit. The story is complicated by her own emotional entanglements, which for our purposes are beside the point. The point is that Chernyshevskii and Vernadskaia were abysmally ignorant about the real world of women of the working classes. Vernadskaia acknowledged the honorable nature of flower making and tailoring but did not trouble herself with the conditions under which flower makers and seamstresses worked. She assumed that women had only to desire such jobs to get them and survive on the wages they paid. Chernyshevskii's heroine, lofty and courageous, achieves personal fulfillment and economic independence through work. But her success is ultimately and decisively dependent on the support of men of her class. The poor women in the novel are dependent on Vera Pavlovna's compassion and initiative to find a better place in the interstices of an exploitative society. Fundamentally, the proponents of this perspective assumed that women's emancipation, predicated on economic indepen-

3. N. G. Chernyshevskii, *What Is to Be Done?* (New York, 1961). First published in 1862.

dence through work, could be achieved through the volition of individual women within the framework of the existing economic structure.

The second perspective on women's emancipation through work, at once more realistic and more abstract, was elaborated in the articles of Iulii Zhukovskii and Peter Tkachev. They took the problem and its solutions out of the realm of individual volition and placed them in the broader context of Russia's economic system. Zhukovskii, a kind of Lasallean socialist, denied the efficacy of piecemeal legalistic solutions that would give women the freedom to choose their mates or to educate themselves. Even more useless, he believed, were the endless debates over women's intellectual and biological equality with men. In the words of Zhukovskii's fictional feminist, "Instead of pondering how our brains are constructed, you would do better to see how our stomachs are constructed. . . . Whether or not our brains are smaller, we experience the same hunger, the same nerves, and the same desire for pleasure [as men] and, in addition, we bear and nourish children!"[4] The source of women's subjugation, then, was an economic system that deprived women of all strata of the right to feed themselves by their own labor. Zhukovskii pointed out that women of the possessing classes, excluded from the world of work, acquired income or capital only as daughters or wives and, at that, were entitled only to a portion of male resources too small for independent survival. Rural women, of course, worked, but were not rewarded by an equitable share of the family income and could not therefore survive independently. Both, however, were better off than urban women workers, who had lost the protection of the family and were obliged to survive as individuals on half of men's wages. Individual solutions, like Vera Pavlovna's, pointed in the right direction insofar as they involved cooperation instead of exploitation. But to transform individual solutions into

4. Iu. Zhukovskii, "Zatrudneniia zhenskogo dela," *Sovremennik* (1863), no. 12, pp. 279–280.

social solutions the entire economic macrocosm had to be altered. In Zhukovskii's opinion, women would achieve economic independence and, consequently, equality with men when the nation's economic life had been reorganized into a society of producers' and consumers' associations. Women's emancipation would accompany the emancipation of all the dispossessed and exploited.

In a similar vein Peter Tkachev, an eclectic socialist and important revolutionary activist, wrote two long essays about women and work.[5] The great thing about the rise of capitalist industrialization, asserted Tkachev, is that it changed work from the symbol of slavery and lowliness of previous epochs into a positive virtue: "[The right to work] is considered so important and valuable that contemporary democracy formally acknowledges it as the necessary condition for human existence."[6] Unfortunately, capitalist industrialization denies some women the right to work and other women the just rewards of work. The upper-class woman is simply not permitted to compete in the marketplace and is thus deprived of both independence and honor. As for women of the lower classes, capitalist industrialization destroys the family, which once provided them with social and economic support. They are forced to compete with men in the male universe of work, but not on equal terms with men. Their lower wages are barely enough for basic subsistence, and in addition, they must endure excessively long working hours, physical deterioration, and insecurity. In Tkachev's opinion, therefore, capitalist industrialization is bad for all women and an un-

5. The first essay was published in a short-lived feminist journal: Peter Tkachev, "Vliianie ekonomicheskogo progressa no polozhenie zhenshchiny i sem'i," *Zhenskii Vestnik* (1866), no. 1–2. The second was a greatly expanded version of the first article. In 1869 two women, M. Trubnikova and N. Stasova, who later became ardent feminists, commissioned Tkachev to translate a book from German and write an introduction to it. The book was A. Daul, *Zhenskii trud v primenenii k razlichnym otrasliam promyshlennoi deiatel'nosti* (St Petersburg, 1869). Tkachev's introduction, "Zhenskii vopros," was intended to correct the book's one-sided celebration of women's equality with men in industrial labor which, in the opinion of the publishers, did not "consider the consequences of such equality under existing conditions of labor" (p. 1).

6. "Zhenskii vopros," p. xxxiii.

equivocal disaster for women workers. But he excoriated the opponents of women's emancipation who used these facts to argue that women should not work. Instead, he concluded, women must be given more right to work rather than less, but in a society transformed by a revolution that would permit Russia to bypass capitalist industrialization and remove labor from "the feudal dependence on capital . . . [to a society in which] . . . capital loses all its privileges."[7]

Zhukovskii and Tkachev shifted the question of women's relationship to work to a plane that made room for the great mass of womankind. Agreeing that work was central to the emancipation of women of all strata, they were grimly aware that the woman who really depended on it for survival was a long way from equality with men and from independence. Work for most women was neither Vernadskaia's sentimental idealization nor Vera Pavalovna's personal fulfillment. Zhukovskii suggested and Tkachev insisted that for the majority of women, industrialization was a curse, creating new and worse conditions for them. The solution, therefore, was to bypass capitalist industrialization and create a new society that would reward the work of all with independence and well-being. The real emancipation of women—ladies as well as workers—could be realized only as a consequence of total economic and social change.

For a decade the potential conflict between these two perspectives lay dormant as women of the intelligentsia groped for practical ways to emancipate themselves. They joined communes, contracted fictitious marriages, and expressed their disdain for traditional roles in their dress and manners. Some circumvented the barriers to higher education in Russia by going abroad to study. Others started women's journals and artels to provide women with remunerative intellectual work. Still others found satisfying outlets for their talents and energy in teaching working women in the Sunday schools of the early 1860s.[8] Those who moved easily

7. Ibid., p. xiv.
8. Stites, chaps. 3 and 4.

among the philanthropic wealthy attempted to influence
the latter to take notice of women of the urban poor. As a
book review in *Zhenskii Vestnik* hinted in 1867, "The needs
of the poor are well known to the educated class, and
among our ladies we would undoubtedly find some who, if
allowed, would surely help the unfortunate of their sex with
the establishment of trade schools and the spread of more
remunerative trades."[9] Wealthy women responded by estab-
lishing institutions such as the Society for Poor Women. It
was founded in St Petersburg in 1865 to "help poor women,
young and adult, to lead honorable and industrious lives"
and "to show concern for their moral condition."[10] The
board consisted of thirty people, including six or seven
noblemen, three priests, and three belle-lettrists, and spent
most of its time fruitlessly soliciting contributions. It opened
a sewing workshop, but was unable to find employment for
the forty-seven poor women it ferreted out in hospitals and
refuges. The Society was typical, in structure and results, of
others that dotted the philanthropic landscape throughout
our period, all designed primarily to "guard girls and
women from the danger of debauchery and to return already fallen women to honorable life."[11]

In whatever disparate ways women of the 1860s and early
1870s sought to liberate themselves or to alleviate the condition of women less fortunate than they, they were not consciously divided by philosophical or tactical differences. In
the early 1870s, however, they began to separate into two
mutually exclusive groups, each guided by one of the perspectives discussed earlier. One group took the path of feminism familiar to us from the history of women's movements
in Western Europe and America. That is to say, they
worked to force existing institutions to change sufficiently

    9. A. S., "Polozhenie rabochei zhenshchiny v Irlandii," *Zhenskii Vestnik* (1867),
no. 7, p. 82.
    10. *Zhenskii Vestnik* (1867), no. 5, p. 70.
    11. *Trudovaia Pomoshch* (1900), no. 2, p. 192. See also *Trudovaia Pomoshch*
(1899), no. 8, pp. 291–292; no. 9, p. 395; (1900), no. 2, pp. 190–192; no. 6, p. 97;
no. 4, p. 430; no. 9, p. 445; M. V. Kechedzhi-Shapovalov, *Zhenskoe dvizhenie v Rossii
i zagranitsei* (St Petersburg, 1902), pp. 152–179.

to accommodate women without challenging the basic structure of society.

The feminists engaged in a multitude of activities to help women achieve higher education, gainful employment, and equitable marital relationships. They wrote, agitated, and lobbied courageously in the face of staunch social and official opposition to the extension of these rights to women. Their most cohesive and successful efforts were devoted to penetrating the world of higher education, and they fought to open existing institutions of higher education to women or to create separate institutions of higher education for women which would parallel men's in quality and legitimacy. By European and American standards of the nineteenth century, they were brilliantly successful, and they sustained their successes by working to provide a sound financial base for women's education.

The activities of the feminists, by their very nature, could not benefit women of the lower classes. But, as women dedicated to helping women, they were concerned with the plight of poor women as well. Before the 1880s factory women were but a small proportion of the urban poor, and in any case, neither feminists nor the wealthy who had some tradition of philanthropy among the poor could distinguish one poor woman from another. By the 1800s, as industrial expansion coupled with visible labor unrest thrust the "worker question" into the public eye, feminists began to sort out the various elements within the amorphous category of "poor women." Two outstanding women scholars and feminists, Aleksandra Efimenko and Mina Gorbunova, did excellent research on peasant women.[12] Other feminists

12. Aleksandra Efimenko, *Izsledovaniia narodnoi zhizni* (Moscow, 1884). Efimenko was the first woman in Russia to receive an honorary doctorate in history. An ethnographer of talent and reknown, she was especially interested in peasant women. A number of her sensitive and compassionate essays on this subject are included in her 1884 book. She taught courses in the institutions of higher education for women and joined in the suffrage movement after 1905. M. K. Gorbunova supported the nonpolitical Populist approach to the problems of industrialization in Russia, and with that in mind conducted a massive research project on peasant women and their crafts, published as *Sbornik statisticheskikh svedenii po moskovskoi gubernii*, t. 7, vyp. 4 (Moscow, 1882).

began to ponder the effects of industrialization on urban women. In the mid-1880s a feminist journal, *Drug Zhenshchin,* published two long and serious studies of women factory workers.

The first was written by V.O. Portugalov, a well-known doctor and publicist with a considerable knowledge of factory conditions. He wished to compensate for men's indifference to female labor by studying the health and sanitary aspects of factory work. Now that women's intellectual equality is an accepted fact, stated Portugalov optimistically, the question of their relative physical abilities should be investigated, especially since industrialization is making new kinds of demands on women of the lower strata: "If we were to list in detail all the illness, all the suffering to which women are subjected in the factories and plants over the expanse of industrial and mercantile Europe, we would not find enough ink, paper, or pens; indeed, one lifetime would not be enough for the task."[13] A litany of the physical horrors experienced by women workers follows, replete with squashed intestines, obstructed digestion, misshapen spines, degenerating eyesight, nervous ailments, and infertility. However, Portugalov did not propose to improve factory conditions. He did not believe they could be improved, since factory work by its very nature destroyed the female organism. He wished rather to prove that "there is not the slightest shadow of a doubt that the female organism is significantly weaker than the male organism in the physical sense in general and specifically for two or three days in each month when they are not entirely healthy and are in a certain mood in which they are much more susceptible to colds than men."[14] To be sure, he hastened to add, he was not recommending idleness for women, for hygienists had proved that idleness could actually damage the female organism. The questions of women's work were where and how. And the answer was never in the factory: "Until now

13. V. Portugalov, "Zhenskii trud v sanitarnom otnoshenii," *Drug Zhenshchin* (1884), no. 1, p. 92.
14. Ibid., p. 90.

social progress has been measured by the degree of women's emancipation in general terms; we can and must also define emancipation as emancipation from physical labor."[15] Portugalov did not make clear how he proposed to reconcile women's need for economic independence, which he supported, with his conclusions that no work was appropriate for women which took her from home and family.[16]

This first contribution from the feminist press to the problem of women workers was a hodge-podge of medical terminology and general confusion. The second article, written by a woman and based on the meticulous research of Dr. F. F. Erisman on workers in Moscow province, was sober and well informed. The author, E. Mikhailova, begins with a simple question: "Why does our peasant woman exchange her deprived, laborious, but free peasant life for the crowded and gloomy factory?" Surely, she answers, the peasant woman does not leave home, like the girl of the privileged classes, to satisfy yearnings stifled by the old patriarchal system. She goes to the factory because the meager peasant allotment will no longer nourish the growing number of mouths. Drawing on Erisman's statistical survey of Moscow province, the author points out that "where women can augment the needs of their families without leaving the family circle, we observe that they participate less in factory work."[17] She then discusses and laments the factory woman's low wages, poor diet, wretched working and living conditions, and long hours of arduous labor. Moreover, she continues, the few civilizing benefits of factory life, like increased literacy, accrue mainly to male workers. But by far the worst consequence of factory life, in the author's opinion, was that "the constant combination of both sexes [in the factory] in the absence of a moral regimen which provides people with a settled domestic life, with mutual shared eco-

15. Ibid., p. 94.
16. Ibid., p. 93.
17. E. Mikhailova, "Polozhenie fabrichnykh rabotnits na moskovskikh fabrikakh i uezdnykh," *Drug Zhenshchin* (1884), no. 5, p. 108.

nomic and domestic concerns, cannot help but contribute to the degeneration of [women's] morals."[18]

In contrast to Portugalov, who would eliminate the problem by taking women out of the factory, Mikhailova looked to labor legislation on the Western European model to mitigate the conditions of a horrid necessity. While feminists waited for legislation, which with few exceptions was not forthcoming, they attempted to help factory women in other, more limited ways. In 1897 the Society for Assisting Young Women Workers was established in St Petersburg, and in 1901 a sister branch appeared in Odessa. In 1899 the Society for the Improvement of Women's Lot opened refuges for women in Moscow and attempted to organize programs to provide primary and technical education to poor women. In 1901 a society to hold gatherings for women artisans was established in Saratov, and between 1900 and 1901 more refuges for women workers were opened in St Petersburg, Sevastopol, Minsk, and Warsaw. Special sewing rooms were opened in Moscow and St Petersburg for working women too poor to buy their clothing. Many other philanthropic organizations, not aimed at women workers specifically but accommodating them among others, cropped up as well.[19]

The Society for Assisting Young Women Workers had the most elaborate program of all the organizations for women workers. It is most illustrative of the attitudes of feminists toward working women. The Society's goal was to "protect young girls, primarily of the working class—artisans, factory workers, servants—from the influence of the morally damaging conditions of their lives." With this in mind the Society held Sunday gatherings for working women in two locations in St Petersburg. The day's activities were divided between serious occupation and "innocent entertainment." Hoping that the women workers who attended would "learn to value mainly spiritual well-being"

18. Ibid., p. 123.
19. Kechedzhi-Shapovalov, pp. 156–164.

instead of "material advantages," the Society offered lessons in sewing, reading, and writing. The women workers heard lectures on hygiene and religion, saw plays, listened to concerts, and danced. The Sunday gatherings attracted about a hundred women at each location every week over a period of four years. The Society also maintained a dormitory with inexpensive accommodations, which housed only nineteen women despite the feminists' struggle to acquire funds for expansion. The gatherings attracted mainly factory women, the dormitory almost none, for in the opinion of the Society, factory girls were too spoiled and dissolute to tolerate the strict discipline of the dormitory; they were not permitted to have male visitors and were forbidden to return home late at night.[20]

These feminists were well intentioned and well informed, at least in general terms, about women workers' lives. However, they assumed that if the Sunday gatherings could "awaken good feelings and a vague desire for something better and more fulfilling" in the woman worker, then she had only to act on that desire to fulfill it.[21] For example, the Society's sponsors believed that women workers suffered in times of illness or unemployment because they lacked the foresight to put aside some of their earnings for hard times. A working woman, they asserted loftily, should be able to live by her own work: "This always raises a person's self-esteem and makes her a useful member of society."[22] When women workers on whom the feminists lavished their compassion and resources did not show signs of improving their lives, the blame fell on them rather than on the conditions of their lives. The daunting obstacles in the woman worker's life to improvement through individual volition escaped the feminists. Knowing what we do about women's wages, we can only conclude that class barriers were too high for fem-

20. M. I. Pokrovskaia, "Peterburgskie voskresnye sobraniia dlia rabotnits," *Mir Bozhii* (1899), no. 3, pp. 4–6; "Obshchestvo popecheniia o molodykh devits v SPb-e," *Trudy vserossiiskogo s'ezda po remeslennoi promyshlennosti v S-Peterburge*, t. 3 (St Petersburg, 1901).
21. Pokrovskaia, "Petersburgskie voskrenye sobraniia dlia rabotnits," p. 13.
22. Ibid., p. 9.

inists to vault. In the end they were satisfied that through their efforts the Sunday gatherings brought to women workers "at least temporary oblivion where everything becomes bright and joyful [for a moment]."[23]

* * *

From among the women who feverishly pursued their own emancipation in the 1860s a second group coalesced along the lines suggested by radical thinkers such as Tkachev. This group despaired of achieving equality for women in a nation whose economy, political structure, and traditions, supported by the coercive power of the state, denied equality to the great mass of Russian people. Women's enslavement to the family and subservience to men was only one manifestation of the system that oppressed the many. These women turned to Populism and to its vision of a revolution that would destroy the autocracy, bypass capitalist industrialization, and create a peasant socialism. Industrialization, they believed, was as dubious a benefactor of women as it was of all the dispossessed. As Sophia Bardina testified in a famous speech before a jury that sentenced her to exile for Populist activity, "As for the family . . . is it not undermined by a social structure that forces the woman to leave her family for work in the factory, where she gets a miserable pittance, where she and her children are inevitably degraded?"[24] The erstwhile feminists of the 1860s who became Populists in the 1870s held that only after the tsarist autocracy had been replaced by peasant socialism would there be a "free field of women's labor; only then will you become productive individuals in a society; only then will you have equal rights with men."[25]

Populist women felt that their duty to women in the present was fulfilled by taking an equal place with men in the

23. Ibid., p. 13.

24. S. O. Tsederbaum, *Zhenshchina v russkom revoliutsionnom dvizhenii, 1870–1905* (Leningrad, 1927), p. 26.

25. "Ot Russkogo Revoliutsionogo Obshchestva k zhenshchinam," *Literaturnoe Nasledstvo*, XL–XLII, pp. 147–150.

revolutionary struggle: the emancipation of other women would have to wait for the success of the revolution in the future. It is not surprising, therefore, that they made no effort to include peasant and working women in the here and now. As we saw in chapter five, however, for a brief moment the revolutionary movement stepped off the millenarian path and made deliberate—and successful—efforts to organize women workers, to include them in the process that was meant to emancipate them in the future. It did so just as Marxist formulations began to compete with Populism for the loyalty of radical intelligentsia and workers. Marxism, in a far more deliberate and sophisticated way, was explicitly cognizant of the oppressed condition of women and designated them, along with the proletariat, as the beneficiaries of the coming socialist society. This was not simply a bit of humanitarian fluff dangling from the periphery of the theory. It was woven into the Marxist analysis, although Marxist theoreticians did not spend a vast amount of time and energy on the issue. The basic canons consist of Frederick Engels's *The Origins of the Family, Private Property and the State* (1883) and August Bebel's *Woman Under Socialism* (1879). Both works were elaborations of scattered references in Marx's writings.[26]

According to an important strand in Marxist thought, women were the first proletarians. The capitalist organization of production, and the division of labor fundamental to it, separated male from female labor in a new way. Men were drawn away from home and artisanal production into wage labor in capitalist enterprises. Women, excluded from wage labor outside the home and deprived of access to earnings, became dependent on and therefore exploited by men, just as the proletariat, deprived of the ownership of the means of production, was dependent on and exploited by the bourgeoisie. Women survived by exchanging their

26. For an excellent analysis of Marxists on women, see Alfred G. Meyer, "Marxism and the Women's Movement," in D. Atkinson, A. Dallin, and G. Lapidus, *Women in Russia* (Stanford, 1977). See also Sheila Rowbotham, *Women, Resistance and Revolution* (New York, 1974).

domestic services (and bodies) for subsistence provided them by their husbands. This, said Marx, Engels, and Bebel, determined the nature of marriage in bourgeois society, which they found a disgusting spectacle of the commercialization of the relations between the sexes. Prostitution was only a blatant and possibly more honest expression of the position of women in capitalist society. As women were not intended to perform productive labor, they were not educated or trained. They spent their days confined to their homes in endlessly repetitive and unproductive domestic tasks; their minds were dulled and their intellectual development retarded.

But capitalism also created important distinctions among women along class lines. Working-class women were the victims of a double oppression. Like women of all classes, they were held in bondage by men, and like all workers, they were exploited by capitalists. Further, capitalism took advantage of the submissive and unskilled woman by paying her less. In a vicious circle, these factors contrived to keep women workers unskilled, conservative, and "backward." However, the portent of progress was inherent in their dismal condition. Working-class women were more independent than bourgeois women because they earned their own keep, and for that reason they had a more equal position within the working-class family. In the factory they became aware of the source of their exploitation just as men did and were thus drawn into the proletarian army. Herein lay their salvation; to work side by side with men for the destruction of class society, which would eliminate all forms of exploitation. The new socialist society would create the conditions for the complete emancipation of women. Child care and domestic tasks would be socialized in nurseries, laundries, food services, and the like, and women would be free to spend their lives in productive labor as part of the universal proletariat which owned the means of production.

Marxists did not speak precisely in unison. Engels was more interested in tracing the historical development of the woman's position from prehistorical epochs, and barely dis-

cussed the details of their contemporary position. When he
did, his conclusions about working-class women were rather
a statement of what ought to be: "And now that large-scale
industry has taken the wife out of the home and onto the
labor market and into the factory, and made her often the
breadwinner of the family, no basis for any kind of male
supremacy is left in the proletarian household, except, perhaps, for something of the brutality toward women that has
spread since the introduction of monogamy."[27] Bebel, however, utilizing an extraordinary range of contemporary
studies on women's biology, sexuality, law, work, and attitudes, wrote in great detail on many facets of the women's
position in his own day. Often he indulged in the same
fantasy about the egalitarian nature of working-class families. But just as often he perceived that even working-class
men savored the advantages that patriarchy offered them.
Following a particularly grim picture of factory conditions
for both husband and wife, he described the working-class
family's life at home after work. The husband, weary and
irritable, takes himself off to the saloon, where he relaxes in
drink and gaming. The wife, also weary and irritable, must
nonetheless apply herself to a multitude of domestic and
child-care tasks: "She must work like a drayhorse; for her
there is no rest or recreation; the husband avails himself of
the freedom that accident gives him, of having been born a
man."[28] To be sure, Bebel hopes that "more favorable relations between husband and wife spring up in the ranks of
the working class in that measure that both realize they are
tugging at the same rope,"[29] but he acknowledges that even
men with the most advanced consciousness are not necessarily free of negative attitudes toward women:

> There are socialists who are not less opposed to the emancipa-
> tion of women than the capitalist to socialism. Every socialist

27. Frederick Engels, *The Origins of the Family, Private Property and the State*
(New York, 1972), p. 135.
28. August Bebel, *Woman Under Socialism* (New York, 1971), p. 103.
29. Ibid., p. 115.

recognizes the dependence of the workman on the capitalist . . . but the same socialist often does not recognize the dependence of women on men, because the question touches his own dear self more or less nearly.[30]

Despite their differences, Engles and Bebel agreed on several basic points. Under capitalism bourgeois women could make some piecemeal advances: they could get the vote, they could get more access to higher education and the right to work in certain professions. These gains were as good as nothing for working-class women. True, the working class could wrest from the bourgeoisie some minimal protective legislation for women workers: limitations on working hours, prohibition of work in dangerous industries, maternity benefits. But real emancipation for women was predicated on the success of the socialist revolution.

And here is the rub. The woman question, like racism and nationalism, derived from the exploitation of the proletariat by capital. For the proletariat a solution to the woman question could not exist apart from struggle to emancipate the entire proletariat. As a derivative phenomenon, it could be resolved only after the first cause was eliminated. To be sure, the working class should be made conscious of the woman question as one example of the consequences of class exploitation. But it was illusory and harmful to expend time and energy on resolving it under capitalist conditions: illusory because it could not be done, and harmful because it divided proletarian women from proletarian men when they should be working together to topple the capitalist order. Women would be emancipated after the revolution—and not one day before.

The founding fathers of Marxism were not generous with suggestions on how to involve backward women workers in the process of building the revolution that would emancipate them, in part because the analysis of the woman question was so abstract. More important than the abstrac-

---

30. August Bebel, *Women in the Past, Present and Future* (San Francisco, 1897), p. 85. In subsequent editions this passage was deleted.

tion, although intimately related to it, was that for Marxists consciousness began at the point of production. They assumed that the worker's experience at the workplace was sufficiently powerful to neutralize and overcome all previous acculturation. In the factory the submissive, timid, and backward woman could automatically develop the requisite class consciousness, and the working-class man would inevitably shed his patriarchal prejudices. The closest the early Marxists came to acknowledging that something more might be needed was to exhort men to "enlighten the woman on her position in society, and to educate her into a fellow combatant in the struggle for the emancipation of the proletariat from capitalism."[31]

Other Marxists, contemporaneous with and subsequent to Engels and Bebel, elaborated on the original pronouncements. Marx's daughter, Eleanor Marx Aveling, agreed with her father and his colleagues that the emancipation of women was contingent on the success of the revolution. But another kind of sensitivity prompted her (and her husband) to point out that "women are the creatures of an organized tyranny of men as workers are the creatures of an organized tyranny of idlers . . . the one [women] has nothing to hope from man as a whole, as the other [workers] has nothing to hope from the middle class as a whole."[32] The German Social Democrat Lily Braun wrote copiously on the emancipation of women as *process* rather than as a sudden transformation by revolutionary magic. She believed that it was necessary and possible to create the preconditions of women's equality in the present and made concrete proposals to free women workers from the double burden of domestic and work obligations in the form of communal households.[33] The German Social Democratic party dismissed her suggestions as excessively feminist, but permitted other Social Democratic women to build a wide and

31. Bebel, *Woman Under Socialism*, p. 90.
32. Eleanor Marx and Edward Aveling, "The Woman Question," *Marxism Today* (1972), March, p. 82. First published in 1887.
33. Lily Braun, *Frauenarbeit und Hauswirtschaft* (Berlin, 1901).

reasonably effective network for recruiting women into Social Democratic activity.[34] Thus, by the time the Russian
revolutionary movement embraced Marxism there were
theoretical and practical alternatives upon which to model
tactics for involving women workers. Most Russian Marxists
chose to adhere rigidly and simplistically to the most abstract elements of an already abstract theory. To be sure,
tactics and priorities were guided not only by theoretical
debates but hammered out in the course of daily struggle as
well. In the absence of a legal and open forum, the formation of a mass movement was undertaken by a tiny group of
dedicated revolutionaries beset by the extreme danger of
engaging in illegal political activity. If in practice Russian
Marxists neglected what their guiding theory in any case
regarded as an important but derivative problem, they were
not unique among Marxists—perhaps just extreme.[35]

The Russian Marxists did not put pen to paper to spell
out their position on women workers until 1899. With the
leisure provided by exile in Siberia, Lenin encouraged his
wife, Nadezhda Krupskaia, to write a brochure on women
workers. It was published illegally as *The Woman Worker*
[Zhenshchina-rabotnitsa] in 1901 and legally in 1905 under
her pen name, Sablina. It was neither original nor a particularly interesting restatement of the basic Marxist position.
She left out all the details and embellishments in Engels,
Bebel, and others and offered the reader the bare bones of
the argument. In simple language she explained the relations between capitalist and worker and pointed out that
since women workers, no less and probably more than men,
were victims of capitalist exploitation, their only hope for
equality and justice was to join men in the workers' struggle.
She vividly and sympathetically catalogued the woman
worker's awesome burdens, in and out of the factory, as

34. See Jean Quataert, *Reluctant Feminists in German Social Democracy, 1885–
1917* (Princeton, 1979).
35. For a discussion of the way European Marxist parties dealt with the
woman question, see Marilyn J. Boxer and Jean H. Quataert, eds., *Socialist Women:
European Socialist Feminism in the Nineteenth and Early Twentieth Centuries* (New York,
1978).

worker and as mother. But: "We have seen that no matter how difficult work in the factory is for the woman, it has its bright side: independent earnings liberate the woman from the man's control."[36] She repeated Engels's fantasy about the position of women workers in the family, where, as a result of her alleged economic independence, she was an equal partner.

Here the argument becomes confused and contradictory, for Krupskaia, Janus-like, turned one face to the male reader and another to the female, contorting her argument accordingly. Surely the woman reader must have wondered where Krupskaia got the information, repeated several times in the article, that "where women's labor has become customary, for example in cotton spinning and weaving, women's wages are only insignificantly lower than men's. . . . Where women do piecework . . . they earn barely less than men."[37] This distortion of reality was necessary to support Krupskaia's fundamental point that participation in productive labor made women independent of men, that therefore the enemy of women's emancipation was not male tyranny but capitalist tyranny. When she addressed the potential male reader, however, Krupskaia turned reality around: "Women normally receive much lower wages than men. Therefore, factory owners are eager to bring them into the factory, sometimes replacing male labor with women workers." The point of this contradiction was to convince the "many [male] workers [who] would like to legally prohibit female labor in the factory" that men would not be rehired to replace cheap female labor.[38] The latter would simply be replaced by even cheaper machines. Instead of trying to push women out of the factory, male workers should demand equal pay for equal work.

Krupskaia's strategy for enticing women into the workers' movement consisted of reproaching them for hindering

36. N. K. Krupskaia, "Zhenshchina-rabotnitsa," *Pedagogicheskie sochineniia*, t. 1, (Moscow, 1957), p. 97.
37. Ibid., p. 78.
38. Ibid., p. 99.

conscious male workers with their hostility and of correcting the mistaken view of men who thought that women "should not participate in the struggle for the workers' cause [because] they do not have the intellect for it; it would be better if only men carried on the struggle." However, she encouraged men to accept women as their comrades, not in the name of egalitarianism, but because to isolate women "is to leave half the workers' army unorganized, to obstruct the success of the revolution."[39]

The book ends with the protective legislation that workers should demand, taken from the resolutions of the 1897 International Workers' Congress in Switzerland: prohibition of night work and of work in dangerous industries, the eight-hour day, and paid maternity leave.[40] The same demands reappeared in the resolutions of the historic Second Congress of the Russian Social Democratic Revolutionary Party in 1903, preceded by the explanation that the party made these demands "in the interest of guarding the working class from physical and moral degeneration and . . . of the development of its ability to participate in the struggle for liberation."[41] Thus, by the turn of the century the Russian Marxists had left the direct interests of women workers by the wayside, in theory as well as practice. Women workers were reduced to keeping the working class healthy for the sake of the success of the revolution.

* * *

Russian Marxists and Populists, other serious disagreements notwithstanding, agreed that the emancipation of women would be achieved only as a corollary to the total transformation of society. The practical consequences of this fundamental conviction was the subordination of concern for women in the present to the task of building for the revolution in the future. Both movements attracted ex-

---

39. Ibid., p. 84.
40. Ibid., p. 100–101.
41. *KPSS v resoliutsiakh i resheniiakh s'ezdov, konferentsii i plenumov,* chast' 1 (Moscow, 1953), p. 41.

traordinary numbers of women. The history of Populist women is well known. The story of Marxist women has yet to be told, but the most cursory glance at the sources reveals that large numbers of educated women were drawn to Marxism and actively participated in all facets of revolutionary activity, although their numbers dwindled markedly at the crowning heights of theoretical and organizational work.[42] Yet neither Populist women, who came directly out of the feminist ferment of the 1860s, nor Marxist women, whose guiding theory explicitly acknowledged the condition of women workers, sought to involve women of the working classes in the process of making the revolution. The women among the Populist and Marxist intelligentsia were, with few exceptions, of the educated and possessing classes. They had themselves achieved a greater, if not perfect, equality in the socialist milieu than they could have found elsewhere in Russian society. It may well be that their own social origins and the degree of equality they experienced left them satisfied with the promise of emancipation of other women after the revolution.

There was less and less interaction between feminists and socialist women as the nineteenth century wore on. In the 1870s and 1880s the divergent paths they chose engendered no hostility; if anything, they regarded one another with some respect. By the 1890s the feminists were encapsulated in concerns for women of their own strata, and the revolutionaries in clandestine revolutionary activity. The spheres of feminist and socialist activity rarely overlapped, and there were no areas of competition. The events of 1905 broke the seal and provoked open and hostile confrontation precisely over the women that both groups had hitherto ignored.

42. See, for example, V. I. Nevskii, *Materialy dlia biograficheskogo slovaria sotsial-demokratov, vstupivshikh v rossiiskoe rabochee dvizhenie za period ot 1880–1905 g*, vyp. 1, A–D (Moscow and Leningrad, 1923); A. A. Osinkin, "Ivanovo-Voznesensk. Sovet rabochikh deputatov v 1905," *Voprosy Istorii KPSS*, t. 65 (1965), no. 4, p. 68; N. K. Krupskaia, "Piat' let raboty v vechernikh smolenskikh klassakh," in *Pedagogicheskie sochineniia*, t. 1, p. 55.

8

BETWEEN FEMINISM AND SOCIALISM

In the five decades between the emergence of the woman question in the thoughts and activities of educated society and 1905 a substantial female intelligentsia had evolved: doctors, feldshers, pharmacists, teachers, writers, as well as educated women without specific professions and careers. This generation was the offspring of its predecessors' success in making higher education and professional work more accessible for women. Yet, Russia's *intelligentki,* like women of all strata, still chafed under the weight of law and tradition which perpetuated great obstacles to further emancipation and to equality with men. It is not surprising then that in 1905 the voice of women could be heard in the great chorus of protest against the old regime.[1] Like other elements in society which opposed the autocratic order, feminists came together in organizations, in their case mainly to influence government and society to grant women the vote. The anticipated elections to the Duma, Russia's first elected parliament, evoked in Russian women the same desire for an equal vote with men, which their European and American counterparts had long coveted and were struggling to attain. This was, and remained, the Russian feminists' most abiding concern. But the younger generation of feminists brought to the women's movement new perspectives and

1. For the Russian feminist movement from 1905 to 1917, see Linda Edmondson, *Feminism in Russia, 1900–1917* (London, 1983); Rochelle Goldberg, "The Russian Women's Movement," Ph.D. diss., University of Rochester, 1976; Stites, *The Women's Liberation Movement in Russia,* chaps. 7–8.

sensitivities. Although their social origins placed them firmly above the working classes of Russia, fewer of them were of gentry origin, and they had a deeper and more realistic interest in peasant and factory women. Thus in 1905 and 1906 the feminist horizon expanded far beyond the franchise to embrace a multitude of aspirations and concerns that attracted and excited peasant women and factory women as well. It was over the allegiance of such women that feminists and socialists were brought into direct confrontation.

A month after Bloody Sunday a small group of liberal women in Moscow organized the All-Russian Union for Women's Equal Rights (Vserossiiskii Soiuz Ravnopraviia Zhenshchin). Branches soon sprouted throughout the empire. Women of the St Petersburg branch went into the factories to help women workers formulate their protest against exclusion from the Shidlovskii committees. Subsequently, a prominent male Bolshevik worker-activist sneered at the "slavish and respectful" tone of the petition, which "wrapped protest in the form of a hope . . . that Shidlovskii's decision [to exclude women workers] was not final," and recognized in this the hand of bourgeois women.[2] But, as we saw in chapter six, neither socialists nor male workers took the slightest notice of the exclusion of women workers nor offered support to them.[3]

Within the next two months the *ravnopravki* (as the members of the Equal Rights Union were called) organized a union of women domestic servants in Moscow and made plans to establish an employment bureau and political clubs for women workers.[4] The employment bureau did not materialize, but by the spring of 1906 there were four women's

2. V. Perazich, "Tekstil'shchiki v Komissii Shidlovskogo," *Krasnaia Letopis'* (1930), 6 (9), p. 48. See also A. Kollontai, *K istorii dvizheniia rabotnits v Rossii* (Khar'kov, 1920), p. 7.

3. See text at n. 5 in chap. six.

4. A. Kollontai, *Sotsial'nye osnovy zhenskogo voprosa* (St Petersburg, 1909), pp. 302–304, 314–315; N. Mirovich, *Iz istorii zhenskogo dvizheniia v Rossii* (Moscow, 1908), pp. 22–27; *Obshcheprofessional'nye organy, 1905–1907 gg*, vyp. 1: Moskovskie zhurnaly 1905 goda (Moscow, 1926), p. 42.

political clubs in St Petersburg. Composed mainly of *intelli-gentki*, socialist and feminist, the clubs attracted women workers as well, especially on Vasilev Island, a district with many factories employing women. Unfortunately, the clubs were closed by the police in the repressive atmosphere fol-lowing the dissolution of the First Duma in July.[5]

The *ravnopravki* reached out to peasant women as well, supporting equal land rights and, of course, equal voting rights for peasant women. Under the influence of vigorous branches in the provinces, peasant women from Iaroslavl and Voronezh provinces sent two remarkable petitions to the First Duma protesting the statement made by a peasant deputy to the Duma that peasant women were not inter-ested in the vote:

> We read in the newspaper that Kruglikov, the delegate from Voronzeh, announced in the Duma that peasant men only ac-knowledged women's work in the family and claim that women themselves do not want any rights. There are no women dele-gates in the Duma who could speak for the women, so how does he know? He is wrong, as he would know if he had asked us. We, the women from Voronezh province . . . understand well that we need rights and land just as men do.[6]

In addition, the Equal Rights Union and other feminist groups launched and sustained a feverish campaign for the vote. They sent literally hundreds of letters to governors of provinces, to city and county governing bodies, to ministers, to the leaders of the coalescing political parties. They circu-lated petition after petition for equal voting rights, signed by thousands of women, including great numbers of women workers.[7] The large number of women workers who signed these petitions clearly showed that the appeal of the equal vote was by no means limited to women of the middle and upper strata.

The *ravnopravki* did not limit their involvement with

5. Kollontai, *Sots. osnovy*, p. 24; Goldberg, p. 110.
6. Mirovich, pp. 47–49.
7. Kollontai, *Sots. osnovy*, pp. 303–306, 345; Stites, pp. 198–210.

working-class issues to women workers, however. They took part in radical demonstrations and came out openly in support of workers' strikes. They opened dining rooms and first-aid detachments, raised impressive sums of money to aid the strike movement, striking and unemployed workers, political exiles and prisoners. In petitions and demonstrations they demanded amnesty for political prisoners and abolition of the death penalty.[8]

The feminists' broad range of sympathies and activities was rewarded when over a thousand women attended Russia's first all women's meeting. Convened in St Petersburg in April 1905, the meeting was attended not only by well-known and rank-and-file feminists, but by Socialist women as well. Some Bolshevik, Menshevik, and Social Revolutionary women were, at this moment, sympathetic to a platform that would unite women of all classes and political allegiances, and "women workers, stirred up by the great events of the moment . . . flooded into the meeting looking for a place for themselves [as well]."[9] Only one dissonant note was sounded at this otherwise euphoric assembly of disparate women seeking a way to work together for common interests. Aleksandra Kollontai spoke boldly against the "idyll of cooperation between revolutionary socialist women and bourgeois feminists." She was not well received. As she later recounted:

> My speech was greeted by a storm of indignation. They yelled at me that I was "playing into the hands of the Black Hundreds, . . . and indulging in hooliganism. . . ." Only one woman worker, a former Gaponovite, supported me.[10]

Kollontai spoke for the Social Democratic theoretical position, but not for its practice. Socialist *intelligentki* and women workers were drawn to feminists because their nat-

---

8. Kollontai, *Sots. osnovy*, pp. 314–315; Mirovich, pp. 23–27.
9. Aleksandra Kollontai, *Iz moei zhizni i raboty: vospominaniia i dnevniki* (Moscow, 1974), p. 101. The women socialists that Kollontai names are Bazarova and Anna Gurevich—Bolsheviks; M. Margulies—Menshevik; and O. Volkenshtein—Socialist Revolutionary.
10. Ibid.

ural allies, the socialist parties, refused to acknowledge the validity of women's aspirations. In Kollontai's words:

> In those days the party did not carry out systematic work among women workers. With the exception of the pamphlet by Sablina [Krupskaia], there was no underground work. I recall that soon after Vera Zasulich arrived in Russia I went to see her specifically to discuss how to conduct work among women workers, where to begin. But she gave me not the slightest support. She considered the endeavor unnecessary, even harmful.[11]

Kollontai was a complex and fascinating woman who defies tidy categorization.[12] She was Russia's most outspoken—sometimes the only—proponent of a socialist women's movement dedicated to the needs and organization of women workers. But Kollontai was in equal parts a passionate and sophisticated feminist and Social Democrat. As sensitive as the feminists to the nuances of women's subjugation which underlay and transcended Marxian economic categories, she was nonetheless convinced that working-class women could achieve equality only as a consequence of socialism. Given the indifference, even hostility, of organized social democracy to incorporating the woman question within a socialist framework, Kollontai found herself fighting on two fronts. She struggled to breathe life into Marxist rhetoric, to transform the promise of future emancipation for women into palpable concern for and organization of women workers in the present. But, perceiving in the blossoming feminism of 1905 a competitor for the loyalties of socialist women and women workers, she struggled simultaneously to expose the false promises, as she saw them, of

11. Ibid., p. 104. Vera Zasulich was a famous Populist of the 1870s. Tried and acquitted for the attempted assassination of the governor of St Petersburg, she later eschewed violence and became an unswerving follower of Plekhanov. See Stites, passim; Barbara Engel and Clifford Rosenthall, eds., *Five Sisters: Women Against the Tsar* (New York, 1975); Vera Zasulich, *Vospominaniia* (Moscow, 1931).

12. Kollontai's life and fortunes have been treated in detail. See Barbara Evans Clements, *Bolshevik Feminist: The Life of Aleksandra Kollontai* (Bloomington, Ind., 1979); Beatrice Farnsworth, *Aleksandra Kollontai: Socialism, Feminism, and the Bolshevik Revolution* (Stanford, 1980).

feminism to satisfy the needs of women workers. To the extent that the conflict between socialists and feminists which had raged for almost half a century in Europe was modestly recapitulated in Russia, it was due largely to Kollontai.

Undaunted by the indifference of her socialist colleagues to the threat of feminism in 1905, Kollontai continued to speak in their name and "absolutely wherever possible to defend the position that for social democracy there can be no separate woman question," to "popularize the principles of socialism in connection with the task of multifaceted emancipation of women."[13] Although she complained that women workers were an evanescent presence in the factories and neighborhood meetings at which she spoke, there were soon signs of women workers' dissatisfaction with feminist formulations. In May 1906 a large meeting of women was held in St Petersburg. Organized by the Equal Rights Union and several other feminist organizations, it was attended by a great many socialist women as well as feminists. A Menshevik woman, M. N. Margulies, was chosen to be presiding officer. The goal of the meeting was an agreement on practical action in support of the vote for women. Divisions among feminists were already emerging and expressed at this meeting, but the fundamental division was between feminists and socialists. In the words of one feminist participant:

> The Social Democrats took the upper hand and turned it from a women's meeting into a Social Democratic meeting. . . . In the opinion of the Social Democrats, only they acknowledge the equal rights of women. But what happened at the meeting proved just the opposite. Thanks to their speeches and to the support of the women workers, who of course listened hungrily to speeches about socialism—which is supposed to create heaven on earth—and about the proletariat—which is supposed to save the world—the Social Democrats undermined the women's meeting and destroyed its ability to do what it had set

---

13. Aleksandra Kollontai, "Avtobiograficheskii ocherk," *Proletarskaia Revoliutsiia* (1921), no. 3, p. 271.

out to do. The proposals to send telegrams to Duma members who support equal rights for women . . . were voted down.[14]

Encouraging as this was to Kollontai, it did not compensate for Social Democratic apathy toward women workers. There was still no sign of Social Democratic commitment to consistent, organized work among women, and the threat of feminist divisiveness remained as powerful as before.

In the autumn of 1906 Kollontai attended a congress of the German Social Democratic Party in Mannheim. There she met with Klara Zetkin and other German Social Democratic women who had successfully organized a separate organization for women workers within the German party. Armed with the German example, she once again approached the Russian Social Democratic Party in St Petersburg for support in taking a first modest step toward organizing women workers under party auspices. Party workers greeted her zeal "with skepticism and indifference. There were some, especially old party women revolutionaries who saw in my proposal a 'dangerous tendency to feminism.' "[15] Kollontai persevered and finally persuaded the Petersburg Committee to provide a place for a first meeting:

> But when several of us assembled at the place for the women workers' meeting not only was the door locked, but someone had attached a deliberately rude note: "The meeting *for women only* is cancelled. Tomorrow there will be a meeting *for men only.*"[16]

When Kollontai went to the Petersburg Committee for an explanation, she found that

> formally, the comrades did not forbid our initiative but they would not support it. More accurately, no one was interested in it. And the threat from the bourgeois feminists had grown. Women Social Revolutionaries joined with and supported

14. "Zhenskii miting," *Zhenskii Vestnik* (1906), no. 5, p. 155. See also, Kollontai, *Sots. osnovy*, p. 426.
15. Kollontai, "Avtobiograficheskii ocherk," p. 271.
16. Ibid., p. 272.

them. The bourgeois women published journals and brochures, held meetings, and attracted women workers and peasants from the provinces with the help of the petition to the State Duma [for equal voting rights]. A counterthrust was necessary. We had lost the *kursistki*, the female working intelligentsia, and had not developed a firm base among women workers.[17]

Once again spurned by the party, Kollontai looked for support elsewhere and found it in the Menshevik-dominated St Petersburg Textile Union. She was not entirely satisfied with this affiliation. Through the union she could reach only women workers who were already conscious and not the masses of women workers she aspired to influence. Nonetheless, she rejoiced in the formation of a small core of about five women workers, who worked with her steadily to organize lectures for women workers and to form a club called the Women Workers' Mutual Aid Society. The Petersburg Committee recognized the club but refused to help with either financial or human resources. In the first months of its year-long existence the club numbered three hundred women, of which one hundred were workers. Relations between the socialist *intelligentki* and the women workers were far from harmonious: the former reproached the club for a "tendency toward feminism" and the latter wished to kick out the *intelligentki*.[18]

By 1907, as the liberation movement in general lost momentum and the government grew bolder and more repressive, the great range of social issues that had commanded the interests and resources of feminist organizations dwindled. Feminists began a slow shift toward purely feminist issues, most important among them the vote. Paradoxically, as feminists achieved greater solidarity over central issues, they drew apart on tactics. The majority of feminists believed their best chance of getting the vote lay in allying with and pressuring the liberals in the Duma, represented

17. Ibid.
18. Ibid., p. 273; Aleksandra Kollontai, *K istorii dvizheniia rabotnits v Rossii*, pp. 16–17.

by the Kadet party. Others regarded any kind of alliance
with men a lost cause. The most extreme among them was
M. I. Pokrovskaia, caricatured by Kollontai as the most conservative of feminists. However, Pokrovskaia is as difficult
to categorize as Kollontai was herself. Unquestionably conservative on some important political issues, Pokrovskaia
had a broad and sophisticated social perspective and an
unswerving concern for women workers, which led her to
expose mercilessly the flaws in socialist mythology of
women workers. It was for this reason that Kollontai singled
her out for especially vitriolic attacks.

In the decade before the 1905 revolution when Social
Democrats said little and did nothing about women
workers, and feminists satisfied themselves with philanthropy, Pokrovskaia, a doctor, practiced among St Petersburg's workers, conducted independent studies of workers'
conditions with special emphasis on women workers, and
tried to present the realities of the factory woman's life to
the attention of anyone who would listen: women of her
own station, her medical colleagues, and the government.[19]
In 1905 she proved to be an iconoclast among feminists,
breaking away from them to form her own Women's Progressive Party and publishing the party's mouthpiece, *Zhenskii Vestnik*, until 1914.

Although Pokrovskaia espoused a vague kind of socialism,
she turned away from socialists as well. In her opinion, the
"selfish possessors of capital" were mankind's greatest enemy, but she did not trust Social Democrats to improve the
condition of women workers.[20] Socialism, she accused, "glis-

---

19. M. I. Pokrovskaia, *Novoe Slovo* (1894), no. 10; "Zhenskii trud po ustroistvu
zhilishch dlia bednykh za granitsei," *Vestnik Evropy* (1898), kn. 8; "Peterburgskie
rabochie i ikh ekonomicheskoe polozhenie," *Vestnik Evropy* (1899), kn. 3; "Peterburgskie voskresnye sobraniia dlia rabotnits," *Mir Bozhii* (1899), no. 3; "Peterburgskaia rabotnitsa," *Mir Bozhii* (1900), no. 12; "Vopros o deshevykh kvartirakh dlia
rabochego klassa," *Vestnik Evropy* (1901), kn. 7; "Obshchestvo popecheniia o molodykh devitsakh v SPb," *Trudy vserossiiskogo s'ezda po remeslennoi promyshlennosti* (St
Petersburg, 1901), t. 3; *Kak ia byla gorodskim vrachem dlia bednykh* (St Petersburg,
1903); *Vrachebno-politseiskii nadzor za prostitutsiei sposobstvuet vyrozhdeniiu naroda* (St
Petersburg, 1902).
20. *Zhenskii Vestnik* (1906), no. 6, p. 175.

tens in the beautiful future; [but] daily life makes itself felt at every step."[21] In daily life Pokrovskaia perceived that socialists were no more concerned with women's equality than were liberals, that indeed socialist and liberal parties (both dominated by men) shared a fundamental duplicity on women's issues. One of her favorite examples was the issue of night work for women. Pokrovskaia believed that the consequences of prohibiting night work for women were simply to diminish their ability to get work, to deprive them of higher wages, and in many cases, to push them into prostitution. If men are so concerned with the harmful effects of night work, why, she asked, do they not "prohibit that night work that destroys the female organism—prostitution? O male hypocrisy! No! Better night work in any harmful industry than the torture of the house of prostitution."[22] The concern for the health of women workers that was allegedly the reason for prohibiting night work was simply a smoke screen:

> The woman [worker's] health must be protected, they reason, to allow women to bear healthy children . . . and to give women time to cater to their husbands' comfort. Thus, the protection of women's work is preached not for the sake of the spiritual and physical health *of the woman herself*, but in the name of state, sexual, and family goals. The woman requires protection, not as a person but as a sexual apparatus, as a slave obligated to serve the needs of others (emphasis Pokrovskaia's).[23]

This kind of analysis, of course, offended both socialists and liberals. From the Social Democratic perspective, worse was to come. Pokrovskaia challenged the Marxian axiom that the industrialization process altered the workers' consciousness. Like Bebel before her, "I often observed, as a doctor in St Petersburg, . . . how the male worker returning from work reads the newspaper, chats with friends, goes to the tavern, while his wife [also a worker] cooks, washes, and

21. Ibid. (1913), no. 10, p. 208.
22. Ibid. (1906), no. 5, pp. 162–163.
23. Ibid. (1906), no. 5, p. 148.

nurses."[24] Further, Pokrovskaia took an undeviating stand
against the strike movement:

> We applaud the heroism of fathers and husbands [in the strike
> movement]. But at the same time we assert that they play the
> hero . . . at the expense of mothers and wives . . . who day in
> and day out, from morning until night, remain with their hun-
> gry children, their hearts torn by the children's cries. We ask,
> who bears the main burden of strikes? Wives and mothers. And
> men have the nerve to call women conservative when they try
> to keep their husbands from striking. Let men sit home with
> children during the hunger that results from strikes and give
> their wives the freedom to get away from the children's tears of
> hunger. Perhaps then they will not so cavalierly reproach
> women with conservatism.[25]

Pokrovskaia agreed with the socialists that "the proletarian woman has many interests in common with the entire
working class, and it is necessary for her to fight with all
workers for the improvement of its position." But, she added, "in this struggle she must not forget her lack of rights as
a woman. . . . She can devote herself to the class struggle
only when she is equal to male workers."[26] A vigorous advo-
cate of unionization as one of the greatest weapons in the
emancipation of the working class in general and women
workers in particular, she pointed out that under the existing state of sexual relations women would not find much
joy in men's unions. Her repeated call to women workers to
form their own separate unions, like her position on strikes,
made her anathema to the Social Democrats.[27]

*   *   *

Until 1908 socialists and feminists had argued among
themselves and with each other at meetings, in clubs, and

24. Ibid. (1905), no. 5, p. 147.
25. Ibid. (1905), no. 12, p. 354. For Kollontai's response to Pokrovskaia's anti-
strike position, see *Sots. osnovy,* p. 332.
26. *Zhenskii Vestnik* (1913), no. 3, pp. 67–68.
27. Ibid. (1906), no. 12, pp. 338–341; (1906), no. 11, pp. 269–270; (1912), no.
7–9, pp. 58–59; (1913), no. 12, pp. 203–209.

on the pages of the feminist press. The socialist press had not participated in the debates. An event in 1908 provided an arena for a great mutual washing of dirty linen in public. The proceedings of the First All-Russian Women's Congress, held December 10–16, exposed not only the fundamental conflict between feminists and socialists, but the conflicts within each camp as well.[28]

The initiator of the Congress was the Russian Women's Mutual Philanthropic Society, which had been organized in 1895 by feminist luminaries of the older generation. The Society petitioned the authorities for a women's congress in 1902, when liberal opposition to the autocracy was in its first tentative stages of bloom, and again in 1905. Finally, in 1908, when many of the aspirations of 1905 had been squashed, "The First All-Russian Congress [appeared] like an original and bright spot against the background of the grey monotony of Russian reality."[29] To the astonishment of the Organizing Committee, instead of the anticipated two hundred participants, over a thousand women registered. The great majority were of the "*raznochinnaia* intelligentsia," women descended from Russia's middle stratum of the so-called free professions: doctors, lawyers, writers, teachers, and artists. About half the women in this group were self-supporting women in these professions. At one extreme was a far smaller group of well-born ladies who belonged primarily but not exclusively to the Organizing Committee and were either themselves philanthropic feminists of the past era or spiritually descended from them. At the other extreme was the Workers' Group, consisting of about thirty women workers and ten radical *intelligentki*, Bolshevik, Menshevik, Socialist Revolutionary, and according to one source, some syndicalists.[30]

28. For discussions of the First All-Russian Women's Congress, see Goldberg, chap. 4, and Linda Edmondson, "Russian Feminists and the First All-Russian Congress of Women," *Russian History* (1976), vol. 3, pt. 2.

29. M. B., "Vserossiiskii zhenskii s'ezd i rabochaia gruppa," *Professional'nyi Soiuz* (1909), no. 21, p. 16.

30. Chlen P. K. [Member, Petersburg Committee], "Rabochaia gruppa na zhenskom s'ezde i sotsial-demokratiia," *Sotsialdemokrat* (1909), no. 4, p. 8; A. Ermanskii, "Vserossiiskii zhenskii s'ezd," *Sovremennyi Mir* (1909), no. 1, pp. 103–105.

The feminists invited women workers to participate through the trade unions and waived the five-ruble registration fee for them. The St Petersburg Textile Union took up the question of sending a delegation of women workers to the Congress and passed it on to the Central Bureau of Unions.[31] It was opposed by some on the grounds that exposure to a bourgeois congress would seduce women workers and confuse their class consciousness. The proponents of a delegation of women workers claimed that, on the contrary, women workers would gain experience and enthusiasm for participation in workers' organizations. The ayes won, and the Central Bureau of Unions began to organize.

In the meantime, the unflagging Kollontai approached the Social Democratic party for permission to organize a delegation of women workers, arguing that it would have "collossal educational value for the female proletarian masses." When the party refused to support what it called a tendency within the party to feminism, Kollontai joined with the Central Bureau of Unions.

Between the spring and December of 1908 the Central Bureau held forty meetings of women workers from a variety of industries: textile workers, waitresses, candy makers, tailors, printing workers, tobacco workers, rubber workers, and domestic servants. The Bureau estimated that the forty meetings attracted about six hundred women workers. The initial meetings were in the form of lectures or discussion on topics such as women in the factory, medical insurance, prostitution, the feminist movement, and the workers' movement. The final meetings decided the methods of choosing delegates from among the unions, workers' clubs, and *intelligentki*. At that point the Petersburg Committee, now the Bolshevik center of the fractionalized Social Democratic party, decided to support the effort and appointed Vera Slutskaia and a male Bolshevik to supervise. The irony in this choice was that Slutskaia, a prominent woman Bolshevik, had been

31. The following discussion of the preparation of a women workers' delegation is taken from M. B., pp. 16–18; Kollontai, *K istorii dvizhenii rabotnits*, p. 18; "Avtobiograficheskii ocherk," pp. 273–279; *Iz moei zhizni*, pp. 111–112.

among the most adamant opponents of a delegation of women workers. She was quite superfluous, however, since the organizing work had already been done. Although with one hand the Petersburg Committee approved the delegation, with the other it circulated a brochure on the Congress, encouraging women workers *not* to attend. But, Kollontai added in her recollection, "When the Petersburg Committee was convinced that we could influence a backward element, they were persuaded to withdraw their position and began working in concert with us."[32] Or, in plainer language, when the women workers' group was a fait accompli, the Bolsheviks wished to ensure that the women workers would pursue a course of unequivocal opposition to solidarity with feminists. As Kollontai put it, "Under our influence [women workers] developed hostility to the *ravnopravki* and an inclination to the Party."[33]

Events at the Congress proved that, indeed, the Workers' Group had a principled "inclination" to the Social Democratic approach to women's emancipation, though not necessarily to the Social Democratic party. But they did not manifest consistent hostility to the feminists. An article written on the eve of the Congress in the Textile Union's journal foretold the conflicts that would emerge within the Group during the Congress. The author of the article was an anonymous woman, whether worker or *intelligentka* is not clear. Throughout the article she reiterated that the struggle for emancipation of the entire proletariat was the woman worker's fundamental commitment and task. At the same time, the author left room for the possibility that all women, regardless of class, had some common problems and goals.

> On December 10 there will be women's conference. There will be women teachers, doctors, writers, plenty of them. And each will discuss her own problems. Their lives are not sweet either. We women workers must send our own to represent us. Let

32. Kollontai, "Avtobiograficheskii ocherk," p. 279.
33. Kollontai, *Iz moei zhizni*, p. 111.

our representatives tell them how difficult our lives are, how all her life [the woman worker] lives, against her will, [under the thumb] of her father, her husband, her brother, or her boss. And let those we send in our name proclaim that the woman worker cannot live like this any more, that she wants to change her life and will struggle for change with all her strength.[34]

One hundred and sixty reports were presented at the Congress, covering every conceivable aspect of women's lives and problems, political, economic, social, and psychological. Fourteen reports, of which all but one were presented by members of the Workers' Group, pertained directly to women workers. Resolutions were passed to support legislative reforms, such as the legal prohibition of all night work and work in the mines, overtime, and the work of women under the age of eighteen, as well as to support maternity protection, the establishment of nurseries in factories, a female factory inspectorate, and subsidized insurance for workers. None took issue with the need for special regulation of women's work.

The great conflict between feminists and the Workers' Group was over two related issues: first, whether all women regardless of class or political allegiance could and should unite to solve common problems, and second, whether women's equality could be achieved within the existing social order. In their prepared presentations representatives of the Workers' Group stated unequivocally that women workers had nothing in common with bourgeois women and that women's equality could be achieved only as the consequence of a social revolution.[35] Feminists, in their pre-

34. TsGIA, f. 150, op. 1, d. 154 (*Stanok Tekstil'shchika* [1908], no. 1, Nov. 18, p. 10).

35. Kollontai's speech, "Zhenshchina-rabotnitsa v sovremennom obshchestve [The woman worker in contemporary society]," was specifically on these two issues. The other reports from the Workers' Group on various aspects of the woman worker's life, all concluded similarly. *Trudy pervogo vserossiiskogo zhenskogo s'ezda, 10–16 dekabria 1908* (St Petersburg, 1909), pp. 792–800 and passim. Because Kollontai was forced by the police to flee Russia in the middle of the Congress, her report was presented by a woman worker.

pared speeches, just as consistently proclaimed the reverse. This fundamental discord intruded even into areas of partial accord, such as the importance of the vote for women. Here the feminists and the Workers' Group collided head on over which of the parties in the Duma was the most sincere and dedicated to giving women the vote. Sparks flew when Anna Kal'manovich, an active and articulate member of the Equal Rights Union, declared a plague on all parties:

> The Liberal party [i.e., the Kadets] placed the equal rights of women in their program for the sake of aesthetics, as a kind of decoration. But wherever possible it does not permit the realization of these rights. . . . [The Social Democrats] claim that they always sincerely wanted equal rights for women, that they alone incarnated all justice. I hope to prove that here too the [issue of] equal rights for women serves only to adorn their program . . . that regardless of what men call themselves—liberals, conservatives, or social democrats—they cannot be depended upon to give women freedom.[36]

Kal'manovich's report unleashed a vitriolic exchange over whether bourgeois feminists or socialists were the first and best proponents of women's emancipation. She offended women of both camps with her militant separatist position; predictably, the disputants remained unshaken from their respective political allegiances.

The second aspect of the franchise issue was, in a sense, more sensitive and even more divisive along class lines. Although the Congress ultimately adopted a resolution calling for equal, direct, secret, and universal suffrage without regard to sex, nationality, or religion, the so-called seven-tailed franchise, it became clear that some feminists would settle for less—to the detriment of working-class women. "It is easier to achieve the vote for women if [initially] you accept [a vote with property qualification]," declared one Kadet feminist, referring to the American example. She was supported by another, who pointed out that the British Socialists had

36. *Trudy zhenskogo s'ezda*, p. 784.

come out against the female franchise.[37] The implication of their remarks, clearly understood by the Workers' Group, was that to push for nothing less than universal suffrage would stand in the way of achieving even limited female suffrage because, among other reasons, even Social Democrats did not consistently support the voting rights of working-class women.

On many other issues, however, the Workers' Group manifested a far greater propensity for cooperation with feminists than their statements of principle implied. It was only the Bolsheviks who remained intransigent. Wishing to influence the Workers' Group to declare opposition to feminists and demonstratively walk out of the Congress immediately and without provocation, the Petersburg Committee sent a Bolshevik man to supervise. Subsequently this person, who identified himself only as "Chlen P. K." [Member of the Petersburg Committee], reported on the results of his efforts. "Imagine how I felt," Chlen wrote, "sitting in the general assembly, listening to a whole series of speeches about the unity of all women, a better future, the unimportance of class, etc., and I do not hear a single speech in the name of women workers who should have introduced dissonance into this 'mood of solidarity.' . . . As a representative of the party organization, I demanded from the leaders of the women workers that someone speak out. They answer me: it is awkward, not the right moment, etc."[38]

The Workers' Group was not at all inclined to succumb to Bolshevik dictates: "We will listen to the unions who chose us and to no one else."[39] Hostility to Bolshevik pressure erupted over a number of issues. The most infuriating to Chlen was a resolution on peasant women. Kollontai, in the name of the Workers' Group, had forced a postponement on the resolution, demanding that an open debate on the whole peasant question should take place first. Although the entire assembly agreed, the discussion was not held, and

37. Ibid., p. 523.
38. Chlen P. K., p. 5.
39. Ibid., p. 5.

the various factions went to work on their resolution. Chlen attempted to force the Workers' Group to draw up a resolution on the destruction of "feudal caste relations, transfer of all land to the peasants, etc.," which barely mentioned the peasant women. "I actually *dictated* several points to them against their will. As I was not on the editorial committee, it was necessary for me to force it, to bind them to my position without paying attention to their curses and agitation."[40]

A "colossal noise and protest" greeted Chlen, not so much over the substance of his position as over his attempt to force the Group to declare the resolution a reflection of the Bolshevik position: "Dictator, schismatic, disrupter. That is all one can expect from the Petersburg Committee, was heard from all sides."[41] To Chlen's chagrin, while the group bickered, a resolution was formulated by Kuskova, an erstwhile Social Democrat (anathema to the Bolsheviks for the "Economist" *Credo* she had written in 1899) but now a peripatetic socialist and feminist and a member of the Workers' Group. However, her reading was interrupted by the police, who closed the session on the grounds that the agrarian question was not on the Congress's agenda.[42]

Chlen's blood pressure rose higher yet when E. A. Kuvshinskaia, a Menshevik, stated that although women's organizations must remain within the boundaries of their own class groups, "there can be, in exceptional circumstances, a temporary agreement. The Congress has played a great role in awakening a political awareness [among women] and for that we must be very thankful to it."[43] No one from the Workers' Group objected.

On the last day of the Congress the Workers' Group made a demonstrative exit, but not in a manner that would win Chlen's approval. At the last general session the Organizing Committee put forth a resolution intended to present to the public the political consensus of the entire Con-

40. Ibid., p. 9.
41. Ibid., p. 8.
42. *Trudy zhenskogo s'ezda*, p. 390; Chlen, p. 9.
43. *Trudy zhenskogo s'ezda*, p. 495; Chlen, p. 8.

gress. It stated that the principal goal of women must be the establishment of democracy on the basis of universal suffrage without distinction of sex, religion, or nationality. Further, it stated that the goal was to be achieved by working with existing organizations and through the creation of a separate women's organization, a Women's Council, composed of women regardless of class. The resolution ignored the insistence of the Workers' Group on full, "seven-tailed" suffrage and their opposition to pan-class organizations. But, mainly, the Organizing Committee had unabashedly violated its own rule that the Congress could vote only on resolutions that had been earlier passed at individual sessions of the Congress. When Kuskova, speaking for the Workers' Group, pointed this out, the Organizing Committee responded that the resolution had, in fact, come out of one of the sessions, but had not been read out there "out of simple absentmindedness." This high-handed manipulation was too much for the Workers' Group and it walked out. Or rather, most members of the group trickled out. Some, still seeking a compromise, stated that it was not the content of the resolution but the way in which it was presented that was at issue and proposed to compromise by reading out the Workers' Group's resolution as well. Turned down, they too left.[44]

The Congress revealed that socialist women did not speak in unison. There were three competing tendencies among them. The Mensheviks came to the Congress to court the female working intelligentsia. This was consonant with their general tactic of seeking a broad democratic coalition of all forces in opposition to the established order. After the Congress, the Menshevik press complained that the Workers' Group had not tapped the support for the socialist position latent within the largest group of women in attendance— the working intelligentsia. As the Mensheviks pointed out, this large center had expressed its sympathy for the Social Democratic position a number of times. Despite its good

44. *Trudy zhenskogo s'ezda*, p. 818–820.

intentions and correct views, reported a Menshevik spokes-
man, the Workers' Group remained insensitive to important
differences between the "philanthropic ladies" and the liberal democratic *intelligentki,* wasting its time on "abstractions
and cliches."[45] It was as if, he concluded, the Workers'
Group's insistence that the struggle for women's rights was
a proletarian monopoly bespoke a latent fear that "suddenly
the women from bourgeois society might turn out to be
more or less democratic."[46]

In 1908 Kollontai was still officially a Menshevik. Caught
between the Scylla of the feminist challenge and the Cha-
rybdis of Social Democratic indifference, she was eager to
involve women workers in the debate with feminists—not,
like her Menshevik colleagues, to work out a compromise
but, by exposing the feminists, to mold a movement of
women workers within social democracy.

The Bolsheviks, who participated in the Congress only
reluctantly in the first place, had no desire to engage in the
debate with feminists at all. This, of course, was consonant
with their larger policy of eschewing any kind of cooperation with nonsocialist elements and, specifically, with their
rigid insistence that the woman question could not be addressed outside the framework of the socialist revolution.
What the Mensheviks saw as insufficiently conciliatory tactics at the Congress, the Bolsheviks judged to be shameful
compromise, which they explained by the backwardness of
the women workers in the group.[47]

Feminists too were divided among themselves before and
after the Congress. But they remained united by the belief
that women of all strata had common problems and should
work in common to solve them, and bewildered by the socialist denial of what seemed to them a simple truth. This
position was well articulated by Kal'manovich on the eve of
the Congress. She defended feminists against the Social
Democratic charge that the women's movement was self-

45. Ermanskii, p. 107.
46. Ibid., p. 110. See also "Zhenskii s'ezd," *Dal'* (1901), no. 1, pp. 23–24.
47. *Sotsialdemokrat* (1909), no. 4.

seeking, interested only in voting rights, which would leave the proletarian woman as oppressed by the politically free bourgeois women as the entire proletariat was oppressed by the entire bourgeoisie. Kal'manovich asserted that the vote was not the final goal of the women's movement, but only a first crucial step on the road to justice for all in all areas of human and social relations. The Social Democrats, in her opinion, refused to admit that they had as much to lose as the bourgeoisie by emancipating women: "Even the proletarian to whom the contemporary order gives so little joy [would lose] a slave; the wife who serves him, brings up his children, cooks and launders. Perhaps this is why [Social Democrats] instinctively and unconsciously do not hurry to realize [their program of equal rights for women], and are willing to bequeath the task to future generations." If this were not the case, she asked, why do they discredit the women's movement, for "even if the women's movement were concerned only with political equality, what is to stop us and the Social Democrats from going toward that immediate goal together? We can just as well split when universal suffrage is achieved."[48]

And what of the women workers in the Workers' Group? It is difficult to concur with the Bolshevik judgment that their behavior was a consequence of backwardness and lack of preparation. They were chosen from among the several hundred women workers who were already sufficiently "conscious" and courageous to join unions and clubs. If, as a group, they fully satisfied neither Bolsheviks nor Mensheviks, it was because, like most rank-and-file workers, women workers were indifferent to the discord that raged among Social Democratic intellectuals in this period. Their reports put them squarely in the Social Democratic camp insofar as they emphasized the divisions between the needs of proletarian women and bourgeois feminists. At the same time,

---

48. A. A. Kal'manovich, "Konechnaia tsel' zhenskogo dvizheniia," *Soiuz Zhenshchin* (1908), no. 9, p. 3.

their behavior acknowledged the possibility of some common interests with women of other strata.

One woman worker delegate, identified as "M. B.," wrote a long description of her experience at the Congress in the Textile Union's journal. Her words belie the accusation that the women workers were unable to distinguish between the conservative high-born ladies and the working intelligentsia:

> What incredible ladies! [*Chudnye eti baryni!*] They have lived for ages on this earth and have never seen a "live" woman worker. They would not believe that we worked in the factory. They thought, well, if we are workers, we should be filthy, unwashed, and uncombed. . . . Of course, not all the women were such ladies. Many were working women of various kinds—teachers, doctors, feldshers. They have education and a different life [from us women workers], but they live by their own labor. It was easy for us women workers to mix with them, and they did not look at us as if we were outlandish creatures.[49]

M. B. even made a distinction between the types of "ladies":

> I do not like the sort that do something worth a kopek and call their deed silver, as if without their services the world would perish. . . . But [even] among them there are good people who work from the heart, expending much energy and resources.

M. B. was able to treat some of the differences with gentle humor. For example, she repeats a discussion she had with "one young thing" over the issue of unequal rights:

> What rights, I ask. Well [answered the "young thing"], take as an example—your father dies and leaves an inheritance. But you, as a daughter can have only one-fourteenth, while your brother gets one-half. Is that fair? How shall I put it, I begin—it depends on the inheritance. When my father died, he left four small children on my hands since I was the eldest. . . . I would have given my brother not only half but all the inheritance with pleasure.

---

49. This excerpt and those that follow are taken from TsGIA, f. 150, op. 1, d. 154, l. 146–149 (*Stanok Tekstil'shchika* [1908], no. 2).

Even on the political issue of party alliances for the vote that had created the greatest uproar at the Congress, M. B. took a principled but moderate position. Although she gives the usual arguments against class collaboration, she adds:

> However, it is perfectly true that women of all classes suffer from great injustices, that they are considered children and are not given the vote even though they work as men do.

Finally, M. B. concluded that the Congress was extremely useful:

> It would have been a great error not to make use of this tribunal. The Women's Congress shook us up a bit, awoke many of us from our somnolence, and we must make sure that we do not fall asleep again.

Unfortunately, those women workers who had been courted or stimulated by feminists and socialists would find no place to put their awakened consciousness. The Women's Congress was the last great confrontation between feminists and socialists. Henceforward, there would be small skirmishes but no battles.

* * *

Between 1908 and the outbreak of World War I, Pokrovskaia was the only feminist to sustain an interest in women workers. She continued to thunder away in the Women's Progressive Party journal, *Zhenskii Vestnik,* which, as before, was full of articles on various aspects of women workers' conditions and the hypocrisy of the liberals and Social Democrats alike toward women workers. The Equal Rights Union, defunct by the end of 1908, was replaced by the Russian League for Women's Equality (Rossiiskaia Liga Ravnopraviia Zhenshchin). The League was a truncated version of the Equal Rights Union, bereft now of socialist and generally more radical women. Like all the remaining smaller feminist organizations, it continued to retreat from broad social issues. This was as much a reflection of a social climate that, to put it mildly, no longer supported the pursuit of great encompassing goals as it was of the narrower composition of the movement and its wilting spirit. After 1908 feminist organizations mainly addressed, in piecemeal fashion, inequities that affected women of the middle and upper strata: inheritance laws and property rights, the passport system, access to higher education and the professions.[50] But they made episodic forays into areas that touched on the lives of women workers and momentarily reignited the sparks of antagonism between socialists and feminists.

The first such encounter took place in 1910 at the First All-Russian Congress on Prostitution, organized by the Society for the Protection of Women. A workers' delegation was invited and accepted; it consisted of three men and three women, representatives of four unions and one workers' club. The union representatives were pugnacious, having come, naturally, with the intention of pushing the Social Democratic position that capitalist exploitation was the sole cause of prostitution and continually bringing up issues that the feminist organizers considered irrelevant to the question of prostitution. With the ubiquitous police present at the Congress, seizing every opportunity to threaten the meetings with closure, the feminists grew nervous and irate over the union representatives' disregard for the danger.[51] Thereafter, feminists were wary of inviting union delegations. In October 1912 the League for Women's Equality held a meeting to plan a conference on women's education and refused to sanction a union delegation to speak for women workers, on the grounds that unions were only involved in informal education. However, it agreed to allow the workers' clubs to send representatives.[52] Since workers' clubs as well as unions were involved in informal education, this was a clear attempt to circumvent the possibly more politicized unions. However, a group of union representa-

50. Goldberg, chap. 5.

51. *Trudy pervogo vserossiiskogo s'ezda po bor'be s torgom zhenshchinami i ego prichinami* (Moscow, 1911), vyp. 1–2, passim; TsGIA, f. 154, d. 154, l. 187.

52. *Pravda* (1912), Oct. 17, no. 145, p. 3; Nov. 27, no. 178, p. 3; Dec. 12, no. 191, p. 4.

tives turned up on the eve of the first session and engaged in an acrimonious exchange with the feminist organizers. The upshot was that one Menshevik and one Bolshevik woman, unaffiliated with either unions or clubs, were given a place on the formal agenda.[53]

The last interaction between feminists and socialists took place over the feminists' plan to lobby for the creation of a female factory inspectorate. It is especially illuminating because it involved the liberal parties and the government as well. The idea of a female factory inspectorate to supervise the conditions of female labor and attend to the complaints of women workers was not new. In 1899 Mirovich had brought it up before the newly founded Society for the Improvement of Women's Lot.[54] Pokrovskaia had advocated it at the All-Russian Congress on Artisanal Production in 1900.[55] In response to a petition from the Society in 1902 the Department of Industry and Trade had requested that factory inspectors submit data on women and girls working in factories in the Kingdom of Poland. By 1904 nothing more substantial had come forth, and yet another organization, the Society for the Preservation of Women's Health, petitioned the Ministry of Finance, which, in 1905, put together a cumbersome proposal for a female inspectorate that would attend to children as well as women workers, to questions of child-rearing and education as well as factory problems.[56] But the project did not materialize, and the issue was thrown back into the public arena.

The main arguments for a female inspectorate were that women workers had problems that male inspectors could neither understand nor cope with, and that, in any case, women workers were too shy with male inspectors to discuss their problems with them—a point that had often been veri-

53. *Trudy pervogo vserossiiskogo s'ezda po obrazobaniiu zhenshchin* (Petrograd, 1915), t. 2, pp. 424–442.

54. Kechedzhi-Shapovalov, p. 157.

55. *Trudy vserossiiskogo s'ezda po remeslennoi promyshlennosti v S-Peterburge* (St Petersburg, 1901), t. 3, p. 209.

56. D. P. Nikol'skii, "Zhenskaia fabrichnaia inspektsiia i neobkhodimost' ee v Rossii," *Trudy zhenskogo s'ezda*, pp. 730–740.

fied by observation.[57] The venerable I. I. Ianzhul, one of the most ardent supporters of factory legislation in the past, made the first public argument against a female inspectorate. Ianzhul claimed that such legislation was premature. England, for example, had established a female inspectorate only ninety years after the first factory legislation. But he also advanced a more original and somewhat bizarre objection. Ianzhul insisted that the Russian woman worker was not, in fact, reluctant to discuss her problems with male inspectors; Russian factory conditions led to such debauchery and dissoluteness that the factory woman had long ago lost her modesty and delicacy. A female inspectorate was not only unnecessary, but was a harmful diversion from the struggle for truly important labor legislation: "It is impossible, or at least pointless, to embroider our Russian canvas with a new modish design like a female inspectorate."[58]

Ianzhul's position was attacked with passion and indignation by D. P. Nikol'skii, a doctor with an impressive record of concern for the social problems of workers. To Ianzhul's point about prematurity based on the English example, Nikol'skii retorted sarcastically, "If we accept Mr. Ianzhul's opinion, we must wait yet another seventy years to establish a female inspectorate."[59]

Nikol'skii took even greater umbrage at Ianzhul's claim that Russian women workers were too callous to require women inspectors. Ianzhul, he said, as a former factory inspector should know better than most people that "the factory stud [is] an ulcer of factory life from which the Russian woman worker suffers more than she does from the work itself."[60]

The issue was discussed with fervor once again at a con-

---

57. For example, see L. Katenina, "K voprosu o polozhenii rabotnits v tekstil'noi promyshlennosti," *Obshchestvenny Vrach* (1914), no. 3, passim; M. K. Valitskaia, *Issledovaniia zdorov'ia rabochikh na tabachnykh fabrikakh* (St Petersburg, 1889), pp. 14, 23. For the debate on women factory inspectors in the West and Russia, see V. D. Belikov, *Zhenshchina v promyshlennoi inspektsii zapada* (Tver', 1914), chap. 5.

58. Quoted in Nikol'skii, p. 739.

59. Ibid.

60. Ibid.

gress of factory doctors in 1911.[61] Finally, in the last months of 1912 the League for Women's Equality and a group of factory doctors decided to raise the question of a women's factory inspectorate with sympathetic Duma members.[62] They made no effort to elicit the cooperation of socialists or unions. As *Pravda* complained, "In the ardor of their 'love for the people' they have decided to resolve these questions . . . among themselves. They have not considered it necessary to consult with workers' organizations . . . nor with women workers."[63] A year later the League called a meeting attended by three hundred people, among whom were sixty men and women workers. The chairwoman denied their request to give reports, on the grounds that the police would not permit it—which was undoubtedly true, although the feminists were undoubtedly pleased to have an excuse. The workers' group then asked to be allowed to submit questions that could be answered as part of the formal speakers' presentations. After the first three speakers did not respond to its questions, the workers' group made a demonstrative exit.[64]

On February 29, 1913, thirty-three members of the Fourth Duma—twenty-nine Kadets and four Octobrists—submitted a petition to the Ministry of Trade and Industry for a female inspectorate that would perform the duties of the existing Inspectorate in factories employing women and children. Women inspectors, it stated, should have higher education and be entitled to the same service and pension rights as male inspectors.[65] The ministry flatly refused to consider the petition.[66] In spite of the ministry's opposition, the petition was put to the Duma as a legislative proposal on April 24, 1913. M. Novikov, the Kadet who introduced the

61. *Trudy vtorogo s'ezda fabrichnykh vrachei i predstavitelei fabrichno-zavodskoi promyshlennosti* (April 14–11, 1911), vyp. 1 (Moscow, 1911), pp. 69–76; vyp. 4, pp. 74–75; *Zhenskii Vestnik* (1911), no. 7–8, pp. 155–156.
62. *Pravda* (1912), Nov. 21, no. 174, p. 3.
63. Ibid., Dec. 7, no. 187, p. 3.
64. *Za Pravdu* (1913), Dec. 3, no. 50, p. 4.
65. TsGIA, f. 23, op. 20, d. 881, l. 1.
66. Ibid., l. 20.

bill, emphasized three points from the petition: first, that the increase in women workers who "from feelings of modesty do not express their needs to male inspectors and try to hide their mortifications from male eyes" justified a female inspectorate; second, that women inspectors in other "cultured" nations have met with the approval of entrepreneurs as well as male inspectors and workers; and, third, that Russia had enough educated and well-trained women to undertake the task.[67]

The Bolshevik Roman Malinovskii spoke for the Social Democrats in support of the proposal. He began with a sensitive description of the woman worker, the most poorly paid and defenseless among workers, a worker who did two jobs:

> She does not return home from the factory to rest. On the contrary, she must cook for the husband at whose side she has worked the entire day; she must wash and sew the children's clothes. This alone is enough to tell us that the woman [worker's] lot is more difficult.

But most of Malinovskii's speech was about the flaws of the factory inspectorate in general. He concluded that the Social Democratic fraction would support the proposal in question, inadequate as it might be to reform the Factory Inspectorate.[68]

Litvinov-Filanskii, the director of the Ministry of Trade and Industry and a former factory inspector, spoke in no uncertain terms against introducing women into the Factory Inspectorate. Completely ignoring the issues brought up by Novikov and Malinovskii, he insisted that the only function of factory inspectors was to inspect and make decisions on technical aspects of industry: "We can scarcely expect to find enough women in Russia to whom we could fearlessly assign

---

67. *Gosudarstvennaia Duma. Stenograficheskie otchety* (1913), chast' 2. Chetvertyi sozyv, sessiia 1, zasedanie 37, pp. 533–536.

68. Ibid., pp. 536–539. Malinovskii, a former member of the Metal Workers' Union and a Bolshevik, was also a police agent. In public he diligently espoused Bolshevik policy.

these technical obligations." He then diverted the discussion to a vague promise of extending the Factory Inspectorate to small industrial and artisanal establishments where the majority of women worked, "not in the near future, but perhaps in the not-too-distant future." Then, and only then, it would be appropriate to talk about women inspectors.[69]

Novikov and Rodzevich, another Kadet, objected to the way Litvinov-Filanskii denigrated the abilities of Russian women, and to his attempt to divert attention from the issue at hand with questionable promises of an expanded Inspectorate in the indeterminate future.[70] Once again Malinovskii took the floor to accuse the existing Inspectorate of not even attending to the technical aspects of industry, as Litvinov-Filanskii had insisted, but of serving a purely punitive and police function against workers. While Malinovskii was expanding on the decisive role of workers in provoking any kind of factory legislation, the conservatives in the Duma protested loudly, and amidst growing tension on the floor the discussion was closed. Nevertheless, the legislative proposal was approved in principle by a vote of 77 to 64 and sent to the Duma Committee on Workers' Problems.[71] In the spring of 1914 this committee approved legislation to establish a female inspectorate that mirrored the existing Inspectorate in all but one aspect: since by law women were not entitled to rank in the civil service, women inspectors would not be entitled to receive medals, honors, personal or hereditary nobility, and other kinds of rewards reserved for men. It was then passed on to the Budget Committee, which repeatedly delayed ratification. The Revolution of February 1917 rendered the issue irrelevant.[72]

There were two issues at stake in the debate over the establishment of a female factory inspectorate: the needs of women workers, and the competence of educated women to fill these needs as factory inspectors. Somewhere in the

69. Ibid., pp. 539–542.
70. Ibid., pp. 543–547.
71. Ibid., p. 550.
72. TsGIA, f. 1278, op. 5, d. 670, l. 22–24.

course of the debate women workers, as the raison d'être of a female factory inspectorate, got lost. The Ministry of Trade and Industry denied the validity of both claims. Feminists, and later Kadets in the Duma, defended the project by emphasizing the qualifications of educated women. However sincere their concern for women workers, the real issue for them was the opening of another profession to Russia's educated women, to "give . . . women an equal social position." "When women inspectors appear in the factory, I will consider that the era of true emancipation is upon us," stated a participant in the Congress of Factory Doctors in 1911.[73] In October 1913 the Women's Mutual Philanthropic Society wrote an angry letter to Litvinov-Filanskii to protest his speech in the Duma. Scarcely mentioning women workers, the letter was devoted to convincing him that "at the present time there is a contingent of women competent to fulfill all the obligations of the factory inspector."[74]

Social Democrats had no interest in the proposal at all and responded to it only when provoked by feminists and liberals. Malinovskii's support was lukewarm, and his goal was rather to use the debate to make broader points about the relationship of workers to the state.[75]

The most authentic concern for women workers was expressed by Dr. Nikol'skii, who stood apart from the major protagonists in the battle. His report to the Women's Congress was almost entirely devoted to the female factory inspectorate as an instrument of improvement in the lives of women workers, and along these lines he offered a suggestion more radical and to the point than any that had been expressed before, although it was subsequently imitated by Social Democrats:

> We must not forbear to express the hope that the female factory inspectorate will include representatives of women

73. *Trudy . . . fabrichnykh vrachei*, pp. 69, 74–75.

74. TsGIA, f. 23, op. 20, d. 881, l. 32.

75. The only evidence for Social Democratic initiative is a brochure published in 1917. The author was Eva Broido, a Menshevik woman. See *Zhenskaia inspektsiia truda* (Petrograd, 1917).

workers. This has been done in other countries. Only then . . . will it be possible to effect a rapprochement between workers and the institutions established to defend their interests and rights. Although at this moment under prevailing conditions there can be no thoughts of such a rapprochement, let us . . . strive for better times.[76]

* * *

After the Women's Congress in 1908 the Social Democrats lost virtually all interest in women workers, with the exception of those individuals or small groups that turned up at the congresses initiated by feminists. Kollontai was forced to flee into exile, leaving behind her the first Social Democratic publication on women since Krupskaia's brochure in 1899. *The Social Basis of the Woman Question* was not what its title implied, but rather a narrative and an evaluation of the women's movement and the socialist response to it since 1905. As a chronicle of events, it was detailed, thorough, and accurate. As an evaluation, it was generous to the Equal Rights Union's early activities and intentions regarding women workers in 1905 and 1906, verged on the vicious regarding the conservative wings of the feminist movement such as the Women's Mutual Philanthropic Society, and was positively vituperative toward the likes of Pokrovskaia. The point of this long and sometimes circuitous work, however, was to show that the democratic tendencies among some feminists were ephemeral. In the end, feminists would show their true colors; they would abandon women workers and adhere ever more to the struggle for the vote, which would benefit mainly women of their own class. On the other hand, Kollontai described the Social Democrats as unswerving and united zealots in the pursuit of emancipation for women workers. There is no mention of or allusion to the resistance and opposition that she had encountered in her efforts to bring women workers to the attention of her comrades. By the time the book appeared, however, it ex-

76. Nikol'skii, p. 740.

cited little response in either the feminist or the socialist camp.

To be sure, the Bolshevik postmortems of the Women's Congress acknowledged that "there seems to be an interest in working among the female proletariat. There are discussions of a special women's organization."[77] In May 1909 the Petersburg Committee brought the question up before the Central Committee of the Bolshevik party, which responded that separate organizations for women workers were permissible as long as it was understood that they were temporary—a transition toward joint organization of male and female workers.[78] This guarded resolution was never put into practice.

Until 1912, of course, the Social Democrats, like the feminists, were in a state of disarray. When the strike movement was catalyzed in 1912 by the massacre of striking workers at the Lena Goldfields, the Social Democrats, too, came back to life, organizing in the unions, around the Duma elections and the factory insurance legislation, and with legal newspapers—the Bolshevik *Pravda* and the Menshevik *Luch*. But the earlier promise to work among the female proletariat was honored only with feeble gestures. In 1912 Social Democrats formed two clubs for women, one in St Petersburg and one in Moscow. The St Petersburg club was a revival of the 1907 Society for Women's Mutual Aid. Located in an apartment in a factory neighborhood inhabited by large numbers of women workers, the club had a good library and gave evening courses in literacy. Attendance was small and limited to women, workers and *intelligentki,* despite the efforts of male Social Democrats to take over the leadership.[79] The Moscow club, called the Third Women's Club, was an organization for women in name only. A group of Social Democratic *intelligentki* decided to utilize the charter of a women's club that had been organized in 1907 as a counterweight to two feminist clubs (the

77. Chlen P. K., p. 10.
78. *Sotsialdemokrat* (1909), no. 5, p. 19.
79. *Zvezda* (1912), Jan. 5, no. 2 (38), p. 30.

First and Second Women's Clubs). The charter of the 1907 club had a loophole that permitted men to participate. Male and female workers were drawn into both the leadership and the rank-and-file attendance, and the club was lively and popular, but organization of women workers was not its goal.[80]

The year 1913 marked a modest departure from the previous indifference to women workers. It began with the celebration of International Women's Day. Two years earlier Kollontai had attempted to prod Russian Social Democrats into observing the day, already established as a working-class holiday on a level with May 1 by socialists abroad. But, she recalled, "the party leadership saw no importance in holding a women's day, and my insistence provoked no response."[81] At the end of 1912 several women prominent in Bolshevik and Menshevik circles picked up the idea and gained party approval.[82] The coming celebration was announced at a large meeting in St Petersburg in January, and on February 17 the Kalashnikov Exchange was packed to capacity with an audience that had come to hear speeches by feminists, Menshevik and Bolshevik *intelligentki,* and women workers.[83] If the celebration was intended to demonstrate implacable hostility to feminism, as articles in *Pravda* claimed in the days preceding the celebration, it was not entirely successful.[84] The resolution taken at the end of the meeting called for women workers to join in the campaign for universal suffrage, with the weak caveat that beyond that point socialists parted ways with feminists.[85] The day was marked as well by a celebration at the Third Women's Club, a special talk at one of the workers' clubs,

80. Z. Krzhizhanovskaia, "Iz zhizni odnogo kluba," in S. E. Chernomordik, ed., *Put' k oktiabriu.Sbornik statei, vospominanii i dokumentov* (Moscow, 1923), pp. 130–135; T. Sapronov, *Iz istorii rabochego dvizheniia* (*po lichnym vospominaniiam*) (Leningrad and Moscow, 1925), pp. 16, 134.

81. Kollontai "Avtobiograficheskii ocherk," p. 283.

82. Clements, pp. 76–80.

83. *Pravda,* (1913), Jan. 5, no. 4, p. 1.

84. Ibid., Feb. 1, no. 26, p. 3; Feb. 15, no. 38, p. 4.

85. Ibid., Feb. 22, no. 44, p. 2.

and small meetings elsewhere in Russia.[86] *Pravda* and *Luch* devoted several pages to articles on the socialist women's movement in other countries, on women workers in various industries, and on arguments that International Women's Day was not a concession to female separatism.[87] After February 17, reportage on women workers dwindled considerably, although, until the outbreak of World War I, it was considerably greater than it had been in 1912, when only six articles on women workers were published in 204 issues.[88]

The most interesting development in the press was not, however, the editorials about women workers, but the remarkable increase of letters and reports from women workers. This was unquestionably due to the greater use that women workers were willing to make of the workers' press. But since editorial decisions were made about which letters and reports to print, it was evident that the Bolsheviks were making a conscious decision to provide space for women workers in their press.

In 1914 International Women's Day was celebrated with more vigor and, consequently, met with great official repression. Because St Petersburg's city governor forbade a large meeting at the Fedorova Hall, many small gatherings were held in factory neighborhoods. Despite the prohibition, large crowds gathered at the Fedorova Hall, the overflow milling around in the surrounding streets, watched by police on foot and on horses. Three of the five speakers were arrested, and when the remaining two finished, the

---

86. Ibid., Feb. 24, no. 46, p. 3; March 6, no. 54, p. 3.

87. Ibid., Feb. 17, no. 40, pp. 1–3.

88. Soviet treatments of the Bolshevik interest in women in 1913 and 1914 are unreliable. In these years there was no regular women's page in *Pravda*, as they claim. Nor did *Pravda* and *Luch* publish special issues to commemorate International Women's Day, although the first three pages of the six-page daily were almost entirely devoted to articles on women workers. Neither the influence of Menshevik women in planning International Women's Day, nor the resolution passed in the 1913 celebration are mentioned. See A. V. Artiukhina, et al., eds., *Zhenshchiny v revoliutsii* (Moscow, 1959); S. N. Serditova, *Bol'sheviki v bor'be za zhenskie proletarskie massy* (Moscow, 1959); *Vsegda s vami: Sbornik posviashchennyi piatidesiatiletiiu "Rabotnitsa."* (Moscow, 1964).

crowd from the hall mingled with people on the street to sing revolutionary songs.[89] Moscow Social Democrats also attempted to arrange a celebration but were successfully prevented by the authorities.[90] Fifty women workers attended a celebration held in Moscow by the League for Equal Rights, but according to the report in *Pravda,* the feminist speakers deliberately dragged out their speeches on the unity of women's goals, until the police closed their meeting as well, leaving the workers with no time to speak.[91]

The second celebration of International Women's Day was accompanied by the appearance of two Social Democratic newspapers especially for women. *Golos Rabotnitsy,* the Menshevik newspaper, survived only two issues before it was suppressed by the police. *Rabotnitsa,* the Bolshevik newspaper, put out seven issues before its editorial board was arrested. The idea appears to have arisen almost simultaneously in both camps among women in the higher echelons of party leadership. Although Kollontai argued for going one step farther and organizing a special bureau for women workers, both fractions settled on a newspaper as sufficient.

The pages of *Rabotnitsa,* like those of *Pravda,* revealed a curious imbalance between the content of the letters and reports from women workers and the content of the editorials written by Bolshevik *intelligenty* (male and female). Provided with a forum—and one in which they could express themselves anonymously—women workers wrote incessantly and openly about the hostility they endured from male workers, making it clear that this hostility was as much a feature of the normal daily exchange between men and women workers as was the humiliating treatment they endured from male supervisory personnel. But when the woman worker complained that male workers greeted her presence in workers' organizations with "Quiet, fool. This is not your business. It is not a woman's affair (*ne bab'e delo*),"[92]

89. *Put' Pravdy* (1914), Feb. 25, no. 21, p. 2.
90. Ibid., Feb. 28, no. 24, p. 4; March 2, no. 26, p. 5.
91. Ibid., Feb. 25, no. 21, p. 3.
92. *Rabotnitsa* (1914), Feb. 23, no. 1, p. 11.

Bolshevik agitators replied that although male workers had been hostile to women in the past, "as workers' consciousness heightened they understood that it is as useless to fight against female labor as against mechanization," and exhorted women workers to join unions and serve on insurance committees.[93] To the ubiquitous complaints about male workers' indifference to women workers' needs at best and about brutality and sexual humiliation at worst, *Pravda* and *Rabotnitsa* editorials responded with silence. When women workers called out to their sisters to "acknowledge that the time has passed when the woman was only a mother," and to their male co-workers that "the woman worker . . . just like you must earn her bread,"[94] the response was "We know that you have the heavy but great burden of raising and educating the new young generation, strong and staunch proletarian *sons*."[95] One cannot help but wonder whether Bolsheviks, male workers and *intelligenty*, ever actually read the letters that poured in from women workers.

The celebration of Women's Day and the publication of a newspaper for women workers were clear indications that Social Democratic perceptions had begun to change. In part, women workers benefited from a broader Social Democratic response to the great resurgence of workers' discontent in 1912–1914. As Social Democrats sought to stimulate, nourish, and politicize the accelerating strike movement, their field of vision expanded. They grew more sensitive to the potential for activism of all kinds of "backward" workers, among them women workers.[96] Throughout 1912 women

93. *Pravda* (1912), June 14, no. 39, p. 4.
94. *Rabotnitsa* (1914), no. 6, p. 13.
95. Ibid., p. 10.
96. An American historian has suggested that the Social Democratic interest in 1913 was the result of a palpable increase in women workers' strike activity beginning in 1910, of widespread evidence of new militancy among women workers, and of greater solidarity between men and women in strikes. There is no evidence to support this suggestion. The author bases her case on reports of a few strikes (reported mainly in union journals) before 1910 in which women were either weak or defeated. She contrasts this with strikes reported in the Menshevik press, mainly in 1910, in which women workers were assertive. In both cases, the strikes are typical of women's strikes from the 1880s and 1890s. The strikes the author uses as evidence are presented in isolation from the history of women's participa-

workers had taken advantage of the workers' press, a safe
channel for the expression of their discontent, to a degree
that could not but jolt Social Democratics even if they did
not heed the actual content of the letters that poured in
from women workers. More important, the insurance law of
1913 "for the first time . . . makes us [women] equal in law
with men."[97] That is to say, according to the law, women
could serve as representatives on the insurance committees
that factories were legally obliged to set up. On October 30,
1913, the factory manager at Laferm tobacco factory, in
accordance with the insurance law, posted a notice that
elections of workers to the insurance committee were about
to take place:

> We, a group of conscious workers, offer sincere thanks to those
> who devised the Insurance Law and to the person who trans-
> lated it into life, Mr. Iak [the factory manager]. Only thanks to
> him do we witness the most unusual phenomenon—that at La-
> ferm factory almost all the workers have become *politiki*. We
> swear on our own heads that not even the best Marxist agitators
> could have so awakened the mass of two thousand [women]
> workers to political consciousness.[98]

Incidents of this nature could not have escaped the notice
of Social Democrats and impressed upon them the danger
that "backward" women would represent workers whether
Social Democrats and male workers liked it or not. The
importance of influencing women workers was thereby
raised to a new level of importance.

The perception of women workers as worthy of inclusion
in the revolutionary struggle was new. But the manner in
which it was implemented was very much a case of old wine
in new bottles. International Women's Day might have
been, as the Social Democratic press promised, a focal point

---

tion in labor protest and are neither qualitatively nor quantitatively different from
the strikes of the entire period under consideration in this book. See Anne Bobroff, "The Bolsheviks and Working Women, 1905–1920," *Soviet Studies* (1974),
October.

97. *Proletarskaia Pravda* (1913), Jan. 11, no. 8, p. 2.

98. *Za Pravdu* (1913), Nov. 27, no. 3, p. 3.

for organizational work among women. It was not. The celebration of the day was planned and executed by the intelligentsia leadership.[99] In the aftermath of the 1913 celebration there were no further attempts to organize women workers, and International Women's Day of 1914 was arranged just as the first celebration had been. A big party once a year was, in practical terms, nothing more than a nice gesture. Publication of a special newspaper for women workers was certainly an important acknowledgment of the woman worker's existence. It was a poor substitute for consistent and sustained organization.

* * *

Both socialists and feminists considered women workers to be part of their natural constituencies. The Social Democrats were wedded to a formulation that relegated the remedies for women's subjugation, as well as a host of other social ills, to the aftermath of a successful proletarian revolution. However, this formulation did not compel them to neglect women workers in the process of achieving that revolution. That choice was profoundly influenced by their inability to surmount ingrained attitudes toward women as "creatures of a lower order." Feminists were strong where socialists were weak. They understood that class did not affect the position of women relative to men and that the woman worker's subjugation was rooted in attitudes that pervaded the entire society. But feminists were, for the most part, woefully ill-equipped to comprehend class barriers to independence and human dignity. They believed that "the position of a wealthy woman can often be less enviable than the position of the most humble woman worker who is obligated for her existence only to herself and is not forced to buy it at the cost of human dignity. Can you say that a bird in a gilded cage is happier than a free bird?"[100] Thus, Social Democrats were

99. For example, in 1913 only two meetings of women workers were called to discuss International Women's Day. See *Pravda* (1913), Jan. 12, no. 9, p. 4; Jan 20, no. 16, p. 3.
100. Kal'manovich, p. 2.

convinced that the benefits of a future revolution would automatically trickle down to the segment of the proletariat
which they ignored in the present; feminists were as rigidly
fixated on the conviction that women workers automatically
benefited from solutions to the problems of middle- and
upper-class women. Socialists and feminists were like the
blind men and the elephant. Each correctly felt, described,
and analyzed a crucial part of the beast, but neither could
comprehend its totality.

The women workers who wrote in the workers' press testified amply that they needed neither socialists nor feminists
to explain their problems to them. How to solve them was
another question. Clearly, some women workers experienced an enduring awakening. They had higher aspirations
and greater courage in pursuing them. They could rise
above material and psychological obstacles and engage in
protest and activism. They could sign petitions, confront
the foreman on the shop floor, participate in strikes,
unions, and insurance committees, and openly accuse their
fathers, brothers, and husbands of hostility and indifference. But it is too much to expect the experience of a few
years of involvement, however intense and rewarding for
some, to modify radically the fears, expectations, and habits
of the great mass of women workers.

Bibliography

ARCHIVAL SOURCES

Tsentral'nye Gosudarstvennyi Istoricheskii Arkhiv v Leningrade (TsGIA) [Central State Historical Archive, Leningrad]

Fond 20, Ministerstvo Finansov, Departament Torgovli i Manufaktur. Opis'3, delo 1882[a], "Otchety fabrichnykh inspektorov za 1894–1898." Opis'12, delo 265, "Otchet fabrichnogo inspektora Kazan'skoi gubernii po I-mu uchastky, 1897; Otchet fabrichnogo inspectora olonetskoi gubernii, 1896." Opis'13, delo 192, "O proekte obiazatel'nykh postanovlenii o mere dlia okhraneniia zhizni i zdorov'ia rabochikh." Opis'13, delo 870, "Zakonoproekt po rabochemu zakonodatel'stvu, 1906–1907." Opis'13[a], delo 5, zhurnaly zasedanii i kopii opredelenii po ostanovleniiu po fabrichnym delam prisutstviia, 1899–1900." Opis'13[a], delo 214, "Zhurnaly zasedanii i kopii opredelenii po ostanovleniiu po fabrichnym delam prisutstviia, 1899–1900." Opis'13[a], delo 357, "Ob okruzhnykh s'ezdakh fabrichnykh inspektorov moskovskogo okruga, 1899–1902." Opis'13[b], delo 1, "Otchet fabrichnogo inspektora moskovskogo okruga za 1886–1887. Primenenie zakona 3-ogo iiunia." Opis'13[b], delo 22, "Ezhemesiachnye vedomosti fabrichnogo inspektora sankpeterburgskogo okruga." Opis'13[b], delo 24, "Zhurnal zasedanii sankpeterburgskogo stolichnogo po fabrichnym delam prisutstviia, 1889." Opis 13[b], delo 28, "Otchet fabrichnogo inspektora vladimirskogo okruga. Peskov, P. A., Ob osmotrennykh im v 1891 fabrichno-zavodskikh predpriiatiiakh vladimirskoi, kostromskoi, nizhegorodskoi i iaroslavskoi gubernii, 1892." Opis'16, delo 3, "Obzor rabochego dvizheniia po guberniiam i okrugam, 1905."

Fond 22, Ministerstvo Torgovli i Promyshlennosti, Departament Torgovli i Promyshlennost [Ministry of Trade and Industry, Department of Trade and Industry]. Opis'5, delo 161, "Perepiska s kontseliariei Sinoda o dopuske sviashchennikov v promyshlennye zavedeniia, 1900."

Fond 23, Ministerstvo Torgovli i Promyshlennosti [Ministry of Trade and Finance]. Opis'16, delo 23, "O sposobakh vyiasneniia vazhneishikh dannykh o polozhenii rabochikh, 1907." Opis'16, delo 75, "Poiasnitel'nye teksty k svodnym otchetam okruzhnykh

fabrichnykh inspektorov za 1912." Opis'16, delo 118, "Zabasto-
vochnoe dvizhenie v promyshlennykh predpriiatiiakh podchin-
ennykh nadzoru fabrichnoi inspektsii za ianvar', 1914." Opis'20,
delo 881, "Po zakonodatel'nomu predlozheniiu o vvedenii zhenskoi
fabrichnoi inspektsii, 1913." Opis'29, delo 88. "Statisticheskie tab-
litsy o chislennosti rabochikh vo vsekh guberniiakh Rossii po grup-
pam proizvodstva, po zarabotnoi plate i po vozrastno-polovomu
priznaku. Nachalo 1890–okonchanie 1901." Opis'29, delo 90, "Statisticheskie svedenie o chisle i zarabotnoi plate vzroslykh rabo-
chikh-zhenschin, tavricheskoi, tambovskoi, tver'skoi, khar'kovskoi,
khersenskoi, chernigovskoi i iaroslavskoi gubernii, 1914." Opis'29,
delo 100, "Statisticheskie svedenie o chisle i zarabotnoi plate vzroslykh rabochikh muzhchin, ukrainskoi, khar'kovskoi, khersonskoi,
chernigovskoi, iaroslavskoi gubernii, 1914." Opis'30, delo 2, "O
bezporiadakh i stachkakh rabochikh proiskhodivshikh na fabrikakh, zavodakh i manufakturakh, 1893–1895." Opis'30, delo 4, "O
stachkakh rabochikh v fabrikakh i zavodakh vladimirskoi gubernii,
1905." Opis'30, delo 5, "O zabastovkakh, 1907." Opis'30, delo 7,
"Communication from the senior factory inspector regarding a
strike at the Shereshevskii tobacco factory in Grodno, 1900."
Opis'30, delo 10, "O stachkakh rabochikh na fabrikakh i zavodakh
moskovskoi gubernii, 1895–1898"; delo 11, "1898–1899"; delo 13,
"1901–1904"; delo 14, "O stachkakh na fabrikakh i zavodakh
vladimirskoi gubernii, 1895–1898"; delo 17, "T-vo Manufaktury
A. Karetnikova s synom, 1895"; delo 18, "O stachkakh rabochikh
na Gorkinskoi Manufakture, 1896"; delo 19, "O stachkakh na fabrikakh i zavodakh iaroslavskoi gubernii, 1895–1905." Opis'30, delo
23, "O stachkakh rabochikh na fabrikakh i zavodakh riazan'skoi
gubernii, 1896–1905." Opis'30, delo 26, "O stachkakh rabochikh
na fabrikakh i zavodakh sankpeterburgskoi gubernii, 1898–1899."
Opis'30, delo 42. "O stachkakh i bezporiadkakh rabochikh na fabrikakh i zavodakh mogilevskoi gubernii, 1901." Opis'30, delo 43, "O
stachkakh rabochikh na fabrikakh i zavodakh kievskoi gubernii,
1902–1903." Opis'30 delo 48, "O stachkakh rabochikh na fabrikakh i zavodakh orlovskoi gubernii, 1897–1905."
      Fond 91, Statisticheskaia Komissiia Imperatorskogo Vol'nogo
Ekonomicheskogo Obshchestva [Statistical Commission of The
Imperial Free Economic Society]. Opis'1, delo 575, "IVaia Chast-
naia Zhenskaia Voskresnaia Shkola, 1896."
      Fond 150, Peterburgskoe Obshchestvo Zavodchikov i Fabrikan-
tov [Petersburg Society of Factory and Plant Owners]. Opis'1, delo
51, "Zhurnaly zasedanii, 1906–1908." Opis'1, delo 150, "*Fabrich-*

naia Zhizn', 1908, Nos. 2–3; *Fabrichnyi Stanok*, 1908, No. 2; *Stanok*, 1908, Nos. 1–3; *Stanok Tekstil'shchika*, 1909, No. 2." Opis'1, delo 381, "Doklad o deiatel'nosti obshchestva v 1910 godu, 1911." Opis'1, delo 484 i 490, "Piatoe zasedanie, 1905." Opis'1, delo 553, "Ankety o zarabotnoi plate chernorabochikh raznykh predpriiatii, dek. 1909–ian. 1914."

Fond 741, Ministerstvo Narodnogo Prosveshcheniia. Otdel Promyshlennykh Uchilishch [Ministry of Public Education. Department of Industrial Schools]. Opis'2, delo 66, "O kursakh chercheniia-risovaniia, vechernikh i voskresnykh kursakh dlia rabochikh, 1903." Opis'5-zh, delo 2, "Nizhegorodskoe zhenskoe remeslennoe uchilishche." Opis'5-zh, delo 3, "Zhenskoe remeslennoe uchilishche Shelaputina v Moskve, 1911." Opis'5-zh, delo 4, "Roslavskoe zhenskoe remeslennoe uchilishche, 1904." Opis'5-zh, delo 8, "Zhenskoe professional'noe obrazovanie v SPb-e, 1904." Opis'5-zh, delo 9, "O brianskom zhenskom remeslennom uchilishche, 1905." Opis'5-zh, delo 11, "Ob otkrytii zhenskoi professional'noi shkoly, 1904." Opis'5-zh, g.12, "Detskie priiuty v Tule, 1904." Opis'8, delo 11-zh, "O posobii na vvedenie v kuz'minskom uchilishche tsarskosel'skogo uezda zaniatie po kroike i shit'iu, 1906." Opis'8, delo 43, "Perepiska o sushchestvuiushchikh i predpolozhennykh k otkrytiiu kursov dlia rabochikh i remeslennikov v raznykh gorodakh i selakh Rossiiskoi Imperii, 1906."

Fond 1149, Gosudarstvennyi Sovet, Departament Zakonov [State Council, Department of Laws]. Opis'XI-1890a, delo 7, "Ob izmenenii postanovlenii o rabote maloletnykh, podrastkov i lits zhenskogo pola na fabrikakh, zavodakh i manufakturakh i o rasprostranenii pravil o rabote i obuchenii maloletnikh na remeslennykh zavedeniiakh."

Fond 1152, Gosudarstvennyi Sovet. Departament Gosudarstvennoi Ekonomii [State Council. Department of State Economy]. Opis'X, delo 278, "O vospreshchenii nochnoi raboty nesovershennoletnim i zhenshchinam na fabrikakh, zavodakh i manufakturakh, 1885."

Fond 1278, Gosudarstvennaia Duma, 1913–1916 [State Duma]. Opis'5, delo 670, "O vvedenie zhenskoi fabrichnoi inspektsii."

Leningradskii Gosudarstvennyi Istoricheskii Arkhiv (LGIA) [Leningrad State Historical Archive]
Fond 997, Smolenskie Vechernie Voskresnye Shkoly [Smolensk Evening Sunday Schools]. Opis'1, 1895–1914, dela 16, 31, 57, 59.
Fond 1229, Fabrichnaia Inspektsiia Peterburgskoi Gubernii

[Factory Inspectorate of St Petersburg Province]. Opis'1, delo 307, "Bumago-priadil'naia Stal'ia."

PUBLISHED SOURCES

Abramov, Ia. V. *Nashi voskresnye shkoly*. St Petersburg, 1900.

Ainzaft, S. *Pervyi etap professional'nogo dvizheniia v Rossii* (1905–1907 gg). Moscow, 1924.

Aleksandrov, V. A. *Narody evropeiskoi chasti SSSR*. T. 1. Moscow, 1964.

Anderson, Barbara. *Internal Migration During Modernization in Late Nineteenth Century Russia*. Princeton, 1980.

Antonova, S. I. *Vliianie stolypinskoi reformy na izmenenie v sostave rabochego klassa*. Moscow, 1951.

A[rkhimandrit] Mikhail. *Zhenshchina-rabotnitsa*. St Petersburg, 1906.

Artiukhina, A. V., et al., eds. *Zhenshchiny v revoliutsii*. Moscow, 1959.

Arutiunov, G. A. *Rabochee dvizhenie v Rossii v periode novogo revoliutsionnogo pod'ema, 1910–1914 gg*. Moscow, 1975.

A. S. "Polozhenie rabochei zhenshchiny v Irlandii." *Zhenskii Vestnik*, 1867, no. 7.

Atkinson, D., Dallin, A., and Lapidus, G. *Women in Russia*. Stanford, 1977.

B, R-v. "Ianvarskaia zabastovka 1905 v Peterburge (Materialy dlia kalendaria)." *Krasnaia Letopis'*, 1929, 6 (33).

Babushkin, I. V. *Vospominaniia Ivana Vasil'evicha Babushkina, 1893–1900*. Moscow, 1955.

Balabanov, M. *Ocherki po istorii rabochego klassa*. Chast' 2. Kiev, 1924.

Bater, James. "Spatial Mobility in Moscow and St Petersburg in the Late Imperial Era." Paper delivered at conference, The Social History of Russian Labor, University of California, Berkeley. March 1982.

———. *St Petersburg: Industrialization and Change*. Montreal, 1976.

Bebel, August. *Women in the Past, Present and Future*. San Francisco, 1897.

———. *Woman Under Socialism*. New York, 1971.

Belikov, V. D. *Zhenshchina v promyshlennoi inspektsii zapada*. Tver', 1914.

Belousov, I. *Ushedshaia Moskva. Zapiski po lichnym vospominaniiam s nachala 1870 godov*. Moscow, 1927.

Belousov, V. V. *Izuchenie truda v tabachnom proizvodstve*. St Petersburg, 1921.

Benet, Sula, ed. and trans. *The Village of Viriatino*. New York, 1970.

Blackwell, William L. *The Beginnings of Russian Industrialization, 1800–1860*. Princeton, 1968.

———. *The Industrialization of Russia*. New York, 1970.

Blum, Jerome. *Lord and Peasant in Russia*. New York, 1964.

Bobroff, Anne. "The Bolsheviks and Working Women." *Soviet Studies*, 1974, Oct., no. 4.

Bobrovskaia, Ts. S. *Zapiski riadovogo podpol'shchika*. Chast' 1 (1922).

Bochkareva, E., and Liubimova, S. *Svetlyi put'*. Moscow, 1967.

Bogoslovskii, S. M. *Zabolevaemost' fabrichnykh rabochikh Glukhovskoi i Istominskoi Manufaktur bogorodskogo uezda za 1896–1900*. Moscow, 1906.

Boldyreva, A. G. "Minuvshie gody." In Korol'chuk, E. A., *V nachale puti*. Leningrad, 1975.

Bonnell, Victoria. "Radical Politics and Organized Labor in Prerevolutionary Moscow, 1905–1914." *Journal of Social History*, 1979, vol. 12, no. 2.

———. *Roots of Rebellion: Workers' Politics and Organizations in St Petersburg and Moscow, 1900–1914*. Berkeley, 1983.

Boxer, Marilyn, and Quataert, Jean, eds. *Socialist Women: European Socialist Feminism in the Nineteenth and Early Twentieth Centuries*. New York, 1978.

Braun, Lily. *Frauenarbeit und Hauswirtschaft*. Berlin, 1901.

Broido, E. (E. L'vova). *Zhenshchina-rabotnitsa*. Petrograd, 1917.

———. *Zhenskaia inspektsiia truda*. Petrograd, 1917.

Brusnev, M. I. "Vozniknovenie pervykh sotsial-demokraticheskikh organizatsii." *Proletarskaia Revoliutsiia*, 1923, no. 2 (14).

B-skii, A. "Pervoe maia 1906 v Peterburge i okrestnosti." *Krasnaia Letopis'*, 1926, 2 (17).

Bulgakova, E. I. *Stranichka iz zhizni kievskikh rabotnits*. Kiev, 1906.

Bykov, A. N. *Fabrichnoe zakonodatel'stvo i razvitie ego v Rossii*. St Petersburg, 1909.

Chernevskii, V. A. *K voprosu o p'ianstve v vladimirskoi gubernii i sposobakh bor'by s nim* (po ofitsial'nym dannym i otzyvam korrespondentov tekushchei statistiki). Vladimir, 1911.

Chernyshevskii, N. G. *What Is to Be Done?* New York, 1961.

Chlen, P. K. "Rabochaia gruppa na zhenskom s'ezde i sotsial-demokratiia." *Sotsialdemokrat*, 1909, no. 4.

Churilin, N. A. *Doklad v khar'kovskuiu uezdnuiu zemskuiu Upravu o kustarnykh promyslakh po khar'kovskomu uezdu.* Khar'kov, 1891.

Clements, Barbara Evans. *Bolshevik Feminist: The Life of Aleksandra Kollontai.* Bloomington, Ind., 1949.

Crisp, Olga. "Labour and Industrialization in Russia." In *The Cambridge Economic History of Europe,* vol. 7, pt. 2. Cambridge, 1978.

Czap, Peter. "Marriage and the Peasant Joint Family in the Era of Serfdom." In Ransel, David, ed., *The Family in Imperial Russia.* Urbana, Ill., 1978.

————. "Peasant-Class Courts and Peasant Customary Justice in Russia, 1861–1912." *Journal of Social History,* 1967, Winter.

Dannye o prodolzhitel'nosti rabochego vremeni v promyshlennykh predpriiatiiakh po obrabotke khlopka za 1907. St Petersburg, 1909.

Daul, A. *Zhenskii trud v primenenii k razlichnym otrasliam promyshlennoi deiatel'nosti.* Vvedenie i perevod P. Tkachevym. St Petersburg, 1869.

Davidovich, M. "Khoziaistvennoe znachenie zhenshchin v rabochei sem'e." *Poznanie Rossii,* 1909, vol. 3.

————. *Peterburgskie tekstil'nye rabochie.* Moscow, 1919.

————. *Peterburgskii tekstil'nyi rabochii v ego biudzhetakh.* St Petersburg, 1912.

Davydov, K. V. *Otchet za 1885 fabrichnogo inspektora sanktpeterburgskogo okruga.* St Petersburg, 1886.

Dement'ev, E. M. *Fabrika, chto ona daet naseleniiu i chto ona beret.* Moscow, 1893.

Diubiuk, E. "Tobol'skaia polotnianaia fabrika v nachale 19ogo stoletiia." *Arkhiv istorii truda,* 2. Leningrad, 1924.

Dmitriev, K. (Kolokol'nikov, P. N.) *Iz praktiki professional'nogo dvizheniia v Rossii.* Odessa, 1907.

————. *Professional'noe dvizhenie i soiuzy v Rossii.* St Petersburg, 1909.

Doklad v khar'kovskuiu zemskuiu upravu o kustarnykh promyslakh po khar'kovskomu uezdu. Khar'kov, 1891.

Drug Zhenshchin. St Petersburg, 1884–1885.

Druzhinin, N. K. *Usloviia byta rabochikh v dorevoliutsionnoi Rossii (po dannym biudzhetnykh obsledovanii).* Moscow, 1958.

Dubrovina, O. I. "Rabochie Obshchestva samoobrazovaniia v SPb-e." In *Trudy pervogo vserossiiskogo zhenskogo s'ezda 10–16 dekabria.* St Petersburg, 1909.

Dzhabadari, I. S. "Protsess piatidesiati (Vserossiiskaia Revoliutsionnaia Organizatsiia)," *Byloe,* 1907, no. 22 (10).

Dzhervis, M. V. *Russkaia tabachnaia fabrika v XVIII i XIX vekakh.* Leningrad, 1933.

Edmondson, Linda. "Russian Feminists and the First All-Russian Congress of Women." *Russian History,* 1976, vol. 3, pt. 2.

———. *Feminism in Russia, 1900–1917.* London, 1983.

Efimenko, Aleksandra. *Izsledovaniia narodnoi zhizni.* Vypusk pervyi. Moscow, 1884.

Ekonomicheskoe polozhenie Rossii nakanune velikoi oktiabr'skoi sotsialisticheskoi revoliutsii. Dokumenty i materialy. Chast' pervaia. Moscow and Leningrad, 1957.

Engel, Barbara, and Rosenthal, Clifford. *Five Sisters: Women Against the Tsar.* New York, 1975.

Engels, Frederick. *The Origin of the Family, Private Property and the State.* New York, 1972.

Engelstein, Laura. *Moscow, 1905: Working Class Organization and Political Conflict.* Stanford, 1982.

Erisman, F. F. *K voprosu o sanitarno-fabrichnom zakonodatel'stve.* Moscow, 1881.

———. *Pishchevoe dovol'stvie rabochikh na fabrikakh moskovskoi gubernii.* Moscow, 1893.

———. "Pitanie rabochego naseleniia v tsentral'noi Rossii." *Vestnik Obshchestvennoi Gigieny,* 1889, 3, no. 2.

———. *Sbornik statisticheskikh svedenii po moskovskoi gubernii.* Otdel sanitarnoi statistiki. T. 4, chast' 1. Moscow, 1890.

Ermanskii, A. "Vserossiiskii zhenskii s'ezd." *Sovremennyi Mir,* 1909, no. 1.

Fabrichnaia Zhizn'. St Petersburg, 1910–1911.

Fabrichno-zavodskie predpriiatiia Rossiiskoi Imperii. Petrograd, 1914.

Fabrichno-zavodskaia promyshlennost' goroda Moskvy i moskovskoi gubernii, 1917–27. Moscow, 1928.

Farnsworth, Beatrice. *Aleksandra Kollontai: Socialism, Feminism, and the Bolshevik Revolution.* Stanford, 1980.

Fisher, A. *V Rossii i v Anglii.* Moscow, 1922.

Frieden, Nancy M. "Child Care: Medical Reform in a Traditionalist Culture." In Ransel, David L., ed., *The Family in Imperial Russia.* Urbana, Ill., 1978.

Gaponenko, L. S. *Rabochii klass Rossii v 1917 godu.* Moscow, 1970.

Gerasimovich, V. G. *Zhizn' russkogo rabochego. Vospominaniia.* Moscow, 1959.

Gerschenkron, Alexander. *Economic Backwardness in Historical Perspective.* Cambridge, Mass., 1962.

Giffen, F. C. "In Quest of an Effective Program of Factory Legislation in Russia. The Years of Preparation." *Historian,* 1967, vol. 29, no. 2.

———. "Prohibition of Night Work for Women and Young Persons: The Russian Factory Law of June 3, 1885." *Canadian Slavic Studies,* 1969, vol. 2.

Godovoi otchet o deiatel'nosti zhenskikh vechernikh klassov v Nezhine za 1897–1898 g. Chernigov, 1899.

Goldberg, Rochelle. "The Russian Woman's Movement." Ph.D. diss., University of Rochester, 1976.

Golos Pechatnika. St Petersburg, 1906–1907.

Golos Tabachnika. St Petersburg, 1906–1907.

Golos Zhizni. Moscow, 1910–1911.

Goroda Rossii v 1904 godu. St Petersburg, 1906.

Goroda Rossii v 1910 godu. St Petersburg, 1916.

Gorodkov, G. I. *Otchet za 1885 g. fabrichnogo inspektora vilenskogo okruga.* St Petersburg, 1886.

Gosudarstvennaia Duma. Stenograficheskie otchety (1913). Chast' 2. Chetvertyi sozyv, sessiia 1, zasedanie 37.

Grigor'ev, N. I. "O p'ianstve sredi masterovykh v S-Peterburge." *Zhurnal Russkogo Obshchestva Okhraneniia Narodnogo Zdraviia,* 1898, no. 12.

Grinevich, V. *Professional'noe dvizhenie v Rossii.* St Petersburg, 1908.

Gudvan, A. *Ocherki po istorii dvizheniia sluzhashchikh v Rossii.* Chast' pervaia. Moscow, 1925.

Guettel, Charnie. *Marxism and Feminism.* Toronto, 1974.

Gvozdev, S. *Zapiski fabrichnogo inspektora.* Moscow, 1911.

Haimson, Leopold. "The Problem of Social Stability in Urban Russia, 1905–1917." *Slavic Review,* pt. 1 (1964), vol. 23, no. 4; pt. 2 (1965), vol. 24, no. 1.

Hasegawa, Tsuyoshi. *The February Revolution: Petrograd, 1917.* Seattle and London, 1981.

Hogan, Heather. "The Reorganization of Work Processes in the St Petersburg Metal-working Industry, 1901–1914." Paper presented to conference, The Social History of Russian Labor, University of California, Berkeley, March 1982.

Hosking, Geoffrey. *The Russian Constitutional Experiment.* Cambridge, 1973.

Iakovlev, V., ed. *Revoliutsionnaia zhurnalistika 70-kh godov.* Paris, 1905.

Ianzhul, I. I. *Bab'e delo.* St Petersburg, 1898.

————. *Fabrichnyi byt moskovskoi gubernii. Otchet za 1882–1883.*

————. "Fabrichnyi rabochii v srednei Rossii i Tsarstve Pol'skom." *Vestnik Evropy,* 1882, no. 2.

————. *Iz vospominaniia i perepiski fabrichnogo inspektora pervogo prizyva.* St Petersburg, 1907.

————. *Ocherki i izsledovaniia.* Moscow, 1884.

————. *Otchet za 1885 g. fabrichnogo inspektora moskovskogo okruga.* St Petersburg, 1886.

Issledovanie kustarnykh promyslov saratovskoi gubernii. Vyp. 1. Gorod Kuznetska. Saratov, 1904.

Issledovanie kustarnykh promyslov saratovskoi gubernii. Vyp. 5. Balashovskii i serdovskii uezdy. Saratov, 1913.

Istoriia Moskvy. T. 5. Moscow, 1955.

Istoriia odnogo soiuza. Obshchestvo rabochikh chainykh razvesochnykh g. Moskvy. Moscow, 1907.

Ivanov, L. M. *Rabochii klass i rabochee dvizhenie v Rossii, 1861–1917.* Moscow, 1966.

————. *Rossiiskii proletariat: oblik, bor'ba, gegemoniia.* Moscow, 1970.

————. *Vserossiiskaia politicheskaia stachka v oktiabre 1905 god.* Chast' 1. Moscow and Leningrad, 1955.

Ivanov, N. "Maiskaia zabastovka 1901 na fabrike Cheshera." *Krasnaia Letopis',* (1925), 3 (14).

"Iz vospominaniia S. V. Perazicha," *Krasnaia Letopis',* 1923, no. 7.

Johnson, Robert. *Peasant and Proletarian: The Working Class of Moscow in the Late Nineteenth Century.* New Brunswick, N.J., 1979.

Kabo, E. O. *Ocherki rabochego byta: opyt monograficheskogo issledovaniia domashnego rabochego byta.* Moscow, 1928.

Kahan, Arcadius. "Government Policies and the Industrialization of Russia." *Journal of Economic History,* 1967, vol. 27, no. 4.

————. "The 'Hereditary Workers' Hypothesis and the Development of a Factory Labor Force in 18th and 19th Century Russia." In C. A. Anderson and M. J. Bowman, eds., *Education and Economic Development.* Chicago, 1965.

Kaidanova, O. V. *Ocherki po istorii narodnogo obrazovaniia v Rossii i SSSR.* T. 2, vyp. 2. Moscow, 1939.

Kal'manovich, A. A. "Konechnaia tsel' zhenskogo dvizheniia." *Soiuz Zhenshchin,* 1908, no. 9.

Kanatchikov, Semen. *Iz istorii moego bytiia.* Moscow and Leningrad, 1929.

Karelin, A. E. "Deviatoe ianvaria i Gapon. Vospominaniia." *Krasnaia Letopis',* 1922, no. 1.

Karelina, V. M. "Na zare rabochego dvizheniia v S-Peterburge." *Krasnaia Letopis'*, 1922, no. 4.

———. "Rabotnitsy v gaponovskikh obshchestvakh." In P. F. Kudelli, *Rabotnitsa v 1905 g. v S-Peterburge*. Leningrad, 1926.

———. "Rabotnitsa posle 9ogo ianvaria." In Kudelli, above.

———. "Vospominaniia o podpol'nykh rabochikh kruzhkakh brusnevskoi organizatsii." In Korol'chuk, E. A., *V nachale puti. Vospominaniia peterburgskikh rabochikh 1872–1897*. Leningrad, 1975.

Karnovich, E. P. *O razvitii zhenskogo truda v Peterburge*. St Petersburg, 1865.

Kaser, M. C. "Russian Entrepreneurship." In *The Cambridge Economic History of Europe*, vol. 7, pt. 2. Cambridge, 1978.

Katenina, L. "K voprosu o polozhenii rabotnits v tekstil'noi promyshlennosti." *Obshchestvennyi Vrach*, 1914, no. 3.

Kats, A. N., and Milonov, Iu. *1905: Materialy i dokumenty*. Moscow and Leningrad, 1926.

Kats, A. Iu. "Naselenie Pokrovskoi Manufaktury (dmitrovskogo uezda) i ego zhilishchnye usloviia." *Svedenie o zaraznykh bolezniakh i sanitarno-vrachebnoi organizatsii moskovskoi gubernii*, 1910, no. 10.

Kazakevich, R. A. *Sotsial-demokraticheskie organizatsii Peterburga*. Leningrad, 1960.

Kechedzhi-Shapovalov, M. V. *Zhenskoe dvizhenie v Rossii i zagranitsei*. St Petersburg, 1902.

Kir'ianov, Iu. I, *Zhiznennyi uroven' rabochikh Rossii*. Moscow, 1979.

Kniazeva, M., and Inozemtsev, M. "K istorii rabochikh vyborov v komissiiu Shidlovskogo." *Istoriia Proletariata SSSR*, 1935, Sbornik 2.

Koenker, Diane. *Moscow Workers and the 1917 Revolution*. Princeton, 1981.

Kol'be, E. *Ob opredelenii vremeni rabot na fabrikakh dlia zhenshchin, dlia nesovershennoletnikh i detei*. n.p., 1871.

Kollontai, Aleksandra. "Avtobiograficheskii ocherk," *Proletarskaia Revoliutsiia*, 1912, no. 3.

———. *Iz moei zhizni i raboty: vospominaniia i dnevniki*. Moscow, 1974.

———. *K istorii dvizheniia rabotnits v Rossii*. Khar'kov, 1920.

———. *Sotsial'nye osnovy zhenskogo voprosa*. St Petersburg, 1909.

———. "Zhenskoe rabochee dvizhenie," *Nasha Zaria*, 1913, no. 2.

Kolokol'nikov, P., and Rapaport, S. *1905–1907 gg. v professional'nom dvizhenii*. Moscow, 1925.

KPSS v rezoliutsiiakh i resheniiakh s'ezdov, konferentsii i plenumov TsK. Chast' 1. Moscow, 1953.

Kontorovich, Ia. *Zhenshchina v prave.* St Petersburg, 1895.

Korol'chuk, E. A. *Rabochee dvizhenie 70kh godov.* Moscow, 1934.

Korol'chuk, E. A., ed. *V nachale puti. Vospominaniia peterburgskikh rabochikh 1872–1897.* Leningrad, 1975.

Koz'minykh-Lanin, I. M. *Deviatletnii period fabrichno-zavodskoi promyshlennosti moskovskoi gubernii (s ianvaria 1901 goda do ianvaria 1910 goda).* Moscow, 1912.

———. *Fabrichno-zavodskii rabochii vladimirskoi gubernii.* Vladimir, 1912.

———. *Gramotnost' i zarabotki fabrichno-zavodskikh rabochikh moskovskoi gubernii.* Moscow, 1912.

———. "K voprosu o gramotnosti i ekonomicheskikh usloviiakh truda na sukonnykh i bumago-tkatskikh fabrikakh moskovskoi gubernii." *Vestnik Manufakturnoi Promyshlennosti,* t. 25, pt. 1 (1912).

———. *Mekhanicheskoe tkachestvo v moskovskoi gubernii. Obrabotka khlopa.* Moscow, 1912.

———. *Semeinii sostav fabrichno-zavodskikh rabochikh moskovskoi gubernii.* Moscow, 1914.

———. "Ukhod na polevye raboty fabrichno-zavodskikh rabochikh moskovskoi gubernii." *Izvestiia Obshchestva dlia Sodeistviia Ulucheniiu i Razvitiiu Manufakturnoi Promyshlennosti,* 1912, 16, no. 9.

———. *Zarabotki fabrichno-zavodskikh rabochikh v Rossii.* Vyp. 1. Moscow, 1918.

Kratkii ocherk mestnykh i otkhozhikh promyslov naseleniia khar'kovskoi gubernii. Khar'kov, 1905.

Krupianskaia, V. Iu. "Evoliutsia semeino-bytovogo uklada rabochikh." In L. M. Ivanov, ed., *Rossiiskii proletariat: oblik, bor'ba, gegemoniia.* Moscow, 1970.

Krupskaia, N. K. *Pedagogicheskie Sochineniia,* T. 1. Moscow, 1957.

———. "Piat' let raboty v vechernikh smolenskikh klassakh." In *Pedagogicheskie sochineniia,* T. 1. Moscow, 1957.

———. "Zhenshchina-rabotnitsa." In *Pedagogicheskie sochineniia,* T. 1. Moscow, 1957.

Kruze, E. E. *Peterburgskie rabochie v 1912–1914 godakh.* Moscow and Leningrad, 1961.

———. *Polozhenie rabochego klassa Rossii v 1900–1914 gg.* Leningrad, 1976.

Krzhizhanovskaia, Z. "Iz zhizni odnogo kluba." In S. E. Chernomordik, ed., *Put' k oktiabriu. Sbornik statei, vospominanii i doku-mentov.* Moscow, 1923.

Kudelli, P. F. *Rabotnitsa v 1905 g. v S-Peterburge.* Leningrad, 1926.

———. *Vospominaniia chlenov sovieta rabochikh deputatov Peterburga 1905.* Leningrad, 1926.

Kustarnaia promyshlennost' i sbyt kustarnykh izdeliia. Moscow, 1913.

Kustarnye promysly v khar'kovskoi gubernii po dannym issledovaniia 1912 g. Khar'kov, 1913.

Kustarnye promysly nizhegorodskoi gubernii. Nizhnii Novgorod, 1894.

Kuz'min, N. N. *Nizshee i srednee spetsial'noe obrazovanie v dorevoliutsi-onnoi Rossii.* Cheliabinsk, 1971.

Kuznetsov, D. G. *Deiateli peterburgskogo "Soiuz bor'by za osvobozhdenie rabochego klassa."* Moscow, 1962.

L-a, Ia. "Zhenshchina rabotnitsa." *Rabochii Soiuz,* 1906, no. 2.

Laverychev, V. Ia. *Krupnaia burzhuaziia v poreformennoi Rossii, 1861–1900.* Moscow, 1974.

———. *Tsarism i rabochii vopros v Rossii (1861–1917 gg).* Moscow, 1972.

Lenskaia, L. N. *O prisluge.* Doklad chitannyi v 2-m Zhenskom Klube v Moskve v fev. 1908 goda. Moscow, 1908.

Levin, I. D. "Rabochie kluby v Peterburge (1907–1914)." In *Materialy po istorii professional'nogo dvizheniia v Rossii,* 3–4. Moscow, 1926.

Liashchenko, P. I. *History of the National Economy of Russia.* New York, 1949.

Listok Soiuza Rabochikh Portnykh, Portnikh i Skorniakov. St Peters-burg, 1905–1907.

Litvinov-Filanskii, V. P. *Fabrichnoe zakonodatel'stvo i fabrichnaia in-spektsiia v Rossii.* St Petersburg, 1900.

Luch. St Petersburg, 1912–1914.

Lunts, M. G. *Sbornik statei.* Moscow, 1909.

L'vova, E. *Russkaia rabotnitsa.* St Petersburg, 1914.

M. "Zhenskii trud v fabrichno-zavodskoi promyshlennosti Rossii za poslednie 13 let (1901–1913)." *Obshchestvennyi Vrach,* 1915, no. 9–10.

M. B. "Vserossiiskii zhenskii s'ezd i rabochaia gruppa." *Professional'nyi Soiuz,* 1909, no. 21.

Malia, Martin. *Alexander Herzen and the Birth of Russian Socialism.* Cambridge, Mass., 1961.

Marks, K., Engels, F., and Lenin, V. I. *O zhenskom voprose.* Moscow, 1971.

Martov, L. *Zapiski sotsial-demokrata.* Kn. 1. Berlin, 1922.

Marx, Eleanor, and Aveling, Edward. "The Woman Question." *Marxism Today,* 1972, March.

"Materialy dlia istorii russkogo rabochego dvizheniia." *Krasnaia Letopis',* 1923, no. 7.

Materialy dlia otsenki nedvizhimykh imushchestv v gorodakh i fabrichnykh poselkakh kostromskoi gubernii. T. 1, vyp. 2. Kostroma, 1915.

Materialy dlia otsenki zemel' vladimirskoi gubernii. T. 2, vyp. 3. Vladimirskii uezd. Vladimir, 1912.

Materialy dlia otsenki zemel' vladimirskoi gubernii. T. 10, vyp. 3. Shuiskii uezd. Vladimir, 1908.

Materialy dlia otsenki zemel' vladimirskoi gubernii. T. 12, vyp. 3. Pokrovskii uezd. Vladimir, 1908.

Materialy po istorii professional'nogo dvizheniia v Peterburge za 1905–1907. Leningrad, 1926.

Materialy po istorii professional'nogo dvizheniia v Rossii. Sbornik 1, Moscow, 1924; Sbornik 4, Moscow, 1925.

Materialy po statistike narodnogo khoziaistva v s-peterburgskoi gubernii. Vyp. 2. *Shlissel'burgskii uezd.* St Petersburg, 1885.

Materialy po statistike narodnogo khoziaistva v s-peterburgskoi gubernii. Vyp. 5. *Krest'ianskoe khoziaistvo v s-peterburgskom uezde.* Chast' 2. St Petersburg, 1887.

Materialy po statistike narodnogo khoziaistva v s-peterburgskoi gubernii. Vyp. 7. *Krest'ianskoe khoziaistvo v tsarskosel'skom uezde.* St Petersburg, 1892.

Meshalin, I. V. *Tekstil'naia promyshlennost' krest'ian moskovskoi gubernii v XVIII-pervoi polovine XIX veke.* Moscow, 1950.

Menshchikov, L. P. *Okhrana i revoliutsiia.* Moscow, 1925–1932.

Meyer, Alfred G. "Marxism and the Women's Movement." In Atkinson, D., Dallin, A., and Lapidus, G., *Women in Russia.* Stanford, 1977.

Mikhailova, E. "Polozhenie fabrichnykh rabotnits na moskovskikh fabrikakh i uezdnykh." *Drug Zhenshchin,* 1884, no. 5.

Mikhailovskii, A. "Zarabotnaia plata i prodolzhitel'nost' rabochego vremeni na russkikh fabrikakh i zavodakh." In Ministerstvo Finansov, Departament Torgovli i Manufaktur, *Fabrichno-zavodskaia promyshlennost' i torgovli Rossii.* St Petersburg, 1896.

Mikulin, A. A. *Fabrichnaia inspektsiia v Rossii, 1882–1902.* Kiev, 1906.

————. *Fabrichno-zavodskaia i remeslennaia promyshlennost' odesskogo gradonachal'stva khersonskoi gubernii.* Odessa, 1897.

Milonov, Iu. *Kak voznikli profsoiuzy v Rossii.* Moscow, 1929.

―――. *Moskovskoe professional'noe dvizhenie v gody pervoi revoliutsii.* Moscow, 1925.

Miropol'skii, V. I. *Otchet za 1885 g. fabrichnogo inspektora voronezhskogo okruga.* St Petersburg, 1886.

Mirovich, N. *Iz istorii zhenskogo dvizheniia v Rossii.* Moscow, 1908.

Mitskevich, S. E., ed. *Na zare rabochego dvizheniia v Moskve. Vospominaniia uchastnikov moskovskogo rabochego soiuza, 1893–95, i dokumenty.* Moscow, 1932.

―――. *Revoliutsionnaia Moskva, 1888–1905.* Moscow, 1940.

Moskovskaia guberniia po mestnomu obsledovaniiu 1898–1900. T. 4, vyp. 2. Moscow, 1908.

Muralova, S. I. "Iz proshlogo." In Mitskevich, S. I., ed., *Na zare rabochego dvizheniia v Moskve.* Moscow, 1932.

Nash Put'. Moscow, 1910–1911.

Naumov, G. *Biudzhety rabochikh goroda Kieva.* Kiev, 1914.

"Nekrologi: M. D. Subbotina i B. Kaminskaia." *Obshchina,* 1878, no. 6–7.

Nevskii, V. I. *Materialy dlia biograficheskogo slovaria sotsial-demokratov, vstupivshikh v rossiiskoe rabochee dvizhenie za period ot 1880–1905 g.* Vyp. 1. Moscow and Leningrad, 1923.

Nikol'skii, D. P. "Zhenskaia fabrichnaia inspektsiia i neobkhodimost' ee v Rossii." In *Trudy pervogo vserossiiskogo zhenskogo s'ezda. 10–16 dekabria.* St Petersburg, 1909.

Norinskii, K. "Moi vospominaniia." In *Ot gruppy Blagoeva k "Soiuz Bor'by" 1886–1894.* 1921.

Novitskii, I. O. *Otchet za 1885 g. fabrichnogo inspektora kievskogo okruga.* St Petersburg, 1886.

Novosel'skii, S. A. *O razlichiiakh v smertnosti gorodskogo i sel'skogo naseleniia Evropeiskoi Rossii.* Moscow, 1911.

Obninskii, V. P. *Polgoda russkoi revoliutsii.* Moscow, 1906.

Obshcheprofessional'nye organy, 1905–1907 gg. Vyp. 1: Moskovskie zhurnaly 1905 goda. Moscow, 1926.

Obzor vladimirskoi gubernii v sel'sko-khoziaistvennom otnoshenii za 1900. Vladimir, 1903.

"Odin iz voprosov professional'noi gigieny v sekstii akusherstva i zhenskikh boleznei na predstoiashchem IX Pirogovskom s'ezde vrachei." *Promyshlennost' i Zdorov'e,* 1903, no. 8.

Odnodnevnaia perepis' nachal'nykh shkol v Imperii, 18 ianvaria 1911. M.N.P. Vyp. 2. Moskovskii uchebnyi okrug. St Petersburg, 1913.

Oliunina, E. A. *Portnovskii promysl v Moskve i v derevniakh moskovskoi i riazan'skoi gubernii. Materialy k istorii domashnei promyshlennosti v Rossii.* Moscow, 1914.

Opatskii, A. N. *Fabrichno-zavodskaia promyshlennost' khar'kovskoi gubernii.* Khar'kov, 1912.

Orlov, A. C. *Kustarnaia promyshlennost' moskovskoi gubernii.* Moscow, 1913.

Orlov, P. A. *Ukazatel' fabrik i zavodov Evropeiskoi Rossii.* St Petersburg, 1887.

Osinkin, A. A. "Ivanovo-Voznesensk. Sovet rabochikh deputatov v 1905." *Voprosy Istorii KPSS,* 1965, t. 65, no. 4.

Otchet byvshego departamenta neokladnykh sborov, a nyne Glavnogo upravleniia neokladnykh sborov i kazennoi prodazhi pitei za 1895. St Petersburg, 1897.

Otchet chinov fabrichnoi inspektsii vladimirskoi gubernii, 1894–1897. Vladimir, 1899.

Otchet otdela bor'by s alkogolizmom zhenshchin i detei. Obshchestvo okhraneniia zdorov'ia zhenshchin, s noiabria 1903-ianvaria 1905. St Petersburg, 1906.

Ot gruppy Blagoeva k "Soiuz bor'by" 1886–1894. 1921.

"Ot Russkogo Revoliutsionnogo Obshchestva k zhenshchinam." *Literaturnoe Nasledstvo,* t. 40–42, 1941.

"Otsenka zhenskogo i muzhskogo truda na sel'skikh rabotakh." *Zhenskii Vestnik,* 1907, no. 2.

Ozerov, I. Kh. *Politika po rabochemu voprosu v Rossii za poslednie gody.* Moscow, 1906.

Paialin, N. P. *Zavod imeni Lenina 1857–1918.* Moscow, 1933.

Pankratova, A. M., ed. *1905. Stachechnoe dvizhenie.* Moscow and Leningrad, 1925.

Pavlov, F. P. *Za desiat' let praktiki (otryvki vospominanii, vpechatlenii i nabliudenii iz fabrichnoi zhizni).* Moscow, 1901.

Pazhitnov, K. A. "Iz kazennoi ekaterinslavskoi sukonnoi i shelkochulochnoi fabriki." *Arkhiv Istorii Truda.* Leningrad, 1924.

———. *Ocherki istorii tekstil'noi promyshlennosti dorevoliutsionnoi Rossii: sherstianaia promyshlennost'.* Moscow, 1955.

———. "O reglamente i rabotnykh regulakh sukonnym i kazeinym fabrikam." *Trud v Rossii,* 1925, kn. 1.

———. *Polozhenie rabochego klassa v Rossii.* St Petersburg, 1906.

Perazich, V. "Iz materialov po istorii klassovoi bor'by tekstil'shchikov Leningrada." In *Materialy po istorii professional'nogo dvizheniia v Peterburge za 1905–1907.* Leningrad, 1926.

————. "Soiuz viazal'shchikov." In the source above.

————. "Tekstil'shchiki v Komissii Shidlovskogo." *Krasnaia Letopis'*, 1930, 6 (9).

Perepis' Moskvy 1902 goda. Chast' 1, vyp. 2. Moscow, 1906.

Pervaia vseobshchaia perepis' naseleniia rossiiskoi imperii. 1897 g., T. 47 (1903).

Pervyi soviet rabochikh deputatov: gorod Ivanovo-Voznesensk, mai-iiul' 1905. Moscow, 1905.

Peskov, P. A. *Fabrichnyi byt vladimirskoi gubernii. Otchet za 1882–1883.* St Petersburg, 1884.

————. *Otchet za 1885 g. fabrichnogo inspektora vladimirskogo okruga.* St Petersburg, 1886.

————. *Sanitarnoe issledovanie fabrik po obrabotke voloknistykh veshchestv v gorode Moskve.* Vyp. 1–2. Trudy komissii, uchrezhdennoi g. moskovskim General-Gubernatorom, kn. V. A. Dolgorukovym, dlia osmotra fabrik i zavodov v Moskve. Moscow, 1882.

Petrykovskii, S. V. "Polozhenie beremennykh rabotnits na zavodakh," *Trudy vtorogo vserossiiskogo s'ezda fabrichnykh vrachei.* Vyp. 1. Moscow, 1911.

Pogozhev, A. V. "Iz zhizni fabrichnogo liuda v stolitse." *Russkaia Mysl'*, 1885, kn. 5.

————. *Obzor mestnykh obiazatel'nykh postavlenii po fabrichnoi sanitarii v Rossii.* St Petersburg, 1894.

Pogruzov, A. D. *Kustarnaia promyshlennost' Rossii. Ee znachenie, nuzhdy i vozmozhnoe budushchee.* St Petersburg, 1901.

Pokrovskaia, M. I. *Kak ia byla gorodskim vrachem dlia bednykh.* St Petersburg, 1903.

————. "Obshchestvo popecheniia o molodykh devitsakh v SPb-e." *Trudy Vserossiiskogo s'ezda po remeslennoi promyshlennosti v SPb-e 1900.* St Petersburg, 1901.

————. "Peterburgskie rabochie i ikh ekonomicheskoe polezhenie." *Vestnik Evropy*, 1899, kn. 3.

————. "Peterburgskaia rabotnitsa." *Mir Bozhii*, 1900, no. 12.

————. "Peterburgskie voskresnye sobraniia dlia rabotnits." *Mir Bozhii*, 1899, no. 3.

————. "Vopros o deshevykh kvartirakh dlia rabochego klassa." *Vestnik Evropy*, 1901, kn. 7.

————. *Vrachebno-politseiskii nadzor za prostitutsiei sposobstvuet vyrozhdeniiu naroda.* St Petersburg, 1902.

————. "Zhenskii trud po ustroistvu zhilishch dlia bednykh za granitsei." *Vestnik Evropy*, 1898, kn. 8.

Portal, Roger. "The Industrialization of Russia." in *The Cambridge Economic History of Europe*, vol. 6, pt. 2. Cambridge, 1965.

Portugalov, V. "Zhenskii trud v sanitarnom otnoshenii." *Drug Zhenshchin*, 1884, no. 1.

Pravda, 1912–1914. St Petersburg.

Prechistenskie rabochie kursy. Pervyi rabochii universitet v Moskve. Moscow, 1948.

Proekt pravil dlia fabrik i zavou v v S-Peterburge i uezde. St Petersburg, 1860.

Professional'nyi Listok. St Petersburg, 1914.

Professional'nyi Soiuz. St Petersburg, 1905–1906.

Professional'nyi Vestnik. St Petersburg, 1907–1909.

Prokopovich, S. "Biudzhety peterburgskikh rabochikh." *Poznanie*, 1909, 2.

Promyshlennost' i Zdorov'e, 1904, kn. 2.

Promysly krest'ianskogo naseleniia s-peterburgskoi gubernii. S-Peterburgskii uezd. St Petersburg, 1912.

Promysl vladimirskoi gubernii. Vyp. 3. Pokrovskii i Aleksandrovskii uezdy. Moscow, 1882.

Quataert, Jean. *Reluctant Feminists in German Social Democracy, 1885–1917*. Princeton, 1975.

Rabochee dvizhenie b Petrograde v 1912–1917. Dokumenty i materialy. Leningrad, 1958.

Rabochee dvizhenie v Rossii XIX veke: Sbornik dokumentov i materialov. Moscow and Leningrad, 1950–1963. The editor-in chief of vols. 1–3 was A. M. Pankratova; of vol. 4, L. M. Ivanov.

Rabochee dvizhenie vo vladimirskoi gubernii, 1910–1914. Vladimir, 1957.

Rabochii vopros v kommissii V. N. Kokovtseva v 1905. 1926.

Rabotnitsa. St Petersburg, 1914.

Ransel, David. "Abandonment and Fosterage of Unwanted Children: The Women of the Foundling System." In Ransel, David, ed., *The Family in Imperial Russia*. Urbana, Ill., 1978.

———. *The Family in Imperial Russia*. Urbana, Ill., 1978.

Rashin, A. G. *Formirovanie promyshlennogo proletariata v Rossii*. Moscow, 1940.

———. *Formirovanie rabochego klassa Rossii*. Moscow, 1958.

———. *Naselenie Rossii za 100 let*. Moscow, 1956.

———. *Zhenskii trud v SSSR*. Moscow, 1928.

Remeslenniki i remeslennoe upravlenie v Rossii. Petrograd, 1916.

Rimlinger, Gaston V. "Autocracy and the Factory Order in Early

Russian Industrialization." *Journal of Economic History*, 1960, vol. 20, no. 1.

———. "The Expansion of the Labor Market in Capitalist Russia: 1861–1917." *Journal of Economic History*, 1961, vol. 21, no. 2.

———. "The Management of Labor Protest in Tsarist Russia 1870–1905." *International Review of Social History*, 1960, vol. 5.

Romashova, V. I. "Obrazovanie postoiannykh kadrov rabochikh v poreformennoi promyshlennosti Moskvy." In Ivanov, L. M., ed., *Rabochii klass i rabochee dvizhenie v Rossii 1861–1917*. Moscow, 1966.

Roosa, Ruth. "Workers' Insurance Legislation and the Role of the Industrialist in the Period of the Third State Duma." *Russian Review*, 1975, vol. 34, no. 4.

Rossiiskoe Obschestvo Zashchity Zhenshchin. *Ob neobkhodimosti osnovaniia obshchestva zashchity zhenshchin*. St Petersburg, 1896.

Rowbotham, Sheila. *Women, Resistance and Revolution*. New York, 1974.

Rowland, Richard. "Urban In-migration in Late 19th Century Russia." In Michael F. Hamm, ed., *The City in Russian History*, Lexington, Ky., 1976.

Rozanov, M. *Obukhovtsy*. Leningrad, 1938.

Rozhkova, M. K. *Formirovanie kadrov promyshlennykh rabochikh v 60–nachale 80 kh godov XIX v.* Moscow, 1974.

———. "Sostav rabochikh trekhgornoi manufaktury nakanune imperialisticheskoi voiny." *Istoriia Proletariata SSSR*, 1931, 5.

Sablin, V. M., ed., *Protsess 193-kh*. Moscow, 1906.

Sablinsky, Walter. *The Road to Bloody Sunday*. Princeton, 1976.

Sacks, Michael. *Women's Work in Soviet Russia: Continuity in the Midst of Change*. New York, 1976.

S-Peterburg po perepisi 15 dekabria 1890 goda. Chast' 1, vyp. 2. St Petersburg, 1891.

S. Peterburg po perepisi 15 dekabria 1900 goda. Vyp. 2. St Petersburg, 1903.

Sapronov, T. *Iz istorii rabochego dvizheniia (po lichnym vospominaniiam)*. Leningrad and Moscow, 1925.

Sbornik statisticheskikh svedenii po kostromskoi gubernii. T. 2, vyp. 3. *Kinisheiskii uezd*. Kostroma, 1901.

Sbornik statisticheskikh svedenii po moskovskoi gubernii. Otdel sanitarnoi statistiki. T. 4, chast' 1. F. F. Erisman, compiler. Moscow, 1890.

Sbornik statisticheskikh svedenii po moskovskoi gubernii. Otdel sanitar-noi statistiki. T. 5, vyp. 1. E. A. Osipov, compiler. Moscow, 1890.

Sbornik statisticheskikh svedenii po moskovskoi gubernii. T. 7, *Zhenskie promysly.* Vyp. 4. M. K. Gorbunova, compiler. Moscow, 1882.

Sbornik statisticheskikh svedenii po samarskoi gubernii. Otdel khoziai-stvennoi statistiki. Vyp. 1. *Samarskii uezd.* Moscow, 1883.

Sbornik statisticheskikh svedenii po saratovskoi gubernii. T. 3, chast' 1. *Promysly krest'ianskogo naseleniia saratovskogo i tsaritsynskogo uezdov.* Saratov, 1884.

Schneiderman, J. *Sergei Zubatov and Revolutionary Marxism.* Ithaca, N.Y., 1976.

Schwarz, Solomon. *The Russian Revolution of 1905.* Chicago, 1967.

Sel'sko-khoziaistvennyi obzor nizhegorodskoi gubernii za 1907–1908. Nizhnii Novgorod, 1909.

Semanov, S. N. *Peterburgskie rabochie nakanune pervoi russkoi revo-liutsii.* Moscow and Leningrad, 1966.

Serditova, S. *Bol'sheviki v bor'be za zhenskie proletarskie massy.* Mos-cow, 1959.

Shanin, Theodore. *The Awkward Class.* Oxford, 1972.

Shaposhnikov, I. M. "Biudzhety rabochikh odnoi iz fabrik bogo-rodskogo uezda v sviazi s pitaniem i zabolevaemostiu." *Svedenie o zaraznykh bolezniakh i sanitarno-vrachebnoi organizatsii moskovskoi gubernii,* 1910, no. 1.

Shatilova, T. *Ocherk istorii Leningradskogo soiuza khimikov (1905–1918).* Leningrad, 1927.

Shchepkina, A. "Apologiia 'burzhuazok' v knige g-zha Kollontai 'Sotsial'nye osnovy zhenskogo voprosa'." *Soiuz Zhenshchin,* 1904, no. 4.

Shestakov, P. M. *Rabochie na Manufakture T-va "Emil Tsindel" v Moskve.* Moscow, 1909.

Shidlovskii, A. V. *Otchet za 1885 g. fabrichnogo inspektora kazan'skogo okruga.* St Petersburg, 1886.

Shkaratan, O. I. *Problemy sotsial'noi struktury rabochego klassa SSSR.* Moscow, 1970.

Shul'ts-Gavernitz, G. *Krupnoe proizvodstvo v Rossii.* Moscow, 1899.

Shuster, U. A. *Peterburgskie rabochie v 1905–1907 gg.* Leningrad, 1976.

Shuvalov, I. *Rabochee i professional'noe dvizhenie na bumazhnykh fabri-kakh 1750–1914.* Moscow, 1926.

Sidorov, A. L., ed. *Ekonomicheskoe polozhenie Rossii nakanune velikoi oktiabrskoi sotsialisticheskoi revoliutsii. Dokumenty i materialy.* Chast' 1. Moscow-Leningrad, 1957.

Sidorov, N. I., ed. *1905 god v Peterburge.* Vyp. 2. Soviet rabochikh deputatov. Sbornik materialov. 1925.

Smith, S. A. "Spontaneity and Organization in the Petrograd Labour Movement: February to October 1917." Paper presented to conference, The Social History of Russian Labor, University of California, Berkeley, March 1982.

———. *Red Petrograd.* Cambridge, 1983.

Sobolev, M. "Zhenskii trud v narodnom khoziaistve XIX veka." *Mir Bozhii,* 1901, no. 8.

Soiuz Zhenshchin. St Petersburg, 1907–1909.

Sol'skaia, O'lga. *Rabotnitsa i strakhovanie.* St Petersburg, 1913.

Sotsialdemokrat. St Petersburg, 1909.

"Stachka tkachei Ivanovo-Voznesenskoi Manufaktury v 1895." *Krasnyi Arkhiv,* 1955, 5 (72).

Stanok. St Petersburg, 1908.

Stanok Tekstil'shchika. St Petersburg, 1907–1909.

Statisticheskii ezhegodnik g. Moskvy i moskovskoi gubernii za 1914–1925. Vyp. 2. *Statisticheskie dannye po gorodu Moskvy.* Moscow, 1927.

Statisticheskii ezhegodnik kostromskoi gubernii za 1909 g. Vyp. 1. Kostroma, 1912.

Statisticheskii ezhegodnik kostromskoi gubernii za 1910. Kostroma, 1912.

Statisticheskii ezhegodnik kostromskoi gubernii za 1911. Chast' 1. Kostroma, 1913.

Statisticheskii ezhegodnik moskovskogo gubernskogo zemstva za 1893. Moscow, 1893.

Statisticheskii ezhegodnik moskovskoi gubernii za 1889. Moscow, 1889.

Statisticheskii ezhegodnik moskovskoi gubernii za 1904. Moscow, 1905.

Statisticheskii ezhegodnik moskovskoi gubernii za 1911. Chast' 2. Moscow, 1912.

Statisticheskii ezhegodnik S-Peterburga za 1892. St Petersburg, 1894.

Statisticheskii sbornik po iaroslavskoi gubernii. Vyp. 14. *Kustarnye promysly.* Iaroslavl, 1904.

Statisticheskii sbornik po sanktpeterburgskoi gubernii za 1901. Vyp. 1. *Sel'skoe khoziaistvo i krest'ianskie promysly v 1900–1901.* St Petersburg, 1902.

Statisticheskii sbornik po petrogradskoi gubernii. Vyp. 1. *Sel'skoe kho-ziaistvo i krest'ianskie promysly v 1912–1913.* Petrograd, 1914.

Statisticheskoe opisanie iaroskavskoi gubernii. Vyp. 1. *Iaroslavskii uezd.* Iaroslavl, 1907.

Stites, Richard. *The Women's Liberation Movement in Russia.* Princeton, 1978.

————. "Prostitute and Society in Prerevolutionary Russia." (Unpublished article.)

Strakhovanie Rabochikh. St Petersburg, 1912–1914.

Surh, G. "Petersburg's First Mass Labor Organization: The Assembly of Russian Workers and Father Gapon." *Russian Review,* 1981, vol. 40, nos. 3–4.

————. "Petersburg Workers in 1905: Strikes, Workplace Democracy and the Revolution." Ph.D. diss., University of California, Berkeley, 1979.

Sviatlovskii, V. *Professional'noe dvizhenie v Rossii.* St Petersburg, 1907.

Sviatlovskii, V. V. *Fabrichnye rabochie (iz nabliudeniia fabrichnogo inspektora).* Warsaw, 1889.

————. *Otchet za 1885 g. fabrichnogo inspektora khar'kovskogo okruga.* St Petersburg, 1886.

Svod otchetov fabrichnykh inspektorov za 1900–1914. 15 vols. St Petersburg, 1902–1912; Petrograd, 1914–1915.

Svod otchetov professional'nykh obshchestv za 1906–1907. Ministerstvo Torgovli i Promyshlennosti. Otdel promyshlennosti. St Petersburg, 1911.

Tamarchukov, A. N. *Istoricheskii ocherk professional'nogo dvizheniia v voronezhskoi gubernii.* Chast' 1. Voronezh, 1921.

Temnykh, V. "V prokhodnoi. Ocherk iz fabrichnoi zhizni." *Russkoe Bogatstvo,* 1903, no. 3.

The Woman Question. Selections from the Writings of Karl Marx, Frederick Engels, V. I. Lenin, Joseph Stalin. New York, 1951.

Tilly, Louise A. "Urban Growth, Industrialization and Women's Employment in Milan, Italy, 1881–1911." *Journal of Urban History,* 3, 1977, no. 4, Aug.

Tkach. St Petersburg, 1906.

Tkachev, P. N. Vliianie ekonomicheskogo progressa na polozhenie zhenshchiny i sem'i," *Zhenskii Vestnik,* 1866, no. 1–2.

————. "Zhenskii vopros." In Daul, A., *Zhenskii trud v primenenii k razlichnym ostrasliam promyshlennoi deiatel'nosti.* St Petersburg, 1869.

Troinitskii, N. A., ed. *Chislennost' i sostav rabochikh v Rossii na osnovanii dannykh Pervoi Vseobshchei Perepisi Naseleniia Rossiiskoi Imperii, 1897 g.* 1906.

Trudovaia Pomoshch. St Petersburg, 1899–1900.

Trud Tabachnika. St Petersburg, 1907.

Trudy pervogo vserossiiskogo s'ezda narodnykh universitetov i drugikh prosvetitel'nykh uchrezhdenii chastnoi initsiativy. SPb. 21–25 aprelia, 1910. St Petersburg, 1911.

Trudy pervogo vserossiiskogo s'ezda po bor'be s torgom zhenshchinami i ego prichinami. Vyp. 1–2. Moscow, 1911.

Trudy pervogo vserossiiskogo s'ezda po obrazovaniiu zhenshchin. T. 2. Petrograd, 1915.

Trudy vserossiiskogo s'ezda po remeslennoi promyshlennosti v S-Peterburge. T. 3. St Petersburg, 1901.

Trudy pervogo vserossiiskogo zhenskogo s'ezda, 10–16 dekabria 1908. St Petersburg, 1909.

Trudy vtorogo s'ezda fabrichnykh vrachei i predstavitelei fabrichno-zavodskoi promyshlennosti. Vyp. 1–2. Moscow, 1911.

Trusova, N. S. *Nachalo pervoi russkoi revoliutsii. Ianvar'-mart 1905 goda.* Moscow, 1955.

———. *Vtoroi period revoliutsii. 1906–1907 gody.* Moscow, 1963.

Tsederbaum, S. O. *Zhenshchina v russkom revoliutsionnom dvizhenii, 1870–1905.* Leningrad, 1927.

Tugan-Baranovsky, M. I. *The Russian Factory in the 19th Century.* Trans. Arthur and Claora S. Levin. Homewood, Ill., and Georgetown, Ont., 1970.

Turzhe-Turzhanskaia, Evgeniia. *Belye nevol'niki (Domashniaia prisluga v Rossii).* Smolensk, 1906.

1905 g. v ivanovo-voznesenskom raione. Ivanovo-Voznosensk, 1905.

Ustav s-peterburgskogo zhenskogo kluba. St Petersburg, 1908.

Valitskaia, M. K. *Issledovaniia zdorov'ia rabochikh na tabachnykh fabrikakh.* St Petersburg, 1889.

Valk, S. N., ed. *Istoriia rabochikh Leningrada, 1.* Leningrad, 1972.

Varentsova, O. A., ed. *1905 v. ivanovo-voznesenskom raione.* Ivanovo, 1925.

———. *Severnyi rabochii soiuz i severnyi komitet RSDRP.* Ivanovo, 1948.

Vernadskaia, M. N. *Sobranie sochinenii.* St Petersburg, 1862.

Vestnik Rabotnits i Rabochikh Voloknistykh Proizvodstv. St Petersburg, 1907.

Vladimirskie i nikol'skie zhenskie voskresnye shkoly v Peterburge. 1890.

"Vliianie fabrichnoi raboty na rasprostranenie gramotnosti sredi naseleniia v serpukhovskom uezde moskovskoi gubernii." *Promyshlennost' i Zdorov'e,* 1904, kn. 2.

Volin, Lazar. *A Century of Russian Agriculture.* Cambridge, Mass., 1970.

Von Laue, Theodore. "Russian Labor between Field and Factory." *California Slavic Studies,* 1964, vol. 3.

———. "Russian Peasants in the Factory, 1892–1904." *Journal of Economic History,* 1961, vol. 21, no. 1.

———. *Sergei Witte and the Industrialization of Russia.* New York, 1963.

Voprosy Strakhovaniia. St Petersburg, 1913–1914.

Wildman, Allan K. *The Making of a Workers' Revolution: Russian Social Democracy, 1891–1903.* Chicago, 1967.

Zaiats, M. *Tekstili v gody pervoi revoliutsii, 1905–1907.* Moscow, 1925.

Zaretsky, Eli. *Capitalism, The Family and Personal Life.* New York, 1973.

Zasulich, Vera. *Vospominaniia.* Moscow, 1931.

Zelnik, Reginald E. *Labor and Society in Tsarist Russia.* Stanford, 1971.

———. "The Peasant and the Factory." In Wayne S. Vucinich, ed., *The Peasant in Nineteenth Century Russia.* Stanford, 1968.

———. "Russian Workers and the Revolutionary Movement." *Journal of Social History,* 1972–73, no. 6.

———. "The Sunday School Movement in Russia, 1859–1862." *Journal of Modern History,* 1965, vol. 27, no. 2.

Zhak, L. P., and Itkina, A. M. *Zhenshchiny russkoi revoliutsii.* Moscow, 1968.

Zhbankov, D. N. *Bab'ia storona (Statistiko-etnograficheskii ocherk).* Kostroma, 1891.

"Zhenskii fabrichnyi trud." *Drug Zhenshchin,* 1884, no. 5.

Zhenskii Vestnik. St Petersburg, 1867–1868.

Zhenskii Vestnik. St Petersburg, 1904–1917.

Zhenskoe Delo. Moscow, 1909–1917.

Zhenskoe dvizhenie poslednikh dnei. Odessa, 1905.

Zhirnova, G. V. "Russkii gorodskoi svadebnyi obriad kontsa XIX-nachala XX v." *Sovetskaia Etnografiia,* 1969, no. 1.

Zhizn' Tabachnika. St Petersburg, 1907.

Zhukovskii, Iulii. "Zatrudneniia zhenskogo dela." *Sovremennik,*
    1863, no. 12.
Zvanov, A. "Iz praktiki professional'nogo dvizheniia v Peter-
    burge." *Prosveshchenie,* 1913, no. 11.
Zvezda. 1912.

Index

Abandonment of factory work, 140–141

Abilities of women workers, 57; assessment of, 88–89; vs. wage inequality, 107–112. *See also* Physical strength of women workers; Skill

Abortion, 125

Abramov, Ia. V., 136*n*, 137*n*

Absenteeism: fines for, 7, 112, 113; by women factory workers, 113, 122, 124, 125, 127

Abuse of women workers, 141–144; attitudes of government and industrialists on, 145–150; by factory foremen and administrators, 142–144, 211; legislation on, 148–151; by male workers, 204–208. *See also* Sexual harassment; Welfare of women workers

Accident insurance, 10, 214. *See also* Insurance Law of 1913; Labor legislation

Acculturation into factory life, 101, 103

Adolescents, 85, 90; night work by, 146–150

Age of women workers, 11; changes in, 90; compared with male workers, 90–93, 94; and health deterioration, 145; and increase of married female factory workers, 93–96, 102; length of employment influenced by, 101, 102; and literacy, 111; and militant protests, 165; and participation in seasonal migration to the land, 98, 99; of widows, 129–130

Agrarian society: political debates for change of, 259; role of women in the peasant economy in, 29–58; transition to industrial society, 1–4, 17. *See also* Industrialization in Russia

Agricultural labor: by peasant women, 31, 34–35, 43, 44, 47, 50, 97, 108; and the seasonal return of factory workers to the land, 97–99; traditional sexual divisions in, 31, 35, 47–48; and wage inequality, 107; wages for day workers in, 51. *See also* Land

Agricultural production, decline in, 31–32; and the development of peasant wage labor, 31–32, 35, 37–38, 48

Agricultural products, sale of, 45, 70

Alcohol consumption: for entertainment and social interaction, 131–132; and politicized workers, 179; and striking workers, 192

Alcoholism: causes of, 17; compared for male and female workers, 35, 131

Aleksandrova, Elizaveta, 180

Alexander II, 170

All-Russian Congress on Artisanal Production, 266

All-Russian Union for Women's Equal Rights, 243–244, 247, 257

All women's meetings, 245, 247. *See also* First All-Russian Women's Congress

Antisemitism, 212*n*

Apartments: of politicized workers, 176–177; for urban factory workers, 13–14

Apprenticeship, 5; exlusion of women from, 200–201; for silk weaving, 44; of skilled workers, 23, 44; for tailoring, 62, 65–66. *See also* Vocational schools for women

Artels: described and defined, 15–16; for eating, 116, 120; of emancipated women, 225; of unmarried working women, 116

Ascribed female factory labor, 71–73

Associations of workers: legal formation of, 20, 21, 183, 196; protests by, 20–21, 186–187. *See also* Organizations of workers

of workers in, 111, 112; parental occupations of factory workers in, 103; percentage of women in the total factory labor force in, 81; research on workers in, 229; women in the textile industry in, 78, 79

Motherhood, 131, 152; and the definition of women workers, 192

Mothers-in-law, 30

Multiple-family households: decline of, 32–33, 57; domestic obligations of women in, 30; and patriarchal authority, 28–29

Needle trades, 70; wages and working conditions in, 61–66

Newspapers, 273; articles by women workers in, 276–277; protests by women in, 204, 275–277, 278, 280; published for women by the Social Democratic party, 276; reportage on women workers, 275, 276–277; for unions, 196–197, 202–203, 211, 255, 263

Nicholas II, 186, 210

Night work by women and children: criticism of the prohibition of, 251; decline of, 150; effect on family life, 147, 149; legislation to prohibit, 6, 147–150; strikes against the prohibition of, 148, 158–160; in the textile industry, 146–150, 175

Nikol'skii, D. P., 267, 271–272

Nizhnii Novgorod province, 110, 146

Nonindustrial women workers, 59–71. *See also* Women's work in nonindustrial jobs

Norinskii, K., 178

Novikov, M., 268–269, 270

Novyi Aivaz metal-working plant, 206, 207

Novyi Bessner, 206

Novyi cotton-spinning factory, 175

Nuclear families, 33

Nursing of infants: demands of female factory workers, 127, 165, 192; factory contraints on, 127; fines for, 7, 113; and night work, 175; and pacifiers, 128; and union support for maternity benefits, 198

Occupational bonds, 5, 23

Occupational heredity, 3–4, 101–102, 103

Occupations of Russian women, study on, 38. *See also* Women's work

Odessa, 230; women wage earners in, 68–70

Old women, 128

Oliunina, E. A., 62, 63

Orenburg, vocational school in, 134

Organizations of workers, 189–190; in circles for politicization, 173–182, 218; in clubs, 208–210, 265; cooperative efforts among rural peasant women, 54–55; female exclusion from, 189–190, 204–205, 214–215, 243, 276–277; legal formation of, 20, 183, 196; protests by, 20–21, 186–187; separate groups for women workers, 273–274, 275; in soviets, 193–196; in unions, 196–208, 209; women in, 184–188, 195–204, 208–209, 218; and women's equal rights, 243–245

Origins of the Family (F. Engels), 123*n*, 233

Osokin wool factory, 72

Overtime work: sexual inequality in, 200; strikes on, 213; for tailors, 63; and wages, 6

Paper industry, 75, 107

Parental occupations of factory workers, 101–102, 103, 175

Passports, 49

Paternalistic authority, vs. collective action by workers, 19–20

Patriarchal authority, 57; and beating of peasant women, 33–34; Marxist analysis of, 235; in peasant family life, 28–29, 30; and the subordinate status of women, 27–29, 33, 51, 57; vs. wage inequality, 56

Patrilocal marriage, 28

Patternmakers, 7

Peasant economy, 29–58; comparison of male and female workers in, 27, 35, 43–44, 51; crafts produced by women in, 36–45, 48, 50–58; decline of, 31–34, 35, 48;